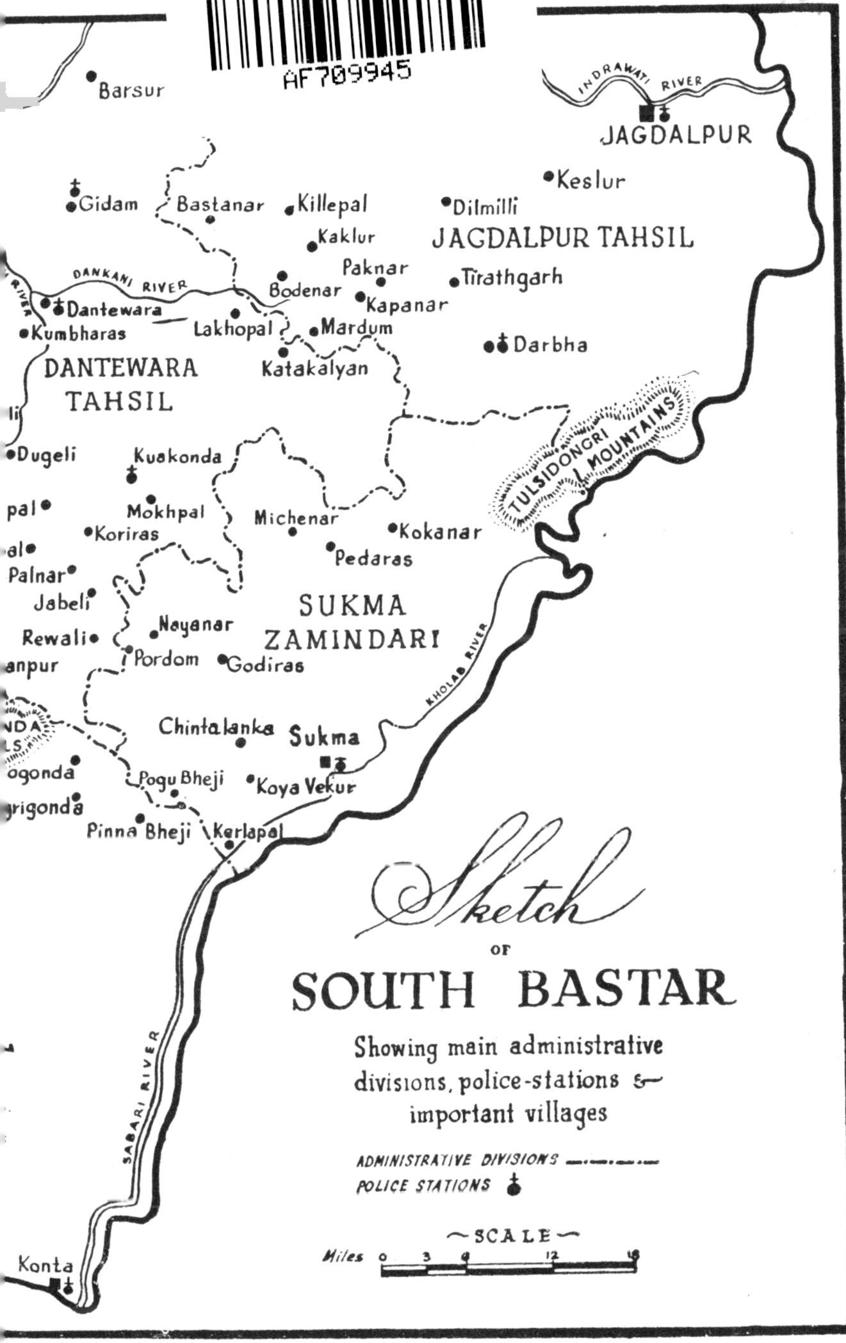

Sketch of SOUTH BASTAR

Showing main administrative divisions, police-stations & important villages

ADMINISTRATIVE DIVISIONS

POLICE STATIONS

SCALE

Miles 0 3 6 12 18

MARIA MURDER AND SUICIDE

Bison-horn Maria drummer

MARIA MURDER AND SUICIDE

BY
VERRIER ELWIN

WITH A FOREWORD BY
the late Sir W. V. GRIGSON

VANYA PRAKASHAN

OXFORD UNIVERSITY PRESS
DELHI BOMBAY CALCUTTA MADRAS
1991

Oxford University Press, Walton Street, Oxford OX2 6DP

New York Toronto
Delhi Bombay Calcutta Madras Karachi
Petaling Jaya Singapore Hong Kong Tokyo
Nairobi Dar es Salaam
Melbourne Auckland

and associates in
Berlin Ibadan

First edition 1943
Second edition 1950
Reprinted 1977
Special reprint for Vanya Prakashan 1991
Second impression 1991

Printed by Rekha Printers Pvt. Ltd., New Delhi 110 020
and published by S.K. Mookerjee, Oxford University Press
YMCA Library Building, Jai Singh Road, New Delhi 110 001

TO

MRS PHIROZA ARDESHIR WADIA

FOREWORD
To Special Vanya Prakashan Reprint

As we take a glimpse at the rich and diverse heritage of this vast country, we discover that the tribal societies have taken an active part in the process of fusion of races and cultures. Their contribution to the creation of the amorphous mass of myths and legends, religious traditions and customs of India has, truly speaking, been phenomenal.

Nevertheless, it is also true that our tribal societies have been undergoing recurrent culture shocks and their absorption in what is considered to be the 'mainstream' is not only a debating point with anthropologists and sociologists but a live issue in determining development strategies.

No society should be disturbed and for tribals even development can assume an intrusive character if undertaken without a thorough understanding of their social and cultural roots. About tribals, even now, so little is known and that too is coloured by our own perceptions. The data available through the Census reports or the studies sponsored by the Anthropological Survey of India, serve a very useful purpose but the studies of field anthropologists alone provide intimate and sympathetic understanding of the tribal way of life.

Verrier Elwin was an outstanding scholar, who explored the tribal areas of Mandla and Bastar districts in his own inimitable style. He lived here for twenty-five years and was able to achieve complete identification with tribals in these parts of the erstwhile Central Provinces.

Vanya feels privileged in bringing out reprints of the rare works of such great scholars as Verrier Elwin, Grigson and others. These works are an enduring testimony to their spirit of adventure, sacrifice and wisdom, and our venture is a humble homage to them. We convey our deep gratitude to all those who helped us in this.

V.G. NIGAM
Chairman, Vanya Prakashan

FOREWORD

It is a privilege to me to write this foreword to Verrier Elwin's book *Maria Murder and Suicide* and to be associated in this way with a man whose great work for the aboriginal of Middle India has made his name known wherever two or three are gathered together to think of India's duty towards her oldest inhabitants, the men of the malaria-belt, the forests and the hills. To his social and philanthropic work he has now added sympathetic and revealing anthropological work of the first order, recording while there is yet time to do so the still distinctive ways of life and culture of many sections of India's twenty-five and a half million tribal population. His researches are providing a scientific basis not merely for social work among the tribes, but above all for the great and complex task of administering the tribal areas in the tribesman's interests. The programme of any wise administration for these areas should be not only to enable the tribesman to hold his own in the world without losing his way of life, his virtues, his dancing, his songs and his laughter, but also, once he has been secured freedom from fear, from want, and from interference, to make his own special contribution to the free India that is to be. That contribution may well be a restoration to the drab village life of the plains of freedom from the puritan and the kill-joy, and the revival of what Mr Elwin in his pamphlet *The Aboriginals*[1] has referred to as the 'art of recreation, an art which is lamentably absent from the ordinary Indian village'. That pamphlet is commended to all who desire to get a clear and sane picture of the whole tribal problem; it states both the creed of one of the finest and best-equipped minds now at work upon the problem, and the case for the scientific approach to it.

To one who has served in Bastar State[2] it must always be a pleasure to read or write anything that will carry his

[1] *Oxford Pamphlets on Indian Affairs*, No 14 (Bombay, 1943).

[2] Bastar is no longer a State, but became in 1948 a District of the Central Provinces.

mind back to that beautiful land and its peoples or contribute to the greater understanding of them. 'Pleasure' may seem inappropriate of a book whose title contains the words 'murder' and 'suicide': but it is the fundamental purpose of the book that should be borne in mind, its desire to reveal the psychology underlying the 'crimes' of violence committed by one of the finest and least spoiled of Indian tribes, and the circumstances that drive its men and women to suicide. Such work can only lead to a wiser handling of the aboriginal accused by the judge or magistrate; and it raises acutely the question of punishment and the prison treatment of tribal convicts. The opening thirty-six pages of the book moreover give a vivid summary of Maria life, even in so short a compass revealing various facets that escaped me in the field-work and inquiries which preceded the writing of my book *The Maria Gonds of Bastar.*[1] In my preface to that book I expressed the hope that other books would be written about the Maria, correcting and supplementing my statements by more systematic field-work, and that my book would tempt trained workers to visit the ethnologically unexplored lands of Bastar and Jeypore. Mr Elwin will agree, I think, that it was talks with me that moved him to visit Bastar, where like many others he has fallen a victim to the beauty and interest of that State.

This short book is the firstfruits of his Bastar researches; although, its subject being what it is, it cannot compare for delight and scientific thrill with his forthcoming *magnum opus, The Muria and their Ghotul*, to me it is of particular interest, both because I was myself the Sessions Judge who tried twelve[2] of the hundred cases summarized in the Appendix and because the book is founded, independently, on an idea I long entertained of a similar book based on an examination of all available sessions trial and other records available from 1915 to 1930. I still have the notes which I prepared on some of these cases, including all those dealt with in this book for the years 1920-30 and fourteen

[1] Oxford University Press, 1938 (re-issued, 1949).

[2] Nos 6, 7, 12, 26, 37, 38, 39, 45, 57, 62, 78 and 83; the murder in No 69 also took place in my time but the trial came after I had left Bastar as the accused had absconded.

others; and I summarized my general experiences of murder in Bastar in pages 94-5 and 226 of *The Maria Gonds of Bastar*. To this study of previous records I was led by my realization, after a year's experience of original and appellate work in Bastar, of the great difficulty of applying to the decision of charges against tribal offenders the general practice as to the appreciation of evidence, court procedure, the assessment of guilt and the imposition of penalties laid down in the commentaries on the Evidence Act, the Code of Criminal Procedure and the Indian Penal Code, all of which had been imposed on the tribal and other areas of Bastar, as of the whole Central Provinces (in which Bastar State was then included), without any thought that any section in these enactments, framed for sophisticated India on European models, might perhaps not suit every part of India. I should have been saved many moments of anxiety as to the justice of my decisions and as to the whole trend of criminal justice in the State had I had at my command so full a study of murder and suicide as Mr Elwin's book, which not only analyses so many actual cases but also links up the results with the conclusions of standard works on crime, penology, psychology and ethnology.

I can almost completely endorse Mr Elwin's analysis of the general causes of Maria murders, though the concept in Chapter XI of fatigue as a cause of crime is one of those things that is startlingly revealing, but has only to be stated to be appreciated as true. Moreover I should perhaps plead guilty to having given currency to what he speaks of (p. 44) as 'the myth that rice-beer is the most important cause of homicide', by writing that 'about half the Bison-horn murders are committed in landa intoxication'.[1] His figures on page 140 show that only 13 of his 100 murder cases were influenced by landa and 6 by other intoxicant liquors. In the further 14 cases of which I still have notes landa intoxication caused 2 murders, and other intoxicants 3. In the earlier years of Bastar's political association with the Central Provinces drunkenness was probably an even more frequent cause of crime, or perhaps a symptom rather than a cause, since often landa or liquor was taken by persons brooding over grievances, and thinking of violent

[1] *The Maria Gonds of Bastar*, p. 94.

action. It may be of interest to classify these 14 murders according to Mr Elwin's categories. Apart from the five intoxication murders, two were prompted by belief that crops had been bewitched, one was a fatigue crime and one was caused by a dispute as to property, one by resentment over being dunned for a debt of one anna and one by a quarrel over failure to repair the skins of a drum broken by a friend who had borrowed it, while three were the result of conjugal infidelity. There were three cases in which the villagers agreed to conceal the crime to avoid the trouble of police and court investigation. The means employed included assault with an axe, a sword, a fencing pole, a stick, a wooden stool and fists, kicking, throttling, shooting with bow and arrow, twisting of neck and stabbing with a knife. In one case the accused committed suicide to avoid the disgrace attendant on the revival of an old scandal caused by his son's association with a blacksmith girl whose murder he and the villagers had hushed up for three years.

Of witchcraft and magic as factors in crime Mr Elwin has written fully in Chapter V, and has illustrated at page 62 a typical clan-god, Anga Pen or Pat Deo (log-god), sometimes used to detect witches in the manner described at page 17, while at pages 186-7 he deals with the Maria view that a witch or a sorcerer should be killed. That view is undoubtedly widely held outside tribal circles, and the power of tribal log-gods to detect black magic is equally strongly believed in by Hindu and Muslim subjects of the State. The reaction of tribal beliefs and practices on the local Hindu rites and ceremonies is very marked, and an example of this is the way in which Raja Bhairon Deo, the great-grandfather of the present Maharaja of Bastar, installed in Jagdalpur a log-god which was either a copy of a famous log-god from Narayanpur in the north-west of the State, or, according to its present Halba Pujari, was brought by a former ruler from Dongar, the old capital, to Narayanpur, and shifted thence by Raja Bhairon Deo. This god is now the Pat Deo of Bastar *par excellence*, and four ceremonies are held in his honour during the Maharaja's Dassara celebrations. His witch-finding function strongly survives, and I well remember my amused astonishment when in 1927 during an inspection of the accounts of the Jagdalpur

Temples managed by the State Court of Wards I found that the villagers around Jagdalpur frequently requisitioned his services for this purpose, paying for them a fee of Rs 5 into the State Treasury. When I wondered whether by lending the log-god the Court of Wards had not been accessory to the killing or beating of witches, the Pujari thus explained the god's conformity to modern law: 'Pat Deo is worshipped to save men from *bhut* and *pret*, and detects *bhut, churel* and witches. If a village needs his detective services, the villagers pay into the Treasury a fee of Rs 5, and then the Manager lets me take the god out. I walk behind Pat Deo, who is carried on the shoulders of four men, none of whom must come from the village which needs his help. Starting from the east side, we take him round the village widdershins, and then enter the village, Pat Deo himself impelling the bearers and then knocking against the house where the evil is hidden or against the actual magician. He will not leave the house till the guilty one comes out. Then in these days the offender kneels before Pat Deo and cries for forgiveness, which is given before Pat Deo goes home; he is not even outcasted now. In my grandfather's time he would have been set on an ass with his face towards the tail and taken in procession round the village; his head would then have been shaved, his front teeth pulled out by a Ghasia, and his hair and teeth buried in an ant-hill, while he would have been excommunicated and driven out of his village. They pulled out his teeth to stop him using them to suck blood and because without them he could not pronounce his spells.' One may be pardoned for scepticism as to the affair even in modern days being closed with Pat Deo kindly forgiving the magician!

This fear of magic as the source of illness and all troubles is strong in many parts of India. Here in Hyderabad belief in the power of *bhanamatti* or black magic is widespread, even among some persons of the highest education and social standing. A detailed investigation was made in 1916 by Mr L. B. Goad, an experienced officer of the Indian Police, then in charge of the State Criminal Investigation Department. His conclusion was that *bhanamatti* was so absolute a scourge in parts of Hyderabad and so utilized as a form of blackmail by its practitioners that special measures were needed to root them out. The evils which he found to have been inflicted on the victims in a series of cases investigated included loss of consciousness, barking and howling like jackals, appearance of black marks on various parts of the body, giddiness with great abdominal pain, setting of the jaws whilst the victim beat the air and ground with hands and feet, immodest and uncontrollable dancing like a prostitute, ape-like antics, violent laughing and hysteria, clothes dropping off the body, vomiting and spitting out of stones, gravel, marking-nuts, needles, thorns and lemons, food turning into excreta, loss of speech, cessation of menstrual periods or their continuance for weeks and months on end, and many others. His report concluded: 'I trust that this report of mine may have the desired effect of proving that the existing state of affairs in those tracts in which *bhanamatti* is prevalent requires special measures to deal with the present evil. If this is not done the populace will take the law into their own hands, as they have done in more than one instance in the recent past, and as they threatened to do when the District Magistrate of Bidar took action in Bidar City with a commendably strong and firm hand last autumn. Having personally witnessed the dreadful trials which women and girls have to suffer under the scourge of *bhanamatti*, I should not hesitate, did the power lie in my hands, to extend the operations of the Criminal Tribes Act to every cowardly blackguard who was known to practise the vile cult of *bhanamatti*.' Even now the Hyderabad District Police retain the services of an official versed in the art of treating the victims of *bhanamatti*. Most of its practitioners are persons of the untouchable castes, but the victims in the 1916 Bidar 'epidemic' of *bhanamatti* included persons of all ranks and professions, even lawyers. Murders of suspected practitioners[1] continue in Hyderabad. Is it to be wondered at that this fear of magic is so common a cause of murder amongst the Maria? It is after all not so long since in Great Britain an Act of Parliament passed in 1736 finally stopped prosecutions for

[1] Two were reported in the *Times of India* of 5 May 1933.

alleged witchcraft.[1] Mr Elwin has pointed out on page 81 that the European superstitions as to crime go far beyond the superstitions of the Maria, and mentions in particular the 'Hand of Glory' ideas; it may be of interest to reproduce an English recipe for making, using and counteracting a Hand of Glory given by Francis Grose in *A Provincial Glossary, with a collection of Local Proverbs and Popular Superstitions*, published in 1787:[2]

> Take the hand left or right of a person hanged, and exposed on the highway; wrap it up in a piece of a shroud, or winding-sheet, in which let it be well squeezed, to get out any small quantity of blood that may have remained in it; then put it into an earthen vessel, with zimat, saltpetre, salt, and long pepper, the whole well-powdered; leave it fifteen days in that vessel; afterwards take it out, and expose it to the noon-tide sun in the dog-days, till it is thoroughly dry; and if the sun is not sufficient, put it into an oven heated with fern and vervain: then compose a kind of candle with the fat of a hanged man, virgin wax, and sisame of Lapland. The Hand of Glory is used as a candlestick to hold this candle when lighted. Its properties are, that wheresoever anyone goes with this dreadful instrument, the persons to whom it is presented will be deprived of all power of motion. . . . The Hand of Glory would cease to take effect, and thieves could not make use of it, if the threshold of the door of the house by which they might enter, were anointed with an unguent composed of the gall of a black cat, the fat of a white hen, and the blood of a screech-owl; which mixture must necessarily be prepared during the dog-days.

Particular attention should be paid to what Mr Elwin has to say in Chapter XVII about the aboriginal prisoner. Whether in Bastar, the Central Provinces or in Hyderabad, I have never felt happy over the subjection of the aboriginal convict to ordinary jail life. Seventeen of the persons convicted in the hundred cases of the Appendix are shown as having died in jail, though, as jails in India go, the Jagdalpur jail was always good. Mr Elwin has summarized the reasons

[1] A useful brief summary of British witchcraft history and folklore is given in Chapter X of *English Folklore* by Christina Hole (London, 1940).

[2] I owe the quotation to my brother Geoffrey Grigson's anthology, *The Romantics* (London, 1942), p. 95.

for the Maria's hatred of jail life, and all who have to handle the aboriginal convict should read, mark, learn and inwardly digest his words. I have always felt that Section 302 of the Indian Penal Code, which prescribes the penalty for murder, is inadequate, in the case of aboriginals, in its recognition of degrees of murder; transportation for life, i.e. life imprisonment, even as reduced by modern practice as to the periodic review of sentences and earned remission, is an intolerable punishment for the average Maria murderer whose crime is committed in a sudden fit of anger and is unpremeditated. Fortunately in the old days such Sessions sentences had to be confirmed by the Political Agent who could also act on the Judge's recommendation to reduce the sentences in the exercise of the royal clemency; this accounts for the frequent reductions of sentences shown in the Appendix as having been ordered in appeal. Let us hope that the new combined High Court for the Eastern States will take as realistic and humane a view of this as the political officers have done, and in their handling of the aboriginal criminal shed the preconceptions and prejudices of the bar and bench of 'civilized' India. The same approach to the imprisonment of the aboriginal is needed in less heinous cases also, and the principle should be, whenever possible, not to send the aboriginal to jail—at least until there are special jails for aboriginals; too often used the Central Provinces jails to be full of unfortunate aboriginal illicit distillers or smugglers. The Central Provinces courts have now begun to realize the undesirability of jailing aboriginals and the need of discretion in inflicting fines proportionate to their slender means; but few policemen and magistrates realize the social cost to the released convict or the acquitted prisoner of the *hathkari dand* (handcuff penalty), and the cost of the ceremony for purging him from the defilement of the jail or lock-up described in pages 196-200. I have always regretted that I was never able in Bastar to experiment with the idea that came to me towards the end of my service there, of a village or camp jail, such as is suggested in the concluding chapter of this book. I see nothing impossible in this, nor in letting the aboriginal prisoner have his singing and dancing, observe his festivals and propitiate his gods; even after a time he might, on promotion to a separate personal hut and holding, be allowed the company of his wife. Agriculture and horticulture would be the ideal occupations in such a jail village, for the average aboriginal remains an agricultural novice.

As to the death sentence there is little to add to Mr Elwin's remarks in Chapter XVIII. Murder and violence were far more frequent in Bastar in the past than they have been since 1910, the Rebellion year, and at one time executions were carried out publicly in Pargana headquarters for deterrent reasons. This possibly had some effect on the vendetta and the bully. My own practice was to impose the death sentence only in cases of premeditated murder or murder with robbery. The very formidable and steady increase of murders and attempted murders in Hyderabad State ever since the virtual suspension of capital punishment is a warning against removal of the fear of death. And though death may be asked for by an occasional Maria in preference to long years of prison, its finality and grimness are realized even by them, and recognized at times as the only appropriate penalty. This happened when I sentenced Marvi Aitá of Paknar (H. Case No 45) to death. The whole trial was impressive. I held it at Paknar, travelling there in the first motor car to use a newly made forest road and followed by a bus bringing assessors, counsel, accused and police escort; we were held up in the few villages through which we passed so that the *perma* and elders might sacrifice cocks and sprinkle blood on the car and bus wheels. The accused had been the village bully, and after the trial, which had added drama from taking place on the actual spot where Aita had deliberately shot Kamlu Masa dead with an arrow as he and his helper neighbours were bringing home his kodon harvest, when I had pronounced sentence, the entire village filed before me to touch my feet in gratitude for freeing them from the perpetual menace of Aita's bullying, and it was then only that I learnt that he had been wrongly acquitted by a former Diwan on a previous murder charge and had been guilty also of yet another killing which the village had been afraid to report.

Let me conclude this Foreword by warmly recommending the book to all whose duties bring them into contact with the aboriginal, though it is so to speak only a study for that full-dress portrait of law and crime in tribal India that is so long overdue. It should also serve to show the ethnologist the wealth of valuable material to be gleaned from the case-records of the Indian courts. The illustrations are a delight, and our warm thanks are due alike to the author and the publishers.

W. V. GRIGSON

Hyderabad, Deccan
20 October 1942

CONTENTS

APPENDIXES

ILLUSTRATIONS

LINE DRAWINGS

MAPS

PREFACE

THIS book is a contribution to social anthropology rather than to the study of crime. For many of the tragedies here are not crimes in any intelligible sense, though in our present state of dealing with such matters we treat them as if they were. Moreover, I have naturally approached the subject from the angle that was most familiar to me. I am neither an administrator, a lawyer nor a policeman. In dealing with crime this is a great disadvantage. It is specially so in India where these simple village crimes offer few problems of detection, and where it is impossible to study the general reaction of society through the columns of the daily press or in such revealing impulses of compassion as petitions for reprieve. It is only rarely that anything like a detective problem with clues and counter-clues is set for the police. It is equally rare for interesting points of law to arise during a trial. In the great majority of cases the accused confesses. But this does not mean that these aboriginal crimes have no importance. It is of absorbing sociological and psychological interest to study the reasons that drive unsophisticated primitive men to kill and wound their fellows; and their behaviour afterwards, as well as the conduct of everyone concerned, is of almost equal importance.

While I was collecting material for my book *The Muria and their Ghotul*, I was greatly struck by the difference in the incidence of crime between the Muria and the great Maria tribe to the south. For homicide the annual incidence to the million is only 21 among the Muria, while it is 69 among the Bison-horn Maria; for suicide it is 22 against 53. In the last 10 years there have only been 21 Muria murders, and a large number of these have occurred either on the boundaries of the State or in the Mardapal Pargana in the extreme south of the Muria area, bordering on the Maria territory. The Muria differ from the Maria in the quite extraordinary absence of jealousy among them, in their lack of attachment to property and personal possessions, in their very strong civic and social instincts, in their gentleness and kindness. I believe that this difference is largely due to the existence among the Muria of the Ghotul or village dormitory,[1] in which the boys and girls of the tribe grow up from childhood under a high degree of discipline and are trained in the tribal virtues. A system of what is practically prenuptial sexual communism teaches them from an early age the impropriety of jealousy. The habit of sharing everything all through childhood and youth in the dormitory weakens their individualistic attachment to personal property. The result is that several of the main causes of murder only lightly press upon them. The Bison-horn Maria probably had a similar dormitory club at one period and traces of it may still be found today. But it no longer exists as a social force, and the result is that the Maria—compared to their northern neighbours—grow up passionate and jealous, strongly attached to individual goods, undisciplined and revengeful. The Muria do not seem to consume any less alcohol than the Maria. Indeed the consumption of mahua spirit per head in the Muria area is higher than in the south. The Maria, however, drink more rice-beer, and there are many more cases of illicit distillation detected among them.

When my friend Mr A. N. Mitchell was Administrator of Bastar, he was troubled by this problem, and one day in conversation about it, one of us—I forget which—suggested that I might make some sort of survey of Maria homicides from my own independent angle. Mr Mitchell, with his unique zeal for everything affecting the life and welfare of aboriginals, gave me all possible facilities for my inquiry, and I was thus able not only to study official documents but also to visit the jail and discuss matters with many criminals.

The first task in my inquiry was to get at the records. I decided to confine myself to the exclusive study of the Bison-horn Maria, and here we were immediately faced by our first difficulty, which was to decide who were to be included under this name. The name has come to be used in Bastar and in anthropology as a result of Mr W. V. Grigson's memorable book, *The Maria Gonds of Bastar*. But it is not, of course, a word that is used by the people of themselves. Many of them now do not call themselves Maria at all. At the 1941 Census, thousands of Maria returned

[1] For a detailed account of this institution, see my *The Muria and their Ghotul* (Bombay, 1947).

themselves as Muria, because they thought it sounded more respectable. Many others in the south have for some time past taken the title of Dorla. Others again are known as Koya, and a few call themselves Gond. When I was in Konta, the very wild Maria there said, 'We are not Maria. That is the name of the uncivilized fellows in Dantewara'. When I was in Dantewara, the equally wild Maria there indignantly rejected the old name which, they said, was only properly given to the savages of Konta. The expression 'Bison-horn Maria' is an obvious linguistic makeshift. Another name for the tribe is Dandami Maria. But I have never heard this used by the people themselves, and many do not know what it means. The name 'Bison-horn Maria' is derived from the tribe's custom of using a magnificent head-dress of bison-horns for their marriage dances, and possibly 'Tallaguda Maria' or even 'Sing Maria' (an expression in actual use) would preserve both the descriptiveness of the title and linguistic propriety. But for the time being I have continued to use the very convenient term, Bison-horn Maria, and throughout this book it will be understood that, wherever the word 'Maria' is used without qualification, it is to the Bison-horn and not the Hill variety of the tribe that I refer.

It will be evident, however, that official records, which are not concerned with scientific classification, were not likely to preserve these nice distinctions between one tribe and another, and I was at first provided with a very large number of files, many of which had nothing to do with the Bison-horn Maria at all. I think it is not unlikely that the bad reputation of this tribe for violence is, to some extent, due to the fact that a number of people who do not belong to it are included when statistics are compiled. However, at last, after much sifting and sorting, I found that I had a collection of 103 records of Bison-horn Maria homicides covering the years 1921 to 1941. During this period there must have been nearly 250 such cases altogether, but some of the files had been eliminated and others for one reason or another were not available. However, 103 was a very fair sample. For convenience I omitted the last 3 cases, and was thus left with a set of 100 taken entirely at random, distributed throughout the period under review and taken from every part of the area.

It was rather more difficult to get records of suicide, for these were not kept at the headquarters of the State, but distributed in the police stations and many of them had been eliminated. But the State Superintendent of Police called in as many aboriginal files as could be found; these were not above three-score in number, and I took the first 50 which were extracted. These extended over a period of 10 years.

Between 1935 and 1942 I made many tours in this enchanting land among these enchanting people. On the earlier tours I was accompanied by my friend Mr Shamrao Hivale whose amazing sympathy and insight helped me to catch my first vision of Maria culture. Later I had the support of my wife who, being herself a Gond, was able to get quickly in touch with the people and immediately established a friendly atmosphere. Particularly in the later tours I tried to see as many scenes of violence as possible, to talk to released convicts and to discover the general attitude of a village towards any crime that had been committed within its boundaries. In Aranpur I stood beside the still warm ashes of the ritually-cremated clothes of Barse Chewa who had recently been hanged in jail. At Khutepal, I watched Oyami Masa's children playing on the very floor once stained by the blood of his murdered wife. In the forest near Jabeli I had a clearing made so that I could photograph the carved pillar erected in memory of a famous murderer. In Rewali I was visited by a ferocious-looking youth who had twice stood on trial for his life and had twice preserved it. Here too I talked with Hemla Bakka who killed his wife for infidelity and was now unable to get another. In Doriras I saw the grave of the murdered Boti which had been desecrated by Ghasia for the sake of the purse of money which had been buried to help the dead man on his journey to the other world. In the same village I visited the home of Kawasi Borga then serving a life sentence, and talked to his fine sons and his sad pathetic wife.

Later I spent many hours in the Jagdalpur Jail talking to Maria who were serving terms of life-imprisonment for homicide. Some of them were as informative as the limits of their psychology allowed, for it must always be remembered that aboriginals are not accustomed to discussing those matters which are of special interest to anthropologists. Other prisoners clearly suspected some trick and told me very little. On the whole I was impressed by the great sadness of their life, even though in the jail they are well and kindly treated. Most of them, I think, felt that an inexplicable tragedy had befallen them. They did not feel like criminals. Their lives had been destroyed by a capricious destiny.

It was naturally more difficult to get information about the suicides, for, in the nature of the case, the person of most interest could not be present to tell his story. Relatives also and the villagers were more reticent, I thought, in discussing this subject, possibly because they feared that any revelations might lead to further police investigation. But even so I was able to get a certain amount of information about the Maria's attitude to self-murder.

But inquiries among the Maria are never easy. The people say that, as a result of Mr Grigson's investigations when he was writing his book on the tribe, their villages have suffered an invasion of man-eating tigers. In one village where I myself took photographs it was declared afterwards that I had made all the women barren. The Maria are friendly people, and I was able to make many friends among them. But particularly on matters which have a police reference they are naturally inclined to be secretive and prefer to claim ignorance rather than expose themselves to possible later difficulties by confiding in the investigator. Moreover, there is undoubtedly throughout aboriginal India a belief that talking about tribal affairs may anger the ancestors of the clan or disturb some godling's peace of mind. It is said of Korava children, members of a criminal tribe in Mysore, that they are taught from infancy to say 'I do not know' in reply to questions put to them.[1] Many Maria adopt the same attitude.

I do not suggest that in this book I have discovered anything new. But the transition from a social order where everything was settled by the tribe to a state of affairs where everything is settled by outsiders and nothing at all by the tribe, is of obvious interest. The tragedies described here

[1] L. K. Ananthakrishna Iyer, *The Mysore Tribes and Castes* (Mysore, 1930), Vol. III, p. 612.

throw light on many aspects of tribal life, and are specially valuable as indicating what things are emotionally disturbing to the Maria mind. When we read a monograph on a tribe, its whole life is laid out before us. Some things are interesting and exciting to the reader, but it is not always easy to discover what is interesting to the people themselves. Supplementary studies like this help us to appreciate the actual realities of, for example, a polygamous household or the real difficulties of the serving-marriage. The impact of witchcraft on the minds of the people, the extent of their attachment to property, their jealousy and desire for revenge are vividly illustrated here.

The value of such a study as this is not, however, only for the student. As the tribal areas are opened up, and as the aboriginals come more and more into touch with the outside world, it will become ever more essential for administrators and magistrates to understand tribal mentality. It is hard enough sometimes to understand any kind of aboriginal action. There is nothing more baffling than aboriginal crime. The Courts are all too ready to save time and energy by accepting a plea of drunkenness as an explanation of what seems incomprehensible. Undoubtedly a proportion of aboriginal crime, like the crime of civilized people, is due to alcohol. But I do not believe the proportion is large and there is reason to suppose that the plea of drunkenness so frequently put forward is often suggested to the accused by his legal adviser.

The importance of anthropological knowledge for the proper evaluation of aboriginal crime hardly needs illustration. One of the most difficult things that a Court has to decide in a case of homicide is whether the deed that it is evaluating comes under any of the Exceptions to Section 300 of the I.P.C. Was the crime premeditated ? Was it provoked by a serious and unbearable insult ? The difficulty here, which every Sessions Judge admits, is that what seems an extreme provocation to him or the Assessors may hardly be noticed by the aboriginal, and incidents that seem quite trifling to the 'civilized' mind may rouse the Maria or Naga to a fit of homicidal rage. The matter is complicated by the fact that the tribes vary greatly from one to another. The Bison-horn Maria, for example, are passionately concerned about female chastity, and a wife's infidelity is constantly a cause of murder. But in this their Gond and Baiga neighbours to the north have a much lower standard. Love is comparatively free. Divorce is easy and a wife's betrayal is readily compensated by the payment of a small fine. It is obvious, therefore, that a Gond or Baiga who suspects his wife of infidelity is not put to anything like the same degree of provocation as that suffered by a Bison-horn Maria under similar circumstances.

Premeditation may be indicated by tribal customs. The Bison-horn Maria express the spirit of implacable revenge by certain dramatic symbols. They pull out their pubic hairs; they remove a few handfuls of grass from an enemy's roof; they whistle loudly the dreaded *sui* whistle. In any case where an accused is proved to have indulged in one or other of these acts, it may be assumed that his crime was premeditated.

A Bastar tragedy, the murder of Tati Hirme by her deceased husband's younger brother Doga, provides an interesting example of how a knowledge of local custom can explain an otherwise meaningless crime. According to tribal practice a younger brother has a right over his elder brother's widow, a right which extends not only to her person, but to her property. This right Tati Hirme refused to Doga, and there is evidence that for a long time the youth bitterly resented her behaviour. On the day of the tragedy he went to her house and asked her for some tobacco. She refused, and he murdered her.

At first sight here is precisely one of those motiveless crimes which have so often puzzled outside observers. It is true that there was hostility between the parties, but the refusal of a small gift of tobacco was hardly sufficient for so disastrous a result. But in Maria practice to ask a woman for tobacco is a symbolic way of inviting her to sexual intercourse, and when the boy asked his elder brother's widow to have congress with him, he was only demanding his right and when she refused it, he found the provocation, both to his pride and his desire, so great that he killed her.

Research, both by medical science and by anthropology, may in time reveal how far the apparently motiveless homicides of aboriginals can be explained as crimes of exhaustion and fatigue. Again and again a man kills his loved wife in a sudden explosion of temper and for no apparent cause. It is probable that in many cases the real reason is not alcoholic intoxication, but extreme fatigue.

A point that often troubles the Courts is the time-element in cases where provocation is pleaded as an excuse. It is often found that there is a lapse of some hours between the actual incident that gave provocation and the subsequent act of violence. It has too often been held that this lapse of time should deprive the accused of gaining the benefit from Exception 1 of Section 300 of the Indian Penal Code. But there can be little doubt that an aboriginal's intelligence does not work so quickly as that of a more sophisticated person, and even in matters of everyday life it often takes an appreciable time for an idea to take root and effect a result in his mind. Laubscher's analysis of the psychology of the Tembu Negroes of South Africa is of some importance here. The Tembu, he says,

> Is not by nature blood-thirsty, but his aggressive instinctive or pugnacious propensities are excitable, easily roused and explosive. His aggressive libido flows outwards, becomes readily externalized, and sudden impulsive assaults, often fatal, are not uncommon. Careful study of the emotional reactions of the participants in stick fights, of course initially playfully performed for my benefit, has shown me how quickly and explosively the native loses his temper and retaliates with death-dealing blows at his opponent. Fatal blows are only avoided by the defensive skill of the opponent. Aggressive impulses are quickly evoked, although there is no apparent bad feeling after such a stick fight. I came to the conclusion that once an emotional impulse is aroused and the stimulus continues to be present, the native just drifts along with the impulse and exercises little or any inhibitory power, unless this inhibition is brought about by the evocation of another impulse, opposite in aim to the first, such as a fear of consequences, but it must be a fear stimulated by something present at the moment. Resultingly, the intellectual mechanisms of foresight, judgement and self-control are readily submerged by the instinctive impulse.[1]

I have not burdened these pages with many cross-references. The two Summaries at the end of the book give the names of the murderers and suicides in alphabetical order,

[1] B. J. F. Laubscher, *Sex, Custom and Psychopathology* (London, 1937), p. 302.

the clan-name in each case coming first. The Summary of homicides enables the reader to trace the sentence and subsequent history of each of the main characters in the book and also to see at a glance the entire outline of Maria crime.

My first friend in Bastar was Mr E. S. Hyde, I.C.S., a life-long champion of the aboriginals. The assistance given by him and Mr A. N. Mitchell was continued by their successor, Mr K. Radhakrishnan, I.C.S. At every stage of my inquiries I had the sympathetic interest of Dr W. P. S. Mitchell, M.B.E. Dr Mitchell was for many years the Superintendent of the Jail at Jagdalpur and was extremely popular among the prisoners. Every ex-convict with whom I talked praised him, and indeed he reminded me of what Dostoevsky said about the good-natured Russian Prison Governor who treated his men as equals. 'They did not love him, they adored him. I do not remember that they ever permitted themselves to be disrespectful or familiar. On the contrary when he met the Governor the convict's face suddenly lighted up; he smiled largely, cap in hand, even to see him approach.' Another popular figure in the Bastar Jail was Dr Satyanarayan who is believed by the Maria to perform some medical magic to free them from erotic desires. The late Rai Saheb Niranjan Singh, Assistant Administrator, who himself had tried and sentenced a large number of Maria criminals, threw much light on the social conditions that give rise to crimes in Bastar. To the police I must give a special word of thanks. Instead of resenting the intrusion of an amateur, Mr A. C. Mayberry, M.B.E., State Superintendent, and his staff gave me every possible assistance. Thakur Manbahal Singh particularly gave me information about the psychology of the homicide which revealed his very deep knowledge of the people. To many other policemen, Circle-Inspectors, Sub-Inspectors and Constables, who aided me in my tours and inquiries, I must express my gratitude. Mr Qudratulla Khan gave me valuable information on Excise matters. Mr Janardhan Joshi and Mr Ramakrishna took great trouble to find records for me, and helped me in every way. Mr S. M. Ishaque's experience of the Maria is unique. He accompanied me on one important tour, and even when lying in great pain in hospital gave me guidance and advice. Mr Q. Huq and Mr M. M. Khirey, who were at the time

Tahsildars of Jagdalpur and Dantewara respectively, exerted themselves in every way to assist me in my tours, and greatly encouraged me by their support.

Mr Sampat Singh acted as my interpreter and teacher in Gondi on most of the later tours. His help was quite invaluable. He himself had been present as a clerk at many murder trials, and was often able to expose the real points at issue. I am very grateful for his company and for the intelligence and energy which he put into a difficult and exacting task. Gulabdas, my assistant, who has been under training for many years and can now be regarded as an expert in his particular sphere of inquiry, did excellent exploratory work, and by his affable and insinuating address won the confidence of many Maria and persuaded them to reveal their secrets.

Part of the expenses of research were covered by a research grant from Merton College: I owe a heavy debt of gratitude to the Warden and Fellows for their assistance. The actual publication of the book was made possible by the enthusiasm and practical assistance of my friend Mr Jehangir P. Patel. The deeper realities of friendship and alliance are not matters for public acknowledgement: this book is itself a token and a proof of them. Mr Patel's share in it has been complete.

Mr Justice C. R. Hemeon, I.C.S., and Mrs Hemeon read the manuscript and made important comments and suggestions. Mr Hemeon adds to an extensive legal and judicial experience an ardent interest in criminology and Mrs Hemeon's unique gifts of understanding and insight make her the kind of critic that an author prays for.

Mrs Maeve Scott made two beautiful drawings (the Anga Pen and the Bison-horn head-dress) and gave much help in the preparation of the maps and half-tones. Mr R. D. Motafram's ready and expert hand was responsible for the other line-drawings. The picture of the Meriah sacrifices was discovered for me by Mr Evelyn Wood.

To Mr C. R. Gerrard I am specially indebted for the dust-cover which takes the book out into the world with beauty and significance.

The late Sir W. V. Grigson first inspired me to visit Bastar and then helped to make it possible for me to stay there. A

CHAPTER ONE

CRIME IN ABORIGINAL INDIA

I

Our knowledge of violent crime in aboriginal India is still elementary. Historically the most sensational conflict between a tribe of aboriginals and Government was over the Meriah sacrifices offered by the Kond up to the middle of the last century. An admirable summary of the ideas underlying the sacrifices and the rites accompanying them is given by Frazer (who bases his story on the records of Campbell and Macpherson) in *The Golden Bough*. 'The sacrifices were offered to the earth goddess, and were believed to ensure good crops, and immunity from all diseases and accidents. In particular, they were considered necessary in the cultivation of turmeric, the Konds arguing that the turmeric could not have a deep red colour without the shedding of blood.' [1]

Infanticide was at one time fairly common among certain aboriginals and has been recorded for, among others, the Irula of the Nilgiri Mountains, the Toda, the Kond and the Kallan. The practices of this last tribe have been described by Thurston.

> It is stated by Orme, on the authority of the Jesuit Father Martin, that the fury of revenge operates so strongly among the 'Collerles' (Kallans) that a man, for a slight affront, has been known to murder his wife and all his children, merely to have the atrocious satisfaction of compelling his adversary to commit like murders in his own family. The former practice of infanticide by the Kallans is dealt with at great length in the Manual of the Madura district, where it is stated, on the authority of the survey account, that 'a horrible custom exists among the females of the Colleries. When a quarrel or dissension arises between them, the insulted woman brings her child to the house of the aggressor, and kills it at her door to avenge herself, although her vengeance is attended with the most cruel barbarity. She immediately thereafter

[1] See Sir J. G. Frazer, *The Golden Bough* (2nd edition), Vol. II, pp. 241 f.; J. Campbell, *A Personal Narrative of Thirteen Years' Service amongst the Wild Tribes of Khondistan* (London, 1864) ; S. C. Macpherson, *Memorials of Service in India* (London, 1865) ; S. C. Roy, 'Ethnography in Old Official Records', *Man in India*, Vol. II (1922), pp. 78 ff. and other works.

> proceeds to a neighbouring village with all her goods. In this attempt she is opposed by her neighbours which gives rise to clamour and outrage. The complaint is then carried to the head Ambalacaur, who lays it before the elders of the village, and solicits their interference to terminate the quarrel. In the course of this investigation, if the husband finds that sufficient evidence has been brought against his wife that she had given cause for provocation and aggression, he proceeds unobserved by the assembly to his house, and brings one of his children, and, in the presence of witnesses, kills his child at the door of the woman, who had first killed her child at his. By this mode of proceeding he considers that he has saved himself much trouble and expense, which would otherwise have developed on him. This circumstance is soon brought to the notice of the tribunal, who proclaim that the offence committed is sufficiently avenged. But, should this voluntary retribution of revenge not be executed by the convicted person, the tribunal is prolonged to a limited period, generally fifteen days. Before the expiration of that period, one of the children of the convicted person must be killed. At the same time he is to bear all expenses for providing food for the assembly during three days '.[1]

The Wynad Paniyan at one time had a bad reputation and it was not unusual for people to come long distances to engage them in the task of carrying out some more than usually desperate robbery or murder. 'Their mode of procedure, when engaged in an enterprise of this sort, is evidenced by two cases which had in them a strong element of savagery. On both these occasions the thatched homesteads were surrounded at dead of night by gangs of Paniyans carrying large bundles of rice-straw. After carefully piling up the straw on all sides of the building marked for destruction, torches were, at a given signal, applied, and those of the wretched inmates who attempted to escape were knocked on the head with clubs, and thrust into the fiery furnace.'[2]

The Bhantu were equally savage in their methods.

> If resistance was shown they were merciless ; indeed, one particular gang sent to Port Blair had committed over fifty murders in one series of outrages. As they were working against time, cruel and violent methods were often adopted

[1] E. Thurston, *Ethnographic Notes in Southern India* (Madras, 1907), pp. 503 ff.

[2] E. Thurston, *Castes and Tribes of Southern India* (Madras, 1909), Vol. VI, pp. 60 f.

> to compel the victims to reveal the hiding-place of their treasure, such as forcing women to sit on burning charcoal. Rape was common. The traditional weapon of attack was a short hard stick, thrown with tremendous force, while the lathi was used for defence. In more recent years, however, guns have been adopted and khaki worn. Having secured their plunder, they buried it immediately in the vicinity to avoid any incriminating evidence and dispersed. In the event of a murder being committed, no serious action is taken, though it is regarded as *pap* or sin, and if a stranger has been murdered, the murderer distributes gur among the brotherhood. This costs Re. 1-4-0. Should one of the tribe, however, be murdered the offender must give a feast costing Rs. 101.[1]

The outlook of the criminal tribes on crime is, however, entirely different from that of the ordinary aboriginal. Ananthakrishna Iyer describes the attitude of the Korava, a criminal tribe of Mysore. 'On a careful examination of the ethics of the Korava and allied tribes, it will be found that theft is a sporting method of making a living, and not a crime as understood by the rest of society. To them it is a love of adventure. If a Korava has bad luck and goes to jail, it is a part of his life which must be endured, but he hopes for good luck in his attempts to escape. He believes it right to steal. When a Korava has committed a theft, he sometimes volunteers to help the police in hunting down the culprit and knowing all the facts, puts them off the scent, and the crime goes unpunished.'[2] This could not be given as a description of, for example, the Bison-horn Maria.

These criminal tribes are distributed throughout India and many of them have been carefully studied by police officers.[3] The Thag stranglers were made the subject of a sensational book by Meadows Taylor. But most of these criminal tribes are not really aboriginals, but offshoots of the lower Hindu castes. One of the few real aboriginal criminal tribes was the Pardhan—but their main interest lay in cheating and theft—and today the great majority of them have settled down to a peaceful and law-abiding life. In Assam, Naga head-hunters have advanced to the savagery of modern Europe

[1] C. J. Bonington in *Census of India, 1931*, Vol. I, Part III-B, p. 37.

[2] L. K. Ananthakrishna Iyer, *The Mysore Tribes and Castes* (Mysore, 1930), Vol. III, pp. 612 f.

[3] A useful brief account is given in B. S. Haikerwal, *Economic and Social Aspects of Crime in India* (London, 1934).

without the help of either education or parliamentary institutions.

The Bhil at one time were greatly feared for their ferocity, and there were some famous Bhil dacoits. It is said that 'in former times when the Bhil seized a whole herd they sometimes offered a human sacrifice to the Mata of the thieves. They then killed the shepherd near the Mata as a sacrifice. The sacrifice was also conducted in another way. The shepherd was taken to the top of a steep hillock. His legs and arms were tied and he was rolled down the hill. These practices have now been abandoned. A common vow taken in honour of the Mata is to burn seven hills or to burn seven houses. When the grass in the jungle is dry they set fire to it in seven different places so as to destroy as much as possible. These acts are done presumably to obtain help of the Mata or to thank her for the success of a plundering expedition'.[1]

Such behaviour was probably due rather to a reaction against the cruel and savage treatment the Bhil suffered at the hands of the Maratha than to any inborn viciousness in the race. So too the rebellions of the Santal, Munda, Maria and other tribes are evidence not so much of their own lawlessness as of the lawlessness of those who oppressed them and drove them to despair.

II

For in India generally the aboriginals have had a high reputation for their pacific and kindly character. Hutton speaks of 'the natural truthfulness and honesty' of the tribesmen. Forsyth declares that 'the aborigine is the most truthful of beings and rarely denies either a money obligation or a crime really chargeable against him'.[2] Majumdar quotes Major Roughsedge as being so pleased with the independent bearing of the Ho that he declared them to be as much superior to their brethren of Chota Nagpur as 'wild buffaloes to the village herd'. Colonel Tickell also was so much impressed with 'their love for truth, their honesty, their obliging willingness and their happy ingenuous disposition, that he would rather see them remain lawless than be brought

[1] C. S. Venkatachar in *Census of India, 1931*, Vol. I, Part III-B, p. 56.
[2] J. Forsyth, *The Highlands of Central India* (London, 1871), p. 164.

under British courts of justice which might end in destroying their virtues '.[1] Of the Kachari, the missionary Endle speaks very highly. Apart from their love of rice-beer, he observes :

> It is pleasing to be able to say that among them are to be found many simple virtues of great price, honesty, truthfulness, straightforwardness and a general trustworthiness deserving of all honour. In illustration of their simple truthfulness, even when involving serious consequences to themselves, the writer recalls a story told him some years ago by an officer in charge of the subdivision of Mangaldai, the late A. J. Primrose, I.C.S. A Kachari of Sekhar Mauza was brought before this magistrate on a charge (manslaughter) involving a very heavy penalty, when he without hesitation admitted his guilt, though the evidence against him was of the slightest, or at least utterly insufficient to secure a conviction. The relations of the sexes too are on the whole of a very sound and wholesome character, far more so probably than in many countries boasting of a higher civilization.[2]

Colonel Ward described the Baiga in 1870 as ' wild as the forests they live in . . . they are independent, high spirited . . . very well behaved, ready to oblige, and deserving every consideration for their orderly manner of life '.[3]

' Excepting the Dhombs ', says R. H. Campbell, ' the Agency hillmen are the most honest and law-abiding people that I have ever had to deal with, and are singularly truthful. In the Gudeme Hills, there are practically no police stations. Thefts and robberies are unknown, and the only crime ever committed is an occasional murder induced by jealousy.'[4]

Unhappily these virtues disappear at the first touch of ' improvement ' and civilization. ' The Bhil ', says C. S. Venkatachar, ' are truthful unless spoilt by being " civilized ".'[5] P. O. Bodding says that the Santal are truthful and honest so long as they speak their own tongue but they ' are especially lying when they use not their own, but the Bengali or Hindi languages which they are taught at school '.[6]

[1] D. N. Majumdar, *A Tribe in Transition* (London, 1937), p. 13.

[2] Sidney Endle, *The Kacharis* (London, 1911), pp. 2 f.

[3] H. C. E. Ward, *Report on the Land Revenue Settlement of the Mundlah District* (Bombay, 1870), p. 36.

[4] R. H. Campbell, 'The Wild Tribes of the Vizagapatam Hills', *Quarterly Journal of the Mythic Society* (Bangalore, 1917), Vol. VIII, pp. 3 ff.

[5] *Census of India, 1931*, Vol. I, Part III-B, p. 56.

[6] ibid., p. 105.

K. Govinda Menon has a sombre picture of the Kadar of Cochin.

> If the physical health of the Kadar has been undermined and ruined almost permanently as a result of their contact with the people of the low country, their moral health has been deeply tainted by the same influence. When the dark avenues of the primeval forests echoed under the tread of the greedy contractor and his assistants, and the screech of the steam-engine of the Forest Tramway first reverberated through the hills and vales, they proclaimed that Civilized Man, the Destroyer, had set his foot within the fair precincts of the Kadar's domains. It was observed that the lust of the people from the plains did not leave Kadar women alone. Promiscuous intercourse for years between the new arrivals and these women has infected the whole tribe with syphilis, the first fruits of civilization. The primitive purity of the Kadar women was tainted for ever and their ideals of chastity have been brought into adjustment with those of the low class people of the plains with whom they were brought into touch. Moral and physical deterioration has followed and the rising generations show mixed and tainted blood. The employment of Kadar labour in the coffee estates of the Nelliampathi Hills has very much aggravated the evil. In the estates the Kadar come into contact with Tamil labourers of the lowest classes. The surroundings, food, and other influences in this new sphere are entirely different from those the Kadar are generally accustomed to. There is free scope to indulge in arrack and opium in the estates, and the Kadar try to ape the filthy ways of the dissolute Tamil labourers. The Kadar children born in the estates are all tainted and cannot be distinguished from the puny and sickly progeny of the Tamil labourer.[1]

C. von Fürer-Haimendorf gives an interesting account of the effect of official interference on the incidence of violent crime among the Chenchu.

> Within the last few years numerous cases of murder and manslaughter committed by the Chenchu of Kurnool have come into court and the majority were crimes passionels, both victims and accused being Chenchu. Rape and attempted rape are by no means rare occurrences and are summarily dealt with by the Foresters in charge of the settlements. Cases of incendiarism out of revenge of personal hate are fairly frequent but they seldom steal from each other.

[1] K. G. Menon in *Census of India, 1931*, Vol. I, Part III-B, pp. 215 f.

It would appear that economic motives play little part in the cases of murder and incendiarism, and we may therefore question how it is that the Chenchu, who in the jungles of Hyderabad are quite capable of settling their quarrels peacefully, should have so many murderers within their ranks in Kurnool. The only answer which presents itself to this disturbing question is that the process of gathering into large settlements has undermined their own social organization and no new system has yet been evolved to replace the old order. In their pristine state they are individualists and any man in disagreement with the other members of his group separates from them and joins another group. Thus friction is avoided and the expedient of flight saves many the bitterness of a long drawn out quarrel, absence of blunting hate and personal jealousies. But in Kurnool the Chenchu are unable and indeed forbidden to leave their villages and settle elsewhere while their traditional customs, which were sufficient to check outbreaks of violence in the case of small groups of closely related families, prove inadequate to govern the relations between the members of large communities. In the old times, for instance, interference with married women was limited by the fact that the women of a man's local group were usually either his clan-sisters or the wives of his brothers or first cousins and that distance rendered intrigues with other women comparatively difficult. Nowadays, however, the inhabitants of a settlement consist of members of many clans between whom there appears to exist little of the cohesion and mutual loyalty necessary for a healthy community life.[1]

III

The Committee for the Study of Suicide established in New York in 1936 included in its aims Ethnological Studies, or 'comprehensive investigation of suicide among primitive races, for this is a rather frequent occurrence among many primitive races still extant and when studied may throw some light on suicide as a psycho-biological phenomenon'.[2] At about the same time, Laubscher in South Africa was also urging the importance of such studies: 'It is generally believed that the rate of suicide increases with civilization. For this reason I consider that whatever evidence can be produced about

[1] C. von Fürer-Haimendorf, 'The Fortunes of a Primitive Tribe', *The Indian Journal of Social Work*, Vol. III (1943), pp. 402 f.

[2] *Medical Review of Reviews* (New York, April 1936), pp. 169 f.

suicide in a primitive culture is of great importance to psychiatry.'[1]

For aboriginal India, however, this subject has been almost entirely neglected. The attention of scholars has been diverted by the better documented and sensational examples of ceremonial or religious suicide. Thus there is ample literature on Sati, the custom whereby a widow devoted herself on her husband's funeral pyre;[2] on the ceremony of Traga, a form of suicide in defence of property or principle;[3] on the process of Dharna, sometimes practised by a creditor to extort his dues from a recalcitrant debtor;[4] on the 'awful rite of Johur' wherein thousands of Rajput women died rather than face captivity; on the ceremonial suicides beneath the wheels of the car of Jagannatha at Puri.[5] A place famous for suicides was the Daitya ka Har, or Devil's Bone, whence those desiring children hurled themselves down and occasionally escaped.[6] Another such place was behind the peak of Kedar, where the Pandava devoted themselves.[7]

But of suicide as the fruit of ordinary despair or domestic tragedy we have few records from India, least of all from among her primitive people. The great volumes of the Ethnographic Survey are practically silent; there is not a word about the subject in the works of Sarat Chandra Roy. For the tribes of peninsular India we not only have no detailed study; there is hardly a hint about the suicide situation. For the tribes on India's borders, we have a little more information. Man declares that suicide was unknown among

[1] Laubscher, op. cit., p. 290.

[2] A full account of the literature will be found in N. M. Penzer, *The Ocean of Story* (London, 1925), Vol. IV, pp. 255 ff.

[3] R. V. Russell and Hiralal, *The Tribes and Castes of the Central Provinces of India* (London, 1916), Vol. II, pp. 259 ff.

[4] ibid., Vol. II, pp. 265 f.

[5] Sir W. W. Hunter, *Orissa* (London, 1872), Vol. I, pp. 305 ff. Hunter rightly contrasts the Cruickshank-illustrated exaggerations of Thackeray, who describes 'the hideous moving palace, the horrible body-crusher, under which unhappy millions were crushed to death' with the 'insignificant' number of actual cases 'registered by the dispassionate candour of English officials'. Another writer who exploited this theme was Charlotte Bronte who speaks of 'the prostrate votary' before the 'annihilating craunch'.

[6] J. Tod, *Annals and Antiquities of Rajasthan* (London, 1829-32), Vol. II, p. 681, who also gives several accounts of the Johur.

[7] W. Crooke, *The Popular Religion and Folk-Lore of Northern India* (Westminster, 1896), Vol. I, p. 256; G. W. Traill and J. H. Batten, *Statistical Sketch of Kumaun* (Agra, 1851), p. 58; E. T. Atkinson, *The Himalayan Districts* (Allahabad, 1882), Vol. II, pp. 773 f.

the Andaman Islanders, until after they had come into contact with 'the alien population', Hindus and Europeans.[1] Among the Vedda, the Seligmans tell us, suicide is rare: they record one case where a wife openly insulted her husband over his intrigue with another woman—he felt so disgraced by the publicity that he shot himself with a gun.[2] Among the Lepcha, however, suicide is said to be 'fairly frequent'. Every one of the six cases recorded by Gorer were 'immediately subsequent to a public reproof'. Five of the six were relatively young men, the sixth was a young girl who drowned herself after being reproved for laziness and promiscuity. Gorer heard of one case of suicide from grief. Women kill themselves by drowning, men generally with the aconite poison they use on their arrows.[3]

In Assam, suicide is common only among the Lhota Naga. Mills speaks of 'the extraordinary readiness' and the extremely trivial grounds of the suicides in this tribe. 'I have known a man hang himself because the elders of his village fined him fifteen rupees—a sum he could well afford to pay. Usually, however, a love affair is the cause, and cases of lovers, who for some reason cannot marry, taking poison together, are common. Little though he knows or cares of the details of the life hereafter, the Lhota never doubts that there is such a life, and lovers die professing their sure faith that they will be united beyond the grave'.[4] The method of suicide is to take poison made from the root of a common flowering plant called rhisa.[5] It is taken in liquor, and death follows intoxication.[6]

Among the other Naga tribes suicide is said to be rare. It is an *apodia* death, accursed and contagious. The body must be buried at the back of the house or in broken ground where men do not walk about.[7] Hutton only knew of three such deaths among the Angami Naga; one of them was that of a man heavily indebted.[8] To the Rengma Naga in their natural

[1] E. H. Man, 'On the Aboriginal Inhabitants of the Andaman Islands', *J.A.I.*, Vol. XII, p. 111.
[2] C. G. and B. Z. Seligman, *The Veddas* (Cambridge, 1911), p. 88.
[3] G. Gorer, *Himalayan Village* (London, 1938), pp. 269 f.
[4] J. P. Mills, *The Lhota Nagas* (London, 1922), p. 20.
[5] ibid., p. 82.
[6] J. H. Hutton, *The Angami Nagas* (London, 1921), p. 229.
[7] J. H. Hutton, *The Sema Nagas* (London, 1921), p. 262.
[8] *The Angami Nagas*, p. 229.

state 'suicide seems to be absolutely unknown'. Mills knew of only one case, that of a Rengma who had become a Baptist Christian.[1] Among the Lakher also, suicide is very rare; after an experience of many years Parry could only recollect one case.[2]

Suicide for erotic causes has been reported for the Badaga girls of the Nilgiri Hills who sometimes poison themselves when betrothed against their will—'very little provocation is needed to induce a Badaga woman to destroy herself',[3] and in old Tamil love-poems there are allusions to an ancient practice of a disappointed lover proclaiming his love in public before committing suicide.[4] And of the Ho, Dalton writes:

> The extreme sensitiveness of both men and women is sometimes very painfully exhibited in the analysis of the numerous cases of suicide that every year occur. A harsh word to a woman never provokes a retort, but it causes in the person offensively addressed, a sudden depression of spirits or vehement outbreak of grief, which few persons would a second time care to provoke. If a girl appears mortified by anything that has been said, it is not safe to let her go away till she is soothed. A reflection on a man's honesty or veracity may be sufficient to send him to self-destruction. In a recent case, a young woman attempted to poison herself, because her uncle would not partake of the food she had cooked for him. The police returns of Singbhum show that in nine years, from 1860 to 1869, 186 men and women committed suicide in that district.[5]

[1] J. P. Mills, *The Rengma Nagas* (London, 1937), p. 221.
[2] N. E. Parry, *The Lakhers* (London, 1932), p. 265.
[3] J. F. Metz, *The Tribes Inhabiting the Neilgherry Hills* (Mangalore, 1864), p. 75.
[4] Kanakasabhai Pillai, *The Tamils Eighteen Hundred Years Ago* (Madras, 1904), p. 123.
[5] E. T. Dalton, *Descriptive Ethnology of Bengal* (Calcutta, 1871), p. 206.

CHAPTER TWO

THE BISON-HORN MARIA

I

THE so-called Maria of Bastar fall naturally into two divisions distinguished by many details of culture and tradition, the Hill Maria of the Abujhmar Mountains and the Bison-horn Maria living to the south of the Indrawati River. A full account of both these tribes has been given by W. V. Grigson, and his book should be read by those who wish to have a fuller background of Maria life than the present volume can supply. In this chapter I will only give a brief summary of the life and customs of the Bison-horn Maria.

The Bison-horn Maria, who are distinguished from the other aboriginals of Bastar by the splendid head-dress they use for their marriage dances, numbered about 156,000 in 1931, and I estimate their present strength at about 175,000. They are distributed all over southern Bastar, among the entrancing hills of Dantewara, in the dry forests of Bijapur, among the hot but lovely lowlands of Konta, in the remote Sukma and Kutru Zamindaris. On the borders of the main Maria stock are a number of communities which really belong to it, the Koya of the extreme south, the Dorla who claim to be a superior caste and the mixed population along the banks of the Indrawati which reaches up towards the Muria country beyond Barsur. The Dorla and Koya dance in Bison-horn Maria fashion; the mixed people to the north combine the customs of the Hill Maria with their own. In the neighbourhood of Jagdalpur, the Maria gradually lose their distinctiveness as they approach the town and merge into the southern Muria.

There are few people in India more attractive than the Bison-horn Maria, physically charming, of good stature, perfect figure, finely featured with carefully tended hair, often a lovely golden-brown in colour. Both men and women are very strong; the men can carry heavy loads great distances, endure long and arduous hunting expeditions and dance all night bearing their great drums. Their health is fairly good, but they are afflicted with yaws, though the work of the

State Medical Department has done much to check the spread of the disease. Malaria, as everywhere in the Indian forests, is endemic, but few suffer from enlarged spleen. Leprosy and the venereal diseases are very rare. Skin diseases are also much less common than among the more elaborately clothed and thus dirtier people of the north.

Men wear a small loin-cloth and sometimes a little turban. The women tie a sort of skirt, very short, round their waists: it hangs down to the knees. The breasts are covered only with ornaments; when visiting a bazaar girls may tie a small piece of cloth round their shoulders. They often wear a thin brass fillet round the hair, and the older women use a large snood which is most becoming. Round the neck are masses of bead-necklaces, and iron or brass torcs. The bright colours of the beads and the shining brass fillets against the rich brown skin make a sight of unforgettable beauty.

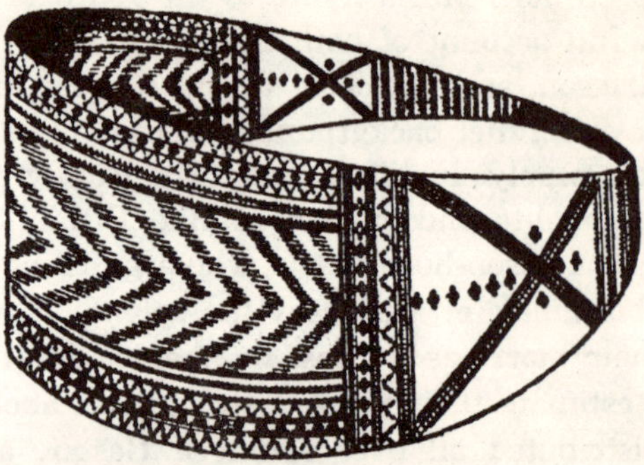

Brass fillet worn by Maria women

The Bison-horn Maria village is laid out on the same lines as the Gond village of the Central Provinces, unlike the communal settlements of the Hill Maria, Baiga or Juang. Each house stands in its own garden which is sometimes a substantial field, and a village may cover a very large area in consequence. Often a village is composed of anything from six to twelve small hamlets, each of which represents the grouping of a family round its patriarchal head. The little huts stand among woods, on rocky hill-sides, in the shade of spreading trees. Sometimes they appear almost submerged by waves of yellow sarson flowers or red jhira vegetable. Each village has a substantial building for the accommodation of travellers and this is used by the unmarried boys as a dormitory. The unmarried girls also sleep together, sometimes in a little house of their own, sometimes in a room lent to them by an old widow. Where there is a separate hut, this is sometimes also used for the segregation of menstruating women. In a few places there are special buildings for this purpose. The houses of the headmen are not built in any special position, but those of the Siraha medicine-men can generally be distinguished by the little huts for patients which are built round them. On the outskirts of the village will be found the shrine of the Village Mother, and in a grove nearby there may be the temple of one of the clan-gods. Beyond is the village burial place and cremation ground. Rows of menhirs in memory of the Dead may be seen in the majority of villages.

There is no standard pattern for the Maria house any more than there is for the Maria village. Most of the houses consist of three rooms, each a separate building with eaves at different levels, which make them look, as Grigson says, 'like card houses'. The first room, which is really a built-in veranda, is the kitchen. It leads into a bedroom and this in turn opens into an inner and secret room mostly occupied by a platform for storing grain and other possessions; in one corner is the Pot of the Departed about which centres the Maria cult of the Ancestors. Frequently two or more such houses are built round a courtyard, part of which is occupied by a more or less open building where people sit to talk and work.

Tops of Maria women's dancing-sticks (*whole stick, 3½' long*)

The houses are generally clean and pleasant, but littered with a great variety of domestic and agricultural impediments. Outside are the pig-sties and cattle-sheds, substantial and carefully tended buildings. Fowls, set in funnel-shaped bamboo stands, share the house with the human beings.

II

The Maria's main source of livelihood is agriculture. The ancient and traditional method is axe-cultivation, whereby the people make clearings in the forest with their axes, allow the felled wood to dry, fire it shortly before the rains and then sow the seed in the ashes. Sometimes this is done in the very place where the trees are cut. Sometimes brushwood is carried to a regular field and spread upon its surface. The Maria, living as they do in settled and often level country, have also many permanent fields which are embanked and irrigated by artificial tanks. The Maria are very proud of these tanks, and they are a frequent cause of dispute which sometimes leads to murder. A great part of the Maria's life is necessarily spent in these fields and clearings, and little field-huts and platforms are erected in which whole families camp for weeks at a time watching the crops at night and cooking and doing their work by day. Everybody helps in the work. Beside the family there may be farm-hands, some of a special kind such as the Lamhada, who serves for his wife instead of paying the bride-price, and the Kabari who is a bond-servant working to repay a loan.[1]

Besides agriculture, the Maria eagerly and successfully exploit the produce of the great forests in which they live. There is nothing edible that they will not eat, fruits, roots, tubers, leaves—they have a profound knowledge of the possibilities of natural produce. They are equally omnivorous in their attitude to meat. In the villages they keep pigs, goats and fowls, and they are fond of pigeons. They still (though they often deny it to outsiders) eat beef on all important and ceremonial occasions. Rats, squirrels and small birds are caught by the children and roasted and eaten with delight. The older people are keen hunters and trappers, though much of the game has disappeared. Simple thorn-traps are placed round the mahua trees to catch bats, and more substantial snares are set for birds, hares and larger animals. Before the great Seed Festival at the end of the hot weather, there

[1] The Kabari system, which is similar to what is called Bhagela in Hyderabad, Kamiauti in Bihar, and Gothi in Orissa and Madras, is open to grave abuses—men working a whole life-time to settle a debt which is not settled even by death, but descends to the sons—and is now controlled by the administration.

a ceremonial hunt at which bows and arrows are worshipped and all the able-bodied men go out to get what game they can, their success or otherwise being regarded as an omen for the coming harvest.

The Maria fish with nets and traps, by baling out water from pools or by poisoning the streams. Small fish, prawns, crabs and frogs are very popular roasted with spices and taken with the refreshing juice of the toddy or sago palm.

The tools and weapons of the Maria naturally figure frequently in their acts of violence. The most common implement of murder is the ordinary *godel* axe which corresponds to the *tangia* in universal use throughout central India. The Maria also use, chiefly for ceremonial purposes, a *pharsi* battle-axe with a crescent blade.

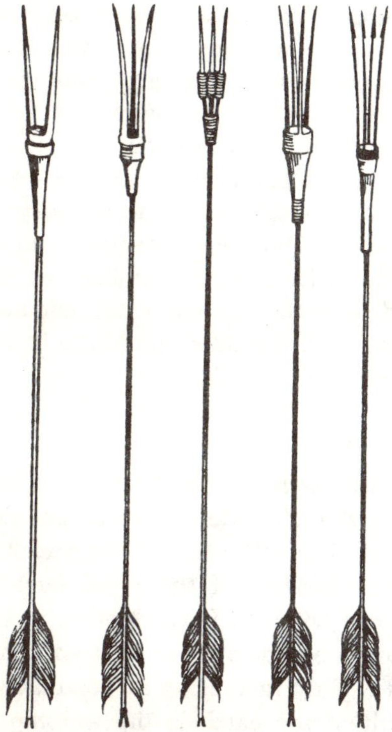

Engram arrows
(*Length about 3'*)

The *banda* or *gagra* is the Maria dao. The *banda* is a large knife with a broad end and rather a short handle used to cut bamboos and young trees. The *gagra* has a much longer handle and sometimes a point and a curved blade. It is not only very useful in the forest; it is a powerful weapon of assault. No spears feature in any of the murders described in this book, but the Maria have a fine spear used for stabbing. Bows and arrows are not unlike those in use elsewhere. The arrows are either pointed or clubbed. Pellet bows are used for killing birds, as is the *engram*, the many-pointed wooden arrow which is illustrated here. The pointed iron arrow is that employed in most of the murders by shooting or stabbing. But the *engram* was used in one or two cases.

Implements of domestic use include the heavy rice-husker which is so constantly in the hands of the women. With this Oyami Masa in a fit of rage battered his cousin to death at Jabeli.[1] The Bison-horn Maria hoe (*korki*) is similar to that common in the plains, and a man once used it to kill his mother in a fit of drunkenness.[2]

The Maria have no subsidiary industries worth the name. Spinning and weaving is taboo to them, though they are allowed to spin rope from hemp and grass. They make baskets of leaves and bamboo, but mostly for their own domestic use. They are expert at making mats, which they either weave with grass and reeds on a frame or plait with bamboo slats. The Maria do their own ironwork and do it well, for there is a plentiful supply of excellent ore. Those Maria who take to smelting and blacksmithery are regarded as inferior by the others, who generally do not intermarry or eat with them. This rule is not, however, absolute and in other ways the Maria blacksmiths live as members of the tribe, join their dances and festivals and share the common life. For statistical purposes I have included the Maria blacksmiths among the other Maria in this book.

III

The religion of the Maria centres round the Earth, the State and the Clan. The Earth is the ultimate source of life and is personified in the Village Mother. The State is represented by Danteshwari, the tutelary goddess of the royal family: she is now sometimes identified with the Earth Mother or the Village Mother, but she often has a shrine or at least an image of her own, and her cult is rapidly increasing in popularity.

Developing out of the cult of the earth is the worship of the clan-god. The traditional theory is that every clan is closely connected with a certain *bhum* or clan-territory. Each *bhum* has its special headquarters where there should be the temple of the clan-god and the residence of the clan-priest. Here members of the clan should bring some token of their Dead and come to celebrate the great clan festivals.

[1] Case No. 62. [2] Case No. 72.

PLATE I. Ancient Scene of Meriah Sacrifice at Goomsur, Khondistan
(From J. Campbell, *A Personal Narrative of Thirteen Years' Service*, 1864)

PLATE II. Tantia Bhil, a famous dacoit (from Russell & Hiralal, *Tribes and Castes of the Central Provinces*, 1916, by courtesy of Messrs Macmillan & Co. Ltd)

The clan-gods are known as Anga or Pen, and are of peculiar shape and character. They consist of three parallel logs attached to one another by cross-bars and decorated with silver bands and peacock feathers, the central log being carved into the rude likeness of a snake or bird. These gods are realistically imagined. They marry and have children; they move from place to place; they have a flair for detecting witches and other criminals. I do not know of any case where the Anga was used to track down a murder, but they are often employed to discover thefts and surprise the secrets of black magic.

The Bison-horn Maria are divided into a number of phratries and clans, resembling those of the Gond and other tribes. Grigson recorded five phratries, the Marvi, the Kuhrami, the Sori, the Markami and the Kawasi. Each of these is connected with a totem, the Marvi with the goat in some villages and the cobra in others, the Kuhrami with the cuckoo, the Sori with the tiger and the Markami and Kawasi with the tortoise. The subordinate clans, of which there are a large number—Grigson did not record quite all of them—are divided among these phratries and are regulated by the usual rule that regards all the clans of one phratry as related to one another and, therefore, barred from intermarriages. As I have said, each clan has its special and separate *bhum* or territory, which should be its exclusive possession. But the neat and tidy arrangements of former days have broken down, and now not only are members of several different clans to be found in one village, but members of the clans are widely dispersed and it is often difficult for them even to visit their clan-god and make the proper sacrifices with the help of the clan-priest, the Waddai, or attend the special festivals for the clan-god.

The Maria year is enriched and diversified by a long series of agricultural and other festivals. At the beginning of the year falls the Bhimul Pandum held in honour of the traditional rain-giver of central India. There follows a ceremony in praise of the mahua tree, before which the new mahua flowers must not be eaten or used for liquor. Then comes a similar ceremony in honour of the mango. This generally falls in March. It may be preceded by a ceremonial fishing expedition. In April, preceded by a ritual hunt, comes the great Seed Festival, the Wijja Pandum, at which the seed then to be sown is consecrated.

At the beginning of the rains many of the Maria now observe the Halba festival of Hareli or Amavas. As the crops ripen, there begins a series of Harvest Festivals or (as a literal translation of their Gondi name would have it) 'New Eating' Festivals. The first of these is for the small millets that ripen early. The next is for the new gourds and cucumbers. It is followed, at about the beginning of November, by the Nuka Nordana Pandum, a festival which falls at about the time of Diwali and is concerned with the new rice. Before this ceremony, the rice of the new harvest must not be husked or washed.

Towards the end of the year comes the Jata Pandum for new beans and pulses, and the Kare Pandum before which no one is allowed to cut grass or bamboo, or begin making clearings for cultivation in the forest.

In addition to this round of celebrations there are the festivals of the clan-gods, the Pen Karsita or Divine Games, which may be held at any time, and the commercial Mandai which are often combined with the clan festivals but are mainly great bazaars.

Dassara is the chief official festival of the State. It lasts fifteen days and is attended by elaborate ceremonies in which each of the aboriginal tribes has its special part to play. All the Maria headmen attend the celebrations in their official capacity, and there is a special Darbar at which they have the opportunity to place their grievances before the administration.

IV

The great dance that has given the Bison-horn Maria their name is really a marriage dance. At its best it is a superb spectacle. The men, in their splendid head-dresses of bison horns and carrying their long drums, move in a large circle with a great variety of turns and changes: the 'bison' charge and fight each other, pick up rings or leaves on the points of their horns, and chase the girl dancers. The girls, each with a dancing-stick in her right hand, form a long line and go round and through the men dancers with many different movements and steps. They do not usually sing, and indeed the tune would be lost in the thunder of the drums. As they go, they beat the ground with their sticks *dum-dum-dum, di-dum, dum-dum*. Masked mummers, clowns dressed in straw, naked acrobats with enormous imitation genitalia, add to the gaiety of the scene. There is no finer dance in India.

The head-dress of bison horns is the chief treasure of a Maria home. It is kept with the utmost care, dismantled, in closed bamboo baskets, and it takes nearly an hour to assemble it. Horns are rare nowadays in Bastar and have to be imported from Jeypore. A Maria may give a bull in exchange for a pair of good horns; they should be white at the bottom turning to black half way up.

A bamboo frame forms the base of the head-dress. The horns are attached to the front and a great tuft of feathers rises behind. Cloth, often old and costly silk, is tied round and round and a tail hangs down behind. Across the front a fringe of cloth adorned with cowries covers the dancer's eyes.

The feathers used are those of the peacock and of domestic cocks specially castrated for the purpose. It is considered unlucky for a feather to fall to the ground during a dance, and before they begin the dancers address the Earth Mother and the Ancestors: 'Save us from the dangers of magic and let none of the feathers fall.'

A man's head-dress passes to his son or brother's son after his death. His bow and arrow and his drum are also heirlooms and are highly valued. The loss of a head-dress drove one Maria youth to suicide, and a dispute about possession of an outfit of buttocks-bells led another to murder.

In the north of the area, many Maria dance both with bison horns and in Hill Maria fashion. The latter wear the skirt, decorated cap and streamers, and buttocks-bells characteristic of the Abujhmar Hills.

The Maria are not very good at musical instruments. They use a small fiddle called *kikir*, a jews'-harp made of iron or bamboo and the usual flute. They are fond of gongs, but these are not now so common as they were. At the great Pen Karsita at Ghotpal in 1942, the dancers used slabs of

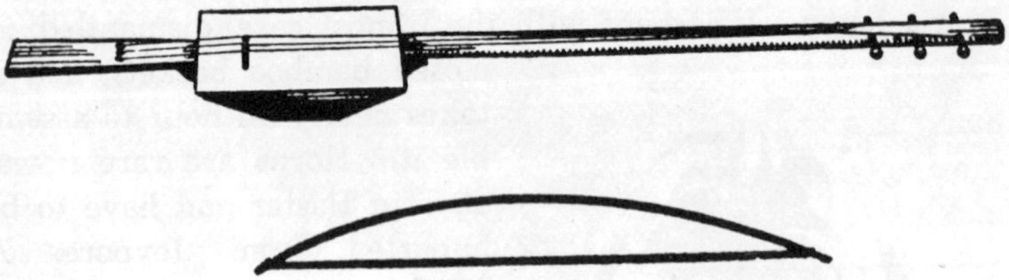

Kikir fiddle
(*Length 2'*)

coloured wood, bits of old tin and indeed anything that would make a noise instead of the traditional gongs. Like the Muria, at festivals and even for amusement the Maria use a hunting horn, either a real horn or one made of brass.

Besides dancing, the chief Maria relaxation is the cock-fight. At the conclusion of all the bigger bazaars, the men retire to a grove of trees and set their cocks against each other. The cocks are armed with sharp and deadly little knives tied to their feet and fights are to the death. The victor has the privilege of taking the defeated bird, but the real excitement comes from the betting.

V

The ceremonies attending birth and marriage are very simple. The pregnant mother is not hampered by many restrictions on her movements. After the birth of the child the placenta is buried in a pit behind the house. Logs are placed above it and the arrow with which the cord was cut is driven into the ground near by. A small shed is made and the mother lives here for some weeks with her child, taking a daily bath above the placenta-pit. At the end of this period of segregation, the husband gives a feast to the neighbours, the child is named and the mother is permitted to return to her household duties. It was to such a feast that the unhappy victim of the Mardum sacrifice was enticed.[1]

There are no ceremonies of initiation at puberty, though a girl's first menstruation is marked by special rites of purification. There is little conscious education of the young who grow up in natural freedom and learn by imitation. Marriage is generally adult but is arranged by the parents, and the cross-cousin marriage is common. Betrothal ceremonies are simple. The boy's father goes with gifts and a traditional formula is used: 'We have heard there is a flower growing in your garden. We have come to pluck it and put it in our hair.' If a boy's family cannot afford the bride-price required, they may send him to serve as a Lamhada in the house of his future wife. His period of service is for three or five years, and the marriage is often celebrated before it is complete. Marriage by capture, which was probably the traditional method, has not yet died out, and occasionally there is a case of the reverse tradition when a girl comes as a Paitu and forces herself upon a man who is bound to marry her. Widow-remarriage is permitted and indeed enjoined, the husband's younger brother having the first claim on the person and property of the widow. Divorce is rare but is available to either husband or wife. The wife usually achieves it by eloping with another man and the husband in most cases accepts a *fait accompli.*

The actual marriage ceremony is also simple. There is no anointing with turmeric or oil, no perambulation of the sacred pole. Customs vary from place to place, but the traditional marriage has probably only three elements—a celebration which includes feasting, drinking and dancing, the pouring of water from the roof of a house or shed onto the bridal pair and the ceremonial consummation of the marriage at which bride and bridegroom are forcibly shut up in a room together.

VI

Funeral ceremonies are more elaborate, and since this book is concerned with death, we will consider them in greater detail.

[1] Case No. 31.

Maria thinking about the destiny and state of the soul after death is as confused as that of more sophisticated people. At least three contradictory views of the subject are held at the same time. I think that the oldest and characteristically primitive opinion is that the soul goes to dwell with the ancestral Dead with whom it is mingled by appropriate ceremonies. These Dead are imagined as being in close touch with their kinsfolk living still on earth and are able to influence their affairs.

But side by side with this belief is a rudimentary theory of transmigration and rebirth, and at every funeral there are special rites to ensure that the soul will be reborn in the same family and will not go elsewhere. This theory is not necessarily inconsistent with the first, though it is not easy to see how once a soul is reborn again on earth it can continue to hold the office and perform the functions of an Ancestor. But the third theory is contradictory of the others. It is borrowed from the graveyard traditions of popular Hinduism. After death the soul is pictured as turning into a dangerous malignant ghost who has to be kept away from the house at all costs and be appeased from time to time with small offerings. We thus have the ridiculous situation that at a funeral some of the rites are directed to bringing the dead man's soul back to the house and settling him there in the Pot of the Departed while others are directed at keeping him at a distance, if possible beyond the village boundary. After death, in fact, the dead man becomes both soul and ghost, and suitable but different arrangements have to be made for each of these aspects of his personality.

We have seen that in the inner room of every Maria house there is kept an earthen pot specially dedicated to the Dead; in the same room is the Hearth of the Departed. It is round this little shrine that there centres an extensive cult of the ancestral Dead. At the end of the funeral ceremonies the soul of the deceased is mingled with the other Dead through ceremonies connected with this Pot. Into it the woman of the house puts a little flour in honour of the Dead when she grinds, and here she cooks new grain at the harvest festivals. The Dead are very touchy and excitable. If the soul of a murdered man or a suicide or anyone who has died by tiger, snake, cholera, small-pox, drowning or a fall from a tree is sent to keep them company, there will be quarrels and in their annoyance they may cause great trouble to the living. They are specially sensitive to any infidelity on the part of the wife, whose special duty it is to tend their shrine. They indicate their will to the living through the Siraha or Waddai and by appearing to them in dreams, and it is considered highly dangerous to ignore their behests.

The necessity for their propitiation has affected every aspect of Maria life. Offerings are made to them at every festival and at every domestic or village ceremony. They are remembered as a matter of routine in every magic formula along with the Earth Mother, Danteshwari and other deities. A few drops of liquor are offered to them every time a Maria drinks. Fire from the hearth of the Pot of the Departed in the Gaita's house is used to light the first fire in the forest clearings and the sacred fires at festivals. The importance of the Ancestors, who remain as a sort of conservative society to safeguard the traditions of the tribe, will appear throughout this book and need not be elaborated now.

VII

Women dying in pregnancy or child-birth are buried, so are the victims of small-pox and of such other diseases as the Siraha may from time to time direct. All others are cremated, a fact which often makes police investigation difficult and even impossible.

At one time (I am not sure how far the custom survives) the Waddai was buried naked and in an upright posture. The first child of a house, if it dies under five years old, is buried in the same erect posture, with face to the east—as there is light there, and beneath a mahua tree—for it is fertile of flowers and fruit, a good omen for the family.

In a funeral the chief actors are the Hanagunda or Hanalgaita, who is the master of ceremonies, and the sister's son or son-in-law of the deceased. The Hanagunda has to tie a thread round the corpse and hang the cow's-tail on the menhir. It is his wife's duty to wash the body, and to take cooked rice and haldi to the pyre. The sister's son has to climb on the roof to beat a drum to summon the relatives: he sits on the uraskal while it is being carried to its place;

he makes the appointed offerings before the stone: he kills the sacrificial and festal cow.

After death the dead man is laid with his head to the east in the living room of his house. His sister's son takes a stick and measures straight upwards from the corpse's chest to the roof, poking the stick through the thatch. Then he climbs up to the roof and makes a hole which is intended symbolically to allow the message of death to spread out through the world. He puts his dhol drum above the hole, waves a stick thrice round his head and then beats his drum with the rhythm *dung dung-dung*. He beats with one hand, though the normal method is to beat with two. After the drumming has continued for a while, he comes down from the roof and continues it on the ground.

The Hanagunda's wife now husks some rice, makes it into four packets with leaves and ties two of these under the arms of the corpse and two at its waist. She applies to the chest black dust from the bottom of one of the cooking utensils so that they may be able to recognize him when he is reborn. The grand-daughter of the dead man, if available, or some girl in the same relationship, passes a string seven times round his three middle fingers and middle toes, again with the intention of ensuring his return.

It will be most convenient if I describe the actual course of a ceremony which occurred at Penta on 10 February 1942. This funeral is of special interest as the mourners had reason to believe that the dead man was the victim of black magic.

Sori Kosa of Penta had a love affair with the daughter-in-law of Markami Bando which resulted in a serious quarrel between the two families. Kosa's father paid the necessary fine and a special ceremony of peace and friendship was performed. But Bando was not really reconciled—and soon trouble began for Kosa's family. His son by his first wife died, shortly afterwards another of his sons died. One day Bando spat on Kosa's father in the bazaar. A week later the old man fell ill and died. Kosa's wife and daughter were also taken ill but recovered. The villagers whispered that this was due to Bando's magic, and described how he had made a small doll of earth, wrapped it up in a leaf-cup and carried it away into the jungle. But there was no case for police interference, and the villagers proceeded with the funeral for Kosa's father.

After the preliminary rites that I have already described, all Kosa's father's relatives assembled. The women brought brass rings and beads and placed them on the corpse; the men brought bits of cloth. The members of the household fasted from the time of the old man's death until he was cremated. The ceremonies were marked by violent manifestations of grief. When the bamboo bier was brought to the house, the wives of the Waddai, Gaita and Hanagunda fell upon it and lay there. They said that this meant that they too wanted to be taken out and burnt, a curious echo of the Sati tradition. Straw was spread on the bier and when the corpse had been placed there, bits of cloth were laid on it by the male relatives present. The women gathered round the corpse again, kissing it and weeping bitterly. It had been lying with its legs towards the door of the house, but now it was lifted up by the bearers and its position changed so that the head was pointing to the door. They touched the door thrice with it saying, 'You made this house, come here again in your next birth'.

Then, led by the drummers, the corpse was carried out to the cremation-ground. The grand-daughter with her hair undone followed immediately behind the bier throwing rice upon it as she went along. As they passed a path that crossed theirs, they dropped a little rice so that if any other ghost came he would eat it and go away. Everyone went to the funeral. Menstruating women are not normally allowed to attend, though sometimes they may come if they stand at a little distance.

When the party reached the pyre, they went round it anticlockwise once and placed the bier on the ground. Once again the women fell upon the corpse weeping and kissing it. They lay down beside the pyre and had to be pushed away before the business of the funeral could proceed.

Then one of the women put a little tobacco in the mouth of the corpse. The body was placed upon the pyre. Some of the bits of cloth with which it was covered were left there; the rest was distributed between the drummers and the relatives by marriage. The Hanagunda removed the packets of rice which had been tied to the waist of the corpse and threw them to left and right. The body was entirely covered with a cloth and the Hanagunda ripped this open just over the mouth. A piece of grass which had been brought from the roof of the house was put into the mouth of the corpse and then thrown aside. It is very important that this grass should not be burnt. The aim of the rite was to ensure that the man would be able to breathe on his journey to the next world, though other informants said that it was to allow the soul to escape. The brother-in-law of the dead man then lit a bundle of grass with fire brought from the house and after taking a turn round the pyre set fire to the pile of wood by the head. Another man went round in the opposite direction and fired the wood by the legs.

After the pyre was well alight, the whole company went to a stream and washed themselves. The grand-daughter soaked part of her sari in water and holding the wet portion in her hand came home and rinsed it out on the very place where the coffin had lain inside the house so that the dead man could drink it.

Early next morning, the dead man's son-in-law went to the cremation-ground to examine the ashes and there found an earthen doll tied in a leaf-cup. This led the Waddai to declare that the death was due to black magic done by Bando and concealed by him in the jungle.

Later in the morning a cow was brought and its legs washed by the deceased's daughter-in-law. After touching its forehead with a little rice she said to it, 'We have given you your share, now don't make us suffer any longer'. One of the drum-beaters touched the cow with his stick and a marriage-relative killed it by a heavy blow with the blunt end of his axe. He then cut the tail, removed the liver and made it into twenty-four pieces in equal shares of six pieces each. Each share was wrapped up in a leaf and roasted. The party took these to the cremation-ground. On reaching the place some of the women picked out the bones from the pyre and kissed them. The dead man's son collected any half-burnt pieces of wood and kicked them towards the centre of the pyre. Then they cleared the ash where the corpse's head had been, cow-dunged the place and put the leaf-cups there.

The packets containing the liver were now opened and three pieces from each packet were placed on the ground and three in each of the leaf-cups. The twelve pieces on the ground were for the Earth and the twelve pieces in the leaf-cups for the Dead. The Waddai made seven piles of rice. He held a piece of wood in his hand and lifting it over each pile several times from right to left uttered charms calling on the soul of the deceased to be content. The dead man's son brought a chicken and made it eat the rice, going from right to left three times. The Waddai passed his stick quickly over the chicken each time. However, when the fowl was eating the rice, it did not follow the proper order, but started to eat the sixth pile after the fourth. The Waddai declared that this was because two persons were involved in the fatal magic. After this had been done three times, the dead man's son passed the chicken between his legs backwards and twisted its neck till it was severed from the trunk. This he threw behind him, holding the head in his hands. He ripped open the head by cutting it through the beak and threw it into the fire. If this was not done, the head might turn into a bird of ill-omen.

They then dug a hole in the earth close to the leaf-cups with a knife and placed a forked saja stick there. The dead man's son stood in front of the stick with his back to it, holding the cow's tail in his hand. He pointed it first at the sun, then to the four corners of the world and lastly to the place where the dead body had been cremated. He did this thrice and then tied the tail to the stick and poured a little landa on it. The dead man's wife offered some mahua liquor in a leaf-cup, because when her husband was alive one day when they were drinking they had agreed to die together. The Waddai, therefore, said as she was giving the liquor, 'Do not also take her away with you; release her from her promise; let her live for a while and look after the other members of the family'. Then the deceased's son and brother-in-law, who had carried the rice and pulse, threw it down near the stick. The dead man's son who had also taken with him a little thatch from the roof of his house now threw this at the stick saying, 'You built the house, now accept this'. Similarly, all the other things of which the old man had been fond when he was alive were thrown there. His son-in-law, however, picked up his bow and arrow and his knife was taken by one of the drummers. The drummers then threw away their drum-sticks into the ashes of the pyre.

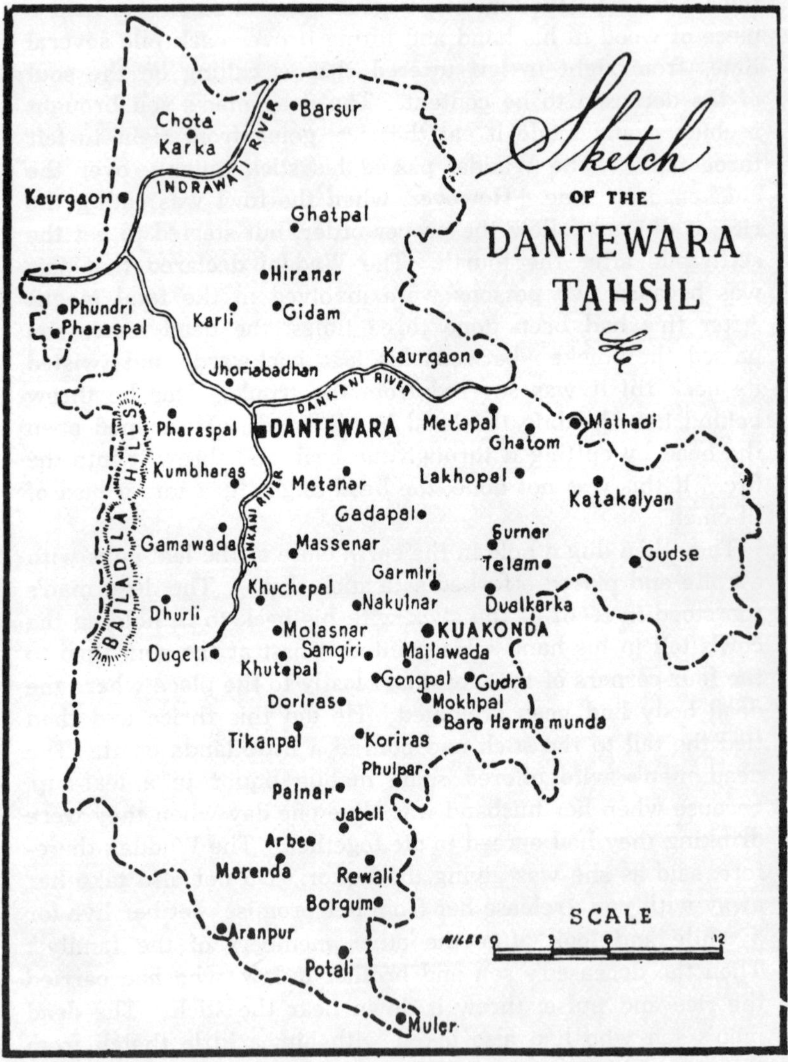

Once again the party went to the stream, but the Gaita and the Waddai stayed behind and addressed the saja stick : 'For one month more you will get nothing, don't go to your house, but stay here.' After a bath they all (with the exception of the drummers) went to the deceased's house. The drummers, who are regarded as unclean for the duration of the ceremony, bathed and washed their drums. They placed some rice on the drums. To them they also sacrificed a chicken and offered the blood and some liquor. The drummers were then given rice, which they cooked separately, and a shoulder of the cow. After eating their food they went to their own houses.

The conclusion of the story is worth recording. A month later, the Waddai went with the villagers to the boundary of the village carrying a chicken, a pig, an egg, egg-shells, a bamboo bow and arrow, burnt earth from below the hearth, charcoal powder, rice, pulse and haldi. All these things were taken in separate leaf-cups. The Waddai arranged them in seven rows and made a chicken eat the rice, calling on Markami Bando's magic to go away. The chicken ate the rice quickly. But this was not sufficient proof that the black magic had really been driven away, 'because every hungry creature will naturally feed upon what it can get'. The Waddai, therefore, tortured the chicken, first by breaking one leg, and still it ate; he broke another leg, and again it ate; then he broke the wings and the fowl though in pain and agony went on eating. It was now beyond doubt that Bando's magic had been dealt with successfully and the chicken was thrown away, still alive, and not sacrificed. The pig was then sacrificed and the Waddai drew a line on the boundary of the village where the seven rows were arranged, spat there and said, 'Away from this line' and they all departed without looking back. In this ceremony the household members did not take part.

The next day the Waddai sacrificed under a mahua tree near the house a white chicken and broke an egg in honour of the ancestral ghost of Kosa's father. After this he entered the house and sprinkled it with a mixture of milk, saja bark, and dab grass to purify it and sacrificed a black chicken for the Ancestors of the family.

Special precautions must, of course, be taken when anyone dies a violent death. The ghost of a man killed by a tiger may possess the animal and drive it to take vengeance on other members of the community: the victim of snake-bite dwells in the snake's tail and drives it to homicidal fury.[1]

Women dying in pregnancy and childbirth become very dangerous after death and their ghosts must be laid by special ceremonies which include the driving of nails into the knees and elbows of the corpse and at the four corners of the grave, over which a herd of buffaloes may sometimes be driven.

VIII

In the neighbourhood of almost every Maria village will be found a row of menhirs erected in memory and for the appeasement of the Dead. Sometimes these stones are very large; sometimes they are quite small and are expected to grow bigger in course of time. The majority of clans erect an upright pillar which is called uraskal. But a number of them place instead a danyakal, a large flat stone supported on four smaller ones.

In the ceremonies attending the bringing of a menhir, the sister's son again plays a leading part. Led by him a party of three drummers and a man beating a gong and twenty or thirty men go out to the quarry where the stone has already been cut out or to some hill where a suitable rock has been observed. The sister's son touches the stone and addresses the dead man. 'In your name', he says 'we are bringing this stone; let it be light, let not the burden be too heavy.' They place poles below and above the stone, lashing them together with rope. Then the sister's son with a drum in his hand climbs on to the stone and begins to drum with a new rhythm which goes *gul-gucha, gul-gucha, gul-gucha.* Some twenty men lift up the stone whistling loudly, *soor, soor, whee, whee,* and swing it to and fro. Then they move towards the place where the menhir is to be erected, the drummers dancing and drumming in front, the sister's son beating his drum above. From time to time they put their burden on the ground to rest, and are refreshed with rice-beer.

[1] Such accidental deaths are far from uncommon. In 1938, in the whole State 55 persons were killed by tigers, 10 by panthers, 4 by bears, 53 by drowning, 102 by snake-bite, 53 by falling from trees (chiefly the tall toddy and sago palms). The great majority of these accidents were to aboriginals and every one involved the relatives in complex and hazardous ceremonies for their protection.

When the party reaches the pit that has been prepared, the drummers throw the castor-sticks which they have been using hitherto on to the pyre, and take new sticks, which may be made of any kind of wood. Before the stone is erected the Gaita addresses the dead: 'You are dead and you must forget your father, your mother, your brother and your family. This is your house. Live here and do not trouble us or our pigs and cattle. We are giving you rice and pulse and everything that you had at home, so that you may be satisfied.'

In the hole which has been dug by the sister's son, the relatives put something or other, rice, small coins, rings or ornaments, whatever they can afford. The bearers untie the stone from its poles and all push and lift it into position. Earth and stones are rammed round the bottom and a small cromlech is placed in front. On this stone offerings are made by the sister's son with his back to the menhir. The women of the household come and put cooked rice and haldi in leaf-cups on the cromlech, and pour upon it grain, roots, or anything that the dead man used to like when he was alive.

Then the whole party returns to the house and one or more cows are sacrificed. These were probably selected by the dead man during his life-time. They remove the liver and cut it in pieces. Rice is prepared in the house of the dead and divided into four portions and put in leaf-cups. These cups, with the tail of the sacrificed cow and a pot of rice-beer, are carried out in a specially-made basket to the menhir. One portion is put on the ground for Mother Earth and the rest for the dead man on the cromlech. The tail is hung over the menhir and rice-beer poured upon it. At the same time a little rice-beer must be offered to the old menhirs. If this is omitted the ancient dead will be angry and will quarrel with the new spirit that has gone to join them.

Rice-beer must be given both to the menhir and to the mourners. It must be made fresh in the room where death occurred and served with a gourd with a long handle that has been specially hollowed out for this purpose. Usually there is no stock of rice-beer at hand and it cannot be made so quickly. The Maria then mix a little mandia flour with water and give this instead.

If for any reason in the course of the ceremony some rite or custom is omitted the spirit of the dead man may attack one or other of the mourners in order to show his displeasure. For example, at Gadapal, Burka Peda told me that they once forgot to give landa to the old menhirs and the insulted Dead attacked his father's sister and she fell down in a fit. They quickly gave both landa and mahua liquor to all the menhirs and she recovered. Again in Mahara-Karka one Kuhrami Eriya was hurled into the fire by the angry ghost and his leg was burnt. If this happens it is a good plan for the victim to run and catch hold of the bamboo poles with which the stone was carried. The Gaita pours water upon him and the angry ghost leaves him alone.

IX

When a very well-known or wealthy man dies his family sometimes erects a carved wooden pillar to his memory. There are very few of these pillars, though the custom of making them is far from moribund, but the expense is great and only the most important people are considered worthy of them.

These pillars are called by Grigson urasgatta, a word that is obviously formed on the same plan as uraskal, from *urasna* meaning 'to bury' and *gatta*—'a pillar'. I have not myself found any Maria using the word or even recognizing it when it has been put to them. It may be that its use has died out. The Maria to whom I have spoken call these pillars either *munde* (Gondi) or *kambha* (Halbi or Hindi).

The pillars are usually erected near a highway—not necessarily a motorable one. It should simply be near any road or path that is constantly used by the people. The pillars are usually made of saja or sarai wood and are erected with ceremonies very similar to those for a stone.

There are not many of these pillars, but they are worth looking at. There is a very fine one near Dilmilli on the main road from Jagdalpur to Dantewara. Near Massenar at the end of a long line of menhirs is the pillar

PLATE III. Girls fetching water at Bastanar

PLATE IV. Girl with sheaf

in memory of the famous Kopa Dhurwa, which has a carving of the old man wearing his jubilee medal. There are others at Chinger, on the way to Chitrakot and in a few other places.

Each pillar attempts to be a biography in wood of the deceased. We see him important carrying the symbols of wealth and power and riding on a horse or elephant; we see the dancers that delighted him and the landa pot which never failed to give him pleasure. We are shown the knives and axes that he used; the animals that he saw or hunted in the forest. The pillar for Oyami Masa, the homicide, had several carvings illustrating his work as a Siraha.

X

Every Maria village has a panel of secular and religious officials. There is the headman (often called the Peda), his assistant (the Kandki) and a Kotwar, who has the duty of reporting to the police all births and deaths within his jurisdiction. Each group of villages belongs to what is called a Pargana, a relic of the older administrative system of the State, and at the head of each Pargana there is a Pargana Manjhi. Each village has its panchayat presided over by the village headman, and each Pargana has a Pargana panchayat which is a Court of Appeal. In 1932, the village panchayats among all the aboriginals in Bastar were entrusted with a certain amount of criminal and civil work. The regular Courts were deprived of jurisdiction over the tribesmen for no fewer than seventeen Sections of the Indian Penal Code, including those dealing with simple hurt and assault, thefts of property up to five rupees, mischief, trespass and adultery. The panchayats were permitted to deal with claims for civil damages that might arise out of the criminal offences, and in other civil claims not exceeding twentyfive rupees. They were permitted to impose fines of not more than twentyfive, and in marriage cases to allow expenses up to fifty rupees. The Kotwar had the business of reporting panchayat decisions to the police. An appeal lay to the Pargana Manjhi and his panchayat which consisted of four headmen chosen from his group of villages.

In the ten years since these panchayats were established, they have done a great deal of work, and on the whole may be said to have functioned very well. A few headmen have abused their positions; there has been a certain amount of diversion of fines to uses for which they were not intended; probably a number of less influential people have not always had the justice that they might have expected. But this might have happened even in the ordinary Courts, and there is no doubt whatever that the establishment of these panchayats has done a great deal to build up the self-respect of Maria and Muria, and has developed leadership among them.

The importance of the panchayat for our subject is obvious. In the first place, it provides a body of semi-official elders in every village whose duty it is to assist the police, and indeed whenever a suspicious death occurs in a village, the investigating officer calls the panchayat for a sort of inquest to which he acts as coroner and they as jury. On the other hand, the establishment of the village elders in a position of considerable authority makes it easy for them, when they wish to do so, to conceal a crime or deal with it themselves. Where a headman is himself the culprit, he may force the people to hush up his guilt; and the solidarity that is created by allowing the village under its own elders to settle many of its own affairs helps the headman to attain this end. This is no argument against the establishment of the panchayat. But it does mean that it is important for the authorities to hold the confidence of the headmen, and to inspire them constantly with a sense of their civic duties.

Side by side with the secular leaders are the religious elders of the village, though there is no reason why spiritual and secular functions should not be, as they often are, combined in the same persons. The priests and medicine-men naturally have more influence than the official headmen, the most powerful combination being when the headman himself is a Waddai or Siraha.

Chief among the religious elders is the Bhum-Gaita or Perma, the priest of the soil whose duty it is to see to all the sacrifices concerned with the village and its festivals, and to perform the worship of the Village Mother. The Pen-Waddai or Waddai is the priest of the clan who fulfils spiritual duties for its members. There may be more than one Waddai in a village or, on the other hand, one Waddai may have jurisdiction over several villages. Everything depends on the distribution of the clan members in the locality. The Waddai is of great importance because of his association with the Ancestors and the Dead. He has to purify offenders against the clan rules, and those who have done anything which might conceivably offend the Dead. The Hanagunda may be the Waddai or some lesser personage. His duty is to act as master of ceremonies at a funeral and to perform the special rites of appeasement for the ghost. He becomes of great importance when anyone has met an unnatural death such as being killed by a tiger or has been executed.

In addition to these regular priests, there are a large number of men who are regarded as being in a special way the servants and interpreters of the gods. These men have the power of falling into ecstasy and in this condition divine the will and proclaim the wishes of unseen beings. They are called Siraha or Gunia. They are chiefly in demand for the cure of disease. Since disease is believed to be the result of supernatural activity on the part of some ghost or demon, it is by supernatural means that it must be diagnosed and cured. The Siraha often has houses round his compound for in-patients, and a celebrated medicine-man may attract sick and anxious people from a wide area.

These men, civil or religious, are the real rulers of the Bastar village. Their influence is more far-reaching, their word is of greater effect than that of the most popular officials. Only the Maharaja, from whom they derive their power, is greater. Today their power is greatly circumscribed, but, as we shall see, it has not altogether disappeared. They can still make unbearable the life of witch or sorcerer; they can still ostracize the social rebel; they can still fine the domestic tyrant and subdue the village bully. The ordeal by fire or burning oil still remains a weapon in their hands, and the threat of excommunication is a greater deterrent than many of the provisions of the Indian Penal Code.

The religious leaders insist on the supernatural dangers of crime, the defilement of jail or handcuffs, the painful death that may follow an unatoned adultery, the offence to the Ancestors of division within the clan. The secular leaders are more concerned with the fatiguing inconvenience of a police inquiry, and the embarrassment and waste of time of going as witnesses to a distant court. Village officialdom, it may be safely said, is anxious to prevent crime. It is equally anxious, when a crime has been committed, to hush it up. But hushing up does not mean that crimes will go unpunished. This might well bring on a village the vengeance of the Dead.

Behind this intense belief and organized activity native to the soil rises the massive and alien structure of the Indian Penal Code. This majestic formulary was first drafted in 1837 by a Law Commission under the presidentship of Lord Macaulay. Its provisions extend throughout India, and it was applied with certain modifications to Bastar. The Civil Code of India is also largely operative in the area. We thus have the remarkable, but not unusual, picture of tribesmen still deeply attached to their own ethical and penal system, still regulating their lives by their own laws of ownership, partition and inheritance, but unable to invoke any sanctions to enforce them and compelled in time of need to turn to a foreign Code that was made without any reference to their traditions and the conditions under which they live. J. H. Hutton has called attention to the result:

> Tribal customs which regulate the ownership, usufruct or transfer of land are normally superseded by a code in the application of which the tribe is deprived of its property, generally in the name of law, either by alienation to foreigners or by transferring the trusteeship of a tribal chief into absolute ownership of a kind quite foreign to the customs of a tribe. This has befallen both the Munda and the hill tribes of Chittagong, while even in Rajputana a somewhat similar process has been at work. A similar application of alien law also usually disturbs the tribal customs of debt. The criminal law of a civilized community is often at variance with what is felt to be just and proper by tribal custom. The complicated system of administration of justice has tended to impair the natural truthfulness and honesty of the people and social solidarity of the tribes and has weakened the authority of the social heads and the respect they formerly commanded.

CHAPTER THREE

THE STATISTICS OF VIOLENT CRIME

I

THE Bison-horn Maria have long had a bad reputation for violence and drunkenness. But before this reputation is accepted as scientific fact we should examine the matter statistically and in detail. I will give first a Table which will show the total homicidal crimes in Bastar under Sections 302 and 304 of the Indian Penal Code during the 10 years 1931 to 1940.

TABLE ONE

NUMBER OF HOMICIDE CASES IN BASTAR (UNDER SECTIONS 302 AND 304 I.P.C.) FOR 10 YEARS, 1931-40

—	Bison-horn Maria	Ghotul Muria of the North	Others (whole State)	Total
1931	8	1	7	16
1932	14	3	10	27
1933	8	1	10	19
1934	19	2	16	37
1935	14	2	7	23
1936	8	—	14	22
1937	8	2	12	22
1938	13	2	13	28
1939	15	1	9	25
1940	14	7	18	39
Total ...	121	21	116	258

The next Table will relate these figures to the estimated population, both for the tribes and for the State.

The striking difference in the number of murders committed by the Bison-horn Maria and their neighbours, the Ghotul Muria, is probably to be explained by the fact that the Muria have in their Ghotul or dormitory system an ideal method of training the youth of the tribe in the civic virtues, in eliminating jealousy and in teaching everyone to live together

TABLE TWO

ILLUSTRATING THE RELATION OF HOMICIDE CASES TO THE ESTIMATED POPULATION

——		Population in 1941	Annual average of homicides	Average annual incidence of homicides to the million[1]
Bison-horn Maria	...	175,000	12·1	69·14
Ghotul Muria	...	100,000	2·1	21·00
Others	...	360,000	11·6	32·22
Total	...	635,000	25·8	40·63

as a family. Even the few murders that do take place among the Ghotul Muria occur, for the most part, in villages which have for one reason or another lost their dormitories. 'Reformers' who would banish the dormitory from tribal India should very carefully consider this fact before they do so.

It is not easy to obtain comparative figures for other tribes or communities in India. There is a Maria (but not Bison-horn Maria) population in the Chanda District: here there were 26 cases of homicide in 10 years among a population of 34,776—which works out near the Bison-horn Maria figure of 69 to the million. In Mayurbhanj State, in 1935-6 there were 25 similar cases from a population of about 890,000 or about 28 to the million. In 1939, there were 184 persons found guilty under Sections 302 and 304 I.P.C. in the Central Provinces and Berar, which gives a figure of approximately 11 to the million. In the same Province, with its total population of some eighteen millions, 53 persons were sentenced to death and 131 to transportation in 1941. The figures for 1942 were 59 and 127.

Against these figures, the incidence of 69 homicides to the million among Bison-horn Maria seems very high, but it must be remembered that the inhabitants of this part of India are among the most peaceful people on this planet.[2] Laubscher

[1] Based on the population estimates for 1941.

[2] With the exception of the small Bondo tribe of Orissa, where the homicide rate is very high—see my *Bondo Highlander* (in press), ch. viii.

gives some comparative statistics from various parts of the world. The rate of homicide among South African pagans was 171 per million in 1935. In 1924, Canada had a homicide rate of 15 per million. In 1926, the rate for England and Wales was 7 per million. In the same year the rate for the U.S.A. was 52 per million for the white population and 454 per million for the Negroes.[1]

In India at least all such calculations are bound to be rough and ready. The population figures for individual tribes and areas are often in doubt: some police statistics include all cases of violent death, some only the 'true' homicides. There can be no doubt that many crimes are concealed from the police. But the figures may serve as a basis of discussion.

Do these figures, such as they are, suggest that one race is more predisposed to crime than another? Bonger,[2] after a full discussion of the evidence, decides against this view:

> To speak of criminal races (in which all the individuals would be criminal) is pure nonsense. No person comes into the world a criminal (if one omits consideration of pathological cases—*insania moralis*). There are differences, though probably exaggerated, between the races, particularly in the psychological sphere. How far are these differences relevant in the study of crime?
>
> First of all, the most flagrant contradiction is sometimes witnessed between criminological facts and what is psychologically known. The Nordic race is pictured, for example, as being violent in its inherent nature, but its aggressive criminality is (with exceptions!) small. The Jewish race, to take another example, numbers very probably a greater percentage of nervous cases than others, but it counts few crimes of violence, although the 'nervous type' is somewhat predisposed to this sort of crime.
>
> On the other hand, there are cases in which there is indeed agreement between criminological and psychological facts. We limit ourselves to the temperament, very nearly the only fact about which we may speak with any certainty. (There is, for instance, not the least shadow of evidence that races show a congenital dis-

[1] Laubscher, op. cit., p. 307. But von Hentig, in a careful analysis of the quantitative aspect of crime, concludes that such statistics must be regarded with caution. 'Comparative statistics for murder, for instance, must be accepted with the greatest reserve'.—H von Hentig, *Crime: Causes and Conditions* (New York 1947), p. 77.

[2] W. A. Bonger, *Race and Crime* (New York, 1943), pp. 105 ff.

> honesty.) As an example, and a striking one, we choose the aggressive criminality of the Mediterraneans. This is great, and their temperament is quick and violent. Naturally this is only true in general; the breadth of variation within one race is ordinarily great, so that one section of a naturally non-violent race is more violent than one section of a naturally violent race: 'overlapping curves.' Here, as I see it, one can speak of a certain predisposition, just as this is the case within one race where the individuals likewise differ in temperament.
>
> Has one the right, now, to qualify this predisposition as criminal? As I see it, this question must be answered emphatically in the negative. There is no question of special predisposition for crime. A lively, violent disposition also predisposes to other deeds, least of all to crime. The phlegmatic type (to name the opposite temperament) are worthy, dutiful burghers in general, but the pioneers of mankind mostly do not belong to this type. In other words, it becomes a question of the circumstances under which a man has lived from birth, and under which he still lives. A choleric temperament is dangerous under quite other conditions. In this connexion it is important to remark that female criminality is generally slight in lands where aggressive crime is frequent, although the women belong to the same race as the men.

We may conclude then that the comparatively high incidence of homicide among the Maria is due to social and economic factors rather than to their racial affiliations.

II

I have already spoken of the 100 files of homicide cases which I have examined. Brief epitomes of these are given in an Appendix. These cases covered a period of 20 years, during which the total number of homicides could not have been more than 250—there were 121 Maria homicides in the last 10 years and the amount of crime was certainly not greater in the first decade than in the second. I have included only those cases which ended in the conviction of one or more of the accused.

The 100 cases involved the conviction of 177 people as follows:

PLATE V. A girl cleans grain in a field at Garmiri: failure in preparing food is sometimes a cause of tragedy

PLATES VI-VII. The famo

son-horn marriage dance

PLATE VIII. Maria girl of Mokhpal. Domestic life is usually happy: the rare infidelities quickly lead to revenge

TABLE THREE

PUNISHMENTS AWARDED IN 100 CASES, INVOLVING THE CONVICTION OF 117 PERSONS

Sentenced to death under S. 302 I.P.C.	21
Executed	18
Transportation for life (14 years' imprisonment under S. 302, I.P.C.)	57
Various terms of imprisonment under S. 304, I.P.C.	39
Acquitted but detained as insane under S. 471, Cr.P.C.[1]	3

The great majority of persons convicted were men, as the next Table shows.

TABLE FOUR

SEX-RATIO IN 100 CASES, INVOLVING 117 CONVICTIONS

Male	112
Female	5

The Bison-horn Maria do not live in complete isolation. They are in contact with other people, what are often called civilized people. But this contact is mainly a business and commercial contact; it is not an emotional one. Normally there are few chances in any relationship between a Maria and a Hindu or Mussalman for the development of those intense and passionate feelings that may lead to murder. This will probably account for the very small number of people murdered who belonged to other communities. Two of these were killed for their possessions in straightforward robbery—very unusual incidents. One of the victims was a Kalar who was going to report a cattle-theft. One was a boy caught in a madman's fury. But it might have been anyone. Another was a Rawat. But the Rawat, who are the herdsmen of the Maria, live so closely with them as to count

[1] This Section provides for the detention in safe custody of a person whose act would 'but for the incapacity found, have constituted an offence'. It does not involve detention in an asylum though it may lead to this. Deaf and dumb persons guilty of murder have been proceeded against under this Section.

almost as members of the tribe. Once during a gambling quarrel a Mahara beat a Maria, a serious matter involving the Maria's excommunication. In one case a Mahara woman was chosen as a human sacrifice. In only one case was a member of another caste involved with a Maria woman. A Dhobi tried to seduce a Maria girl, but it was the girl who was murdered.

TABLE FIVE

ILLUSTRATING CASTE OF VICTIMS IN 107 CASES

Fellow-Maria . . .	99
Members of other castes . .	8

I have heard, however, of another case (not among the 100) where the wife of a Maria, one Poyami Masa, at Kodenar had an intrigue with a Kalar liquor-vendor. One night very late the woman—according to previous arrangement—got up and went behind the house, ostensibly to relieve herself, thinking her husband asleep. But he was really watching and when she did not return, he went in search for her and found her in sexual congress with the Kalar. He returned to the house, got his bow and double-pointed *engram* arrow and killed her. The Kalar made his escape.

III
SEASONAL VARIATIONS

The relative predominance of constitutional factors in crimes of violence and lust are believed by European criminologists to explain the striking differences in the seasonal frequency of these crimes. Sullivan gives a Table based on the police reports of indictable offences for 1909 in England which shows that, while there is comparatively little variation in the frequency of crimes of acquisitiveness from month to month, there is a marked degree of seasonal frequency in crimes of violence and lust, giving a curve of incidence which rises to a maximum in the hot months. This may be explained by the fact that in these forms of delinquency biological factors play an important part.[1] Among the Bison-

[1] W. C. Sullivan, *Crime and Insanity* (London. 1942), pp. 21 ff.

horn Maria seasonal variations, though less striking, do exist, as the following Table shows.

TABLE SIX

SHOWING THE INCIDENCE OF 100 HOMICIDES BY THE TIME OF YEAR	
January	9
February	9
March	5
April	10
May	10
June	3
July	9
August	8
September	10
October	12
November	9
December	6

There is a definite increase in the hottest months of the year, April and May, and a corresponding increase in September and October which are also hot and enervating. On the other hand these variations may not be due entirely to climatic causes. The figure for June and July, for example, is only half that of the figure for September and October, but June and July are the months during which the people are hard at work in their fields. June, in which only 3 murders occurred, is the busiest month of the year and sees the breaking of the monsoon. April and October, which show a heavy incidence of homicides, are festival periods, which are not only occasions for heavy drinking, but by providing opportunities for people to meet together make it possible for disputes to arise and old grievances to be remembered. Yet the influence of festivals must not be exaggerated, as Table Seven will show.

TABLE SEVEN

FESTIVALS AT WHICH HOMICIDES OCCURRED	
January (Bhimul or Gaddi Pandum)	2
February (Irpu Pandum)	1
April (Wijja or Marka Pandum)	3
October (Korta Pandum)	4
November (Nuka Nordana Pandum)	2

Only 12 murders occurred at festivals and not a single one at a marriage—a fact which in itself should dispose of the myth that rice-beer is the most important cause of homicide. For festivals and marriages are the chief occasions when this refreshing but potent drink is brewed and consumed.

IV

METHODS OF MURDER

Maria murders are generally straightforward enough: in only 4 cases were people killed while asleep and in only 6 from behind. There was only 1 case of poisoning. The following Table gives the methods used in 100 cases:

Table Eight

MEANS EMPLOYED IN 100 HOMICIDES	
Beating with godel axe	32
pharsi axe	1
gagra blade	1
log from fire	10
heavy stick	14
rice-husker	2
korki hoe	1
fists	1
Shooting with arrow	17
Stabbing with knife	2
arrow	5
trident	1
Strangling	4
Twisting neck	4
Drowning	2
Cutting throat	1
Poisoning	1
Dashing a child to the ground	1

Table Nine

MEANS EMPLOYED BY WOMEN IN 5 CASES	
Beating and twisting neck	1
Killing husband with axe	2
Killing co-wife with axe	1
Poisoning	1

Among these methods of murder we should especially remark two. Markami Hinga was the Siraha of his village; he had only recently begun his duties and seems to have been very proud of them. One day he had a sudden quarrel with his brother who was annoyed, as not infrequently happens, at having the whole work of the farm thrown upon him as a result of the other's sacred duties. As a result of his abuse Hinga got so angry that he rushed into the temple of his god, took up the trident and chain and stabbed his brother twice in the chest, and so killed him.

There are only 4 cases of murder by throttling in the 100 under review, and it is remarkable that 3 of these occurred within 9 months of one another during the year 1933. The first was on 6 January near Nakulnar, the second on 21 February at Garmiri and the third on 3 August at Kaurgaon. Moreover, in each case the homicide tried to disguise his murder as a suicide by stringing the corpse of his victim to a tree. The first two villages in which these events occurred are close together and the third within gossip distance, and it is obvious that a sort of epidemic of murder by throttling spread among the people and then disappeared.[1]

V

THE STATISTICS OF SUICIDE

In any discussion of violent crime among aboriginals the light thrown by a consideration of suicide must not be ignored. Murder is to the Maria almost a kind of suicide, for discovery is generally inevitable, but a man may willingly ruin his life provided at the same time he destroys his enemy. The Maria, as Table Ten shows, are more prone to suicide just as they

[1] Adam gives an account of unusual methods of murder in the hill areas of Europe. 'In mountainous and other districts where the inhabitants are often endowed with exceptional strength and exceptional brutality, strange things sometimes happen. One day a woodcutter in the midst of a quarrel seized a large piece of wood over nine feet long, part of a tree which he had just cut down, and holding it in front of him like a ram rushed on his assailants, inflicting no fewer than five serious wounds (fracture of ribs, fracture of collar bone, dislocation of hip joint). In a quarrel in a tavern a young man of gigantic height seized the heavy top of the inn table and brandishing it in the air brought it down on the heads of the young men who were fighting with him, inflicting a dozen grave wounds on the skull. —J. C. Adam, *Criminal Investigation* (London, 1924), p. 420.

are more prone to murder than the other tribesmen, and obviously the light hold that life has upon them and their impetuous and passionate temperament is the cause in either case. The reasons for murder or suicide sometimes coincide, and it is interesting to see how one type of personality reacts to a given situation by killing someone else and another type by killing himself. For example, it was a dispute about possession of a dancing outfit that led Wango to murder his betrothed Paike. But when Alami Mata had his splendid bison-horn head-dress, which he loved and cared for with devotion, stolen he did not seek out and kill the thief but was so miserable that he hanged himself. In several cases disputes about the right of a girl to visit her mother's house led to murder. In as many others it led to suicide. Sometimes a girl hangs herself because she is not allowed to go home. Sometimes the husband hangs himself out of loneliness and misery when his wife deserts him for her parents. A public insult caused Marvi Hinga to murder his mother-in-law. Had he been of a different temperament like Markami Pandu, who was abused and insulted by his wife for not working properly, he would have hanged himself. Fatigue drives some Maria to murder in a fit of exhausted rage, but others hang themselves instead.

Some sick people murder the magician who they believe has sent affliction upon them. Others commit suicide in order to escape from him. The Maria themselves identify homicide and suicide in so far that both lead to a violent disturbance of village life. Both involve them in various supernatural dangers, and the ghosts of both can be dealt with in much the same way.

R. S. Cavan discusses the relations of widow suicide and human sacrifice. The voluntary sacrifice of widows at the funeral of their husbands has been recorded in India and China, throughout the central portion of Negro Africa and among certain aristocratic American Indian tribes. These areas are also the areas of human sacrifice.

> In the Orient the sacrifices are a matter of history and are often recorded as accompanying the widow suicide. Among the preliterates, the sacrifices were noted in conjunction with the suicides by early white observers. Moreover, in few parts of the world was human sacrifice

found except in the groups which also had Sati. Human sacrifice and Sati went hand in hand.[1]

The Maria do not have the custom of widow suicide, and human sacrifice is equally rare among them.

I will begin, as in the case of the homicides, with general statistics about suicide in Bastar during the last 10 years.

TABLE TEN

NUMBER OF SUICIDES IN BASTAR IN 10 YEARS, 1931-40

Tribe or Caste	Number of Cases	Annual average of suicides to the million[2]
Bison-horn Maria ...	93	53·14
Ghotul Muria ...	22	22·00
Others ...	130	36·11
Total ...	245	38·58

It is notable again that the highest figure is for the Bison-horn Maria and the lowest for the Ghotul Muria. The Muria, however, are more prone to suicide than murder, which is perhaps what we might expect from a tribe so singularly free of jealousy and passion.

TABLE ELEVEN

METHODS OF SUICIDE USED BY ALL TRIBES AND CASTES (245 CASES)

By cutting the throat . . .	1
By hanging	214
By drowning	15
By poisoning	9
By means not fully reported . .	6

Every case, except one of drowning, of aboriginal suicide in Bastar has been by hanging. This may be due to the fact that the people are not adept at poisons—murder by poison is very rare among them—and because there are few wells in aboriginal villages, and the tanks and streams where they get their water are fairly shallow.

[1] R. S. Cavan, *Suicide* (Chicago, 1928), p. 72.
[2] Based on the population estimates of 1941.

It is said that in India generally, drowning is the most common method of achieving suicide, and then hanging. In England, hanging comes first, then poisoning, then cutting the throat, and lastly drowning. In India men resort to hanging and drowning in about equal numbers but six out of seven female suicides prefer drowning.[1] But this is not so among the Maria. One woman preferred to hang herself even on the very banks of the Indrawati, though the deep waters of the river were at hand.

In the 50 cases of which I have detailed information, 19 suicides were committed inside a building, 16 of them inside the dwelling-place of the family. In 7 other cases death occurred near the house. In the other 24 cases the suicide took place in the jungle, a rope or cloth being attached to the branch of a tree. Among trees the mahua (*Bassia latifolia*, Roxb.) was the most popular with 6 cases, and after it the mango with 3. Otherwise there is a very great variety in the trees selected for this gloomy purpose; there do not seem to be any taboos observed, though I notice the sacred saja (*Terminalia tomentosa*, W. & A.) is not used—but this may be for the entirely practical reason that it does not have suitable overhanging branches.

The method of self-execution seems to be to climb up the tree, to attach and arrange the cord and then jump down. When the suicide occurs inside a house, the person stands on a fish-trap or basket and kicks it away. In many cases, the rope consists of the victim's own loin-cloth, turban or sari, but several different kinds of rope are also used. Rope made of the twisted siari (*Bauhinia vahlii*, W. & A.) creeper is perhaps the most common. Jute cords for tethering cattle, and ropes made of various kinds of bark are also used.

TABLE TWELVE

ANALYSIS OF 50 MARIA SUICIDES BY SEX

Men	26
Women	24

[1] R. Ranchhodas and D. K. Thakore, *The Law of Crimes* (Bombay, 1911), p. 601, in the author's comment on Section 309 of the Indian Penal Code. But in the U.S.A., the order is said to be—for men—firearms, hanging, poisonous gas, corrosives, and—for women—gas, corrosives, firearms, drowning. In Japan, hanging first and then drowning are the favourite methods for both sexes.

(*a*) Dulha of Gadapal with bow and arrow

(*b*) Boys catching a bat at Khutepal

PLATE IX

PLATE X. 'Rice in the mouth and curry in the hand.' Mother and child figure in several murder cases.

The contrast between homicide and suicide in respect of the sex-ratio is very striking; 5 per cent stands against 48 per cent. There may be many reasons for this, chiefly that a woman ought not to kill and often lacks the means of killing —she does not usually learn to be expert with the bow and arrow or with the axe. It is possible that some of the suicides would have been murder, had there been the means and opportunity.

The suicide sex-ratio is remarkable when compared to the situation elsewhere. In Europe and America, there has been over a long period of years a far less equal ratio, varying from one woman to every three or five men. That these figures do vary suggests, however, that 'the propensity of men to commit suicide is probably not inherent in their sex, a conclusion further supported by figures for the Orient. For instance, in Japan the proportion of women who commit suicide is much higher than for Europe or America. The situation in India is yet more at variance with the relations noted for the Occident'.[1]

TABLE THIRTEEN

ANALYSIS OF 50 MARIA SUICIDES BY AGE

Under 15	1
Between 15 and 20	12
Between 20 and 25	9
Between 25 and 30	1
30 and over	5
40 and over	8
50 and over	8
Age not specified	6

There is not anything significant in the above Table except that we should notice that nearly half the suicides were of young people. The older men and women, by the time they have reached some position of dignity in the tribe, have consolations that help them to cling to life. Many of the suicides of the older people are due to insanity and intolerable disease believed to be the result of witchcraft.

[1] Cavan, op. cit., p. 308.

TABLE FOURTEEN

ANALYSIS OF 50 MARIA SUICIDES BY THE TIME OF YEAR

January	3
February	5
March	3
April	2
May	3
June	4
July	6
August	7
September	2
October	3
November	7
December	5

Here again there is nothing very significant, probably because there are not sufficient figures to indicate large variations. But we may note that July and August, which are the most gloomy months of the rains, months also that are filled with heavy and exacting work, show the largest number of suicides. If we take the figures for homicide and suicide together the highest figures are shown by July and August, and then again by October and November.

CHAPTER FOUR

THE CAUSES OF VIOLENT CRIME

I

HOMICIDE

I HAVE divided the crimes rather arbitrarily, and, of course, other divisions in many cases would be possible. For example, some of the murders which I have put down under the heading of 'alcohol' might also be classified as quarrels over property, because it is anxiety about possession which seems to come to the front of a Maria's mind when he becomes intoxicated. 'Family quarrels' is also a large subject. The following Table gives a rough analysis of the causes of murder in 100 cases.

TABLE FIFTEEN

CAUSES OF HOMICIDE IN 100 CASES	
Robbery or accusation of robbery	8
Quarrels over property	15
Suspicion of magic or witchcraft	5
Insanity	5
Resentment at abuse or 'word-magic'	9
Revenge	6
Family quarrels	16
Sex motives	17
Alcohol	19

I have used the word 'cause' rather than 'motive', for motive implies premeditation, and comparatively few of these crimes were premeditated. Indeed some were little more than tragic accidents. For this reason it is not easy to fit many of them into such a scheme as that proposed, for example, by F. Tennyson Jesse who declares that 'every murder falls into one of six classes; it may belong in a greater or less degree to perhaps two of those classes, but in one of them it comes logically to rest'.[1] The six classes are as follows:

[1] F. Tennyson Jesse, *Murder and its Motives* (London, 1924), p. 13.

I. Murder for gain.
II. Murder for revenge.
III. Murder for elimination.
IV. Murder from jealousy.
V. Murder from lust of killing.
VI. Murder from conviction.

Among the Maria there are very few murders for gain, for where is the property to be acquired? It would be laughable to imagine in a Maria village the situation so dear to the writer of detective stories, the murder of an elderly person by his heirs for the sake of his money. Murder for revenge occurs, but in not more than half a dozen cases. I describe later a remarkable case of murder for elimination. Murder from jealousy covers a number of the tragedies which involve relations between husband and wife. I am doubtful whether any of the Maria murders could be included under the heading 'Murder from lust of killing'.

Tennyson Jesse's sixth class 'Murder from conviction' is, I believe, much more common among the aboriginals and leads us to the vexed and difficult problem of how to deal with persons whose ideas of right and wrong vary in certain remarkable respects from those of the modern world. Without exception, every Maria believes that it is the right and proper thing to kill a witch or sorcerer. In this the Maria is not criminal; he is merely out-of-date. Two hundred years ago the best brains in Europe believed the same. Almost all Maria consider that a wife caught in the act of adultery with her lover deserves immediate execution, and here again the Maria are simply out-of-date, though in this case they are rather more behind the times than they are about witchcraft. Kinberg has an interesting passage on this subject.

> A comparison between the judgements passed on one type of action by different peoples, or by one people at different periods of its history, brings out how purely relative moral evaluations are. If a man catches his wife *in flagrante* with her lover and kills them both, he will in Sweden be condemned to a long term of penal servitude for manslaughter and his action will be strongly disapproved. In Latin countries, on the other hand, the same action would in the majority of cases be declared by the jury not to be culpable, and would cause no general moral indignation. Such is the difference in the moral evalua-

> tion of one and the same action in two civilized European countries at the same period. And there have even been times when, if a man has failed in such circumstances to kill both his wife and her lover, this has been so strongly disapproved that he has been punished with loss of life. Such an instance is quoted by Galo Sanchez from the old 14th century Castilian law. In a collection of judgements, one is described in which a knight was condemned to the gallows because, when he surprised his wife *in flagrante*, he was content with castrating the lover. He did not punish his wife at all. He ought to have killed both. This omission brought him to the gallows.[1]

This point has, of course, often been made, and Havelock Ellis quotes one criminologist as suggesting that, 'The criminal of today is the hero of our old legends. We put in prison the man who in another century would have been the dreaded and respected chief of a clan or a tribe', and another as saying, 'How many of Homer's heroes would today be in a convict prison!' It was on a theory of atavism that Lombroso erected his famous structure of criminology. Havelock Ellis properly reminds us that, 'If we are wise we shall be very tender in arousing our indignation against the social habits of lower races, even when these involve such an act as parricide, for the distance between ourselves and even the lowest races is quite measurable. Our social code is not far removed from that of the Maori who considered that it was murder to kill the man to whom he had given hospitality, but not murder to run his spear through the stranger whom he met on his morning walk. We today regard it as a great crime to kill our own fathers or children; but even the most civilized European nation—whichever that may be—regards it as rather glorious to kill the fathers and children of others in war. We are not able yet to grasp the relationship between men. In the same way, while we resent the crude thefts practised by some lower races, we are still not civilized enough to resent the more subtle thefts practised among ourselves which do not happen to conflict with the letter of any legal statute'.[2]

Ten years earlier Stanley Hall had declared in even more striking phrases:

[1] O. Kinberg, *Basic Problems of Criminology* (London, 1935), p. 50.
[2] Havelock Ellis, *The Criminal* (London, 1914), p. 251.

> Extreme views of the abnormality of crime may well make us pause, when we reflect on its relativity. Socrates and Jesus were criminals according to the legal standards of their day. We confine and kill those who in the days of Abraham and Ulysses or in positions of power and influence would be heroes. Of the ten chief crimes of the Hebrews of old, only one is now a crime. Many of the knights and barons of the Middle Ages were brigands, but were not then outlawed by public sentiment as abnormal. There is deep and wide-spread feeling in every community that in extreme hunger all things belong to all. The thought of killing our own fathers or children is monstrous, but we kill the fathers and children of other people with impunity in war. Many of our greatest criminals would have been normal and perhaps eminently useful citizens in other ages and places. Judged by severe and inner standards of morals, most of us have committed every crime.[1]

So also many of the Maria homicides described in this book will be recognized not as anti-social crimes, but as expressions of the strongly social instinct of the murderer. A father seduces the wives of his sons, and in order to enjoy them in freedom drives the boys and their mother out of his house and refuses them support. The murder of such a man expresses a social, rather than an anti-social, instinct. To the Maria the witch is the greatest menace to the order and security of daily life. When he murders a witch, therefore, he is the victim of intellectual error rather than of murderous passion. Adam gives an interesting example from Europe. 'A case is reported by M. Friedmann, of Wiesbaden, of two soldiers who agreed that the one should shoot the head off the other. The victim firmly believed that the survivor could with certain words of sorcery charm his head on again and that after the operation the latter would be able to discover hidden treasure. The first half of the experiment was duly performed and apparently without any difficulty, but the sorcerer dismally failed to replace his comrade's head as agreed upon. It was established that he did not intend to kill his friend, but, with his assistance, expected them both to discover hidden treasure. Nor could he be considered negligent or careless as he did what he did carefully and on purpose, being convinced of the harmlessness of the act. If

[1] G. Stanley Hall, *Adolescence* (London and New York, 1904), Vol. I, pp. 340 f.

he was punished for anything it was for mere ignorance and stupidity. This incident actually took place as recently as 1900.'[1]

Sir Cecil Walsh advances the view that many Indian village crimes are of a 'judicial character', and that the people are driven to commit them by the law's delays.

> A very large proportion of the cases of violence in northern India arise out of hot blood, ungovernable temper, and the natural inclination of the villager, who is generally miles away from any police, to take the law into his own hands and to fight out his quarrel on the spot. There is nothing like this in agricultural districts in England. It has been said that the agricultural classes are not inferior in intelligence to the English peasant. If natural acumen, rapidity of thought, and liveliness of imagination are meant, it may be so. But whether the cause be their lack of education, the narrowness of their religion, the climate, or, as I have often thought, their lack of association with men of attainments superior to their own, the fact is that they fail to use their intelligence, and upon slight provocation lose all power of reasoning and self-control. It is not much good having an equivalent of intelligence if you don't use it when it is wanted. Whether it is a question of cattle trespass, irrigation, family enmity, an old personal grudge, a sexual difficulty, or some quite trivial dispute, the average cultivator will break out at once into abuse, often of the most disgusting character, which develops rapidly into a fight, in which the relations and friends on either side will join in substantial numbers if they happen to be near. If one disputant, finding himself seriously outnumbered, a disadvantage which the villager invariably hopes to impose upon his enemy, should discreetly retire, the fight will take place later on, more or less in cold blood, when both sides are ready. It is impossible to regard these law-breakers and disturbers of the peace as criminals in the ordinary signification of that term. They are probably as honest and industrious as the average respectable citizen in a civilized centre of industry. They want speedy justice, or, what they regard as the same thing, the vindication of their own opinion. They prefer the British variety. But it takes time, and they can't wait. They are great believers in getting in the first blow, and,

[1] Adam, op. cit., p. 262. A remarkable parallel is provided by a case that occurred at Nagpur in 1923, when a constable and a pious friend made a pact to offer their heads to Kali in order to obtain immortality. They mistook a statue of the Virgin Mary for the goddess and the constable stabbed himself to death before it.

> to tell the truth, few of them have learned anything else. And they know that they are pretty certain to get it if they don't give it.[1]

How far this opinion applies to Bastar the reader must judge for himself after a perusal of the cases examined in this book.

II
SUICIDE

On the reasons for aboriginal suicide Briffault has some insufferable words. 'Suicide', he says, 'for all sorts of absurdly frivolous reasons is exceedingly common among all primitive peoples. The chief reason lies probably in the fact that, while the mind of individualistic civilized man is constantly projected into the future and occupied with schemes, primitive man, like the child, is destitute of foresight and lives almost entirely in the present; hence the impulse of the moment, however trifling in itself the object of it may be, determines action uncounteracted by any far-reaching consideration.'[2] Briffault mocks at the idea that primitive people, who (he thinks) usually have little real affection for one another, could possibly kill themselves for love, and he quotes Detzner as saying that every heroic motive is lacking in the records of suicides from Melanesia and Papua. 'The momentary despair caused by the natural or violent death of wife or husband, the complete lack of energy to take up the battle of life singly, alone induce these resourceless people to take the step, and love for the deceased, which in our sense of the word is unknown to them, lends no higher, hallowing significance to the wretched deed.'[3]

To the unsympathetic official without desire to understand or the hurried traveller with no time to inquire, reports of suicides casually heard and indifferently explored must often seem trivial enough. But does it never occur to these reporters that the triviality of motive so often advanced is really a screen to protect the real significance of the deed from official or merely inquisitive eyes? That primitive man does not take suicide lightly is shown by the extraordinary

[1] Sir C. Walsh, *Indian Village Crimes* (London, 1929), pp. 10 f.
[2] R. Briffault, *The Mothers* (London, 1927), Vol. II, pp. 143 ff.
[3] H. Detzner, *Vier Jahre unter Kannibalen* (Berlin, 1920), p. 198.

precautions he takes against the ghost, while the very fact—which Briffault mentions—that suicide can be made a deadly weapon against an enemy indicates what a serious business it is.

For the Maria of Bastar, suicide is a wretched deed; it certainly has no higher, hallowing significance; but it is no light or trivial matter due to lack of foresight. Rather it is caused by an all too clear vision of the future: the leper looks across a wilderness of ever-deepening misery; the widow sees her whole life shadowed by irreparable loss; wife and husband see their home's happiness wrecked about them; a man sees his future darkened by the memory of an unforgivable insult. The people themselves have no desire to glorify the deed, neither do they condemn it. In perhaps the majority of cases psychoneurotic or psychotic symptoms have been recognized by the people themselves, and they regard the unhappy victims as driven to death by their own disordered minds.

The following Table gives the reasons for suicide among all tribes and castes for the 245 incidents in the last 10 years. The classification is one made by the police.

TABLE SIXTEEN

REASONS FOR SUICIDE IN 245 CASES IN BASTAR STATE

Reason	Cases
Insanity	20
Disease	52
Leprosy	6
Grief on account of bereavement	17
Love-affairs	11
Quarrels over property	3
Quarrels between wife and husband	55
Other domestic quarrels	43
Fear of scandal	11
Intoxication	1
Economic: starvation and financial ruin	3
Fear of courts and officials	3
Bad treatment by employers	2
Failing in a school examination	1
Not properly reported	17

When we turn to the 50 sample cases (details of which are given in an Appendix) we find the following.

TABLE SEVENTEEN

REASONS FOR SUICIDE IN 50 MARIA CASES	
Insanity	7
Disease and fear of magic	9
Grief and loneliness	4
Fear of officials	2
Regret for harsh behaviour to someone loved	3
Resentment at a rebuke	7
An intolerable home	4
Antagonism between wife and husband	9
Intoxication	1
Economic causes	1
Special cases	3

There is no evidence for supposing any of the suicides were due to a desire for 'identification with the dead', although in one case a youth slept all night before his death in the granary where the sacred Pot of the Dead was kept. Nor is the desire for revenge specially evident, though it may, of course, have been concealed from the authorities. No doubt the feeling that one's death will cause trouble to one's relatives and so pay them out is often present in suicides that are due to temper. Not one case appears to have been due to sexual jealousy, though several were due to sexual disappointment. The majority seem to have been caused by a desire to escape from a physical or domestic situation that had become intolerable. The insult, as in other primitive cultures, is a very potent stimulus to suicide. This too creates an intolerable situation from which escape is necessary, but I do not notice any stress on the protest which a death makes against those who have done harm.

Suicide has been studied with some care among the Indian tribes of North America. The older view was that it was exceptional among primitive people. Thus Hrdlicka says that it was rare on the San Carlos reservation, 'infrequent' among the Jicarillas: 'among the Navaho rare instances occur from destitution, despondency or drink'. Among the Papago, Pima, Zuni and other tribes suicide was equally rare. Among the Tarahumare occasionally a despondent individual ended his life by hanging. Everywhere it was said to be specially rare among women. Where it occurred it was said to be due to despondency.[1] It was reported as unusual among the Havasupai.[2]

Recent research, however, suggests that the tendency to self-destruction is commoner than was formerly supposed, and Voegelin says that 'modern inquiry into the subject is revealing a growing number of tribes in northeastern California in which suicide was practised'. For both the Klamath and Modoc 'suicide is a romantic gesture, motivated by disappointment in love and, indirectly, jealousy. Women hang themselves, men in some instances drown themselves. Among the Atsugewi, Achomawi and Surprise Valley Paiute, suicide was usually motivated either through jealousy or quarrelling; eating wild parsnip root was one of the more generally accepted modes; the bodies of suicides were accorded the same disposal as the bodies of persons dying natural deaths, but only close relatives wailed'.[3]

Among the Tanaina, suicide is said to have become more common 'when old men lived to see the last of their sons die'.[4] Among the Mohave 'the conflict between longing for the dead and the impossibility of catching up with them should one live too long after they died led to an appalling number of suicides'.[5] Fenton traces the increase to contact with civilization. In a study of the Seneca and Mohawk Indians, he writes, 'Public opinion condemned as cowardice male suicides to avoid physical suffering, such as torture, but condoned cases of women who were mistreated by lovers. The greatest frequency came during the period immediately following white contact when conditions were ripe for social disorganization. The principal motive with women was revenge of mistreatment by husbands who

[1] A. Hrdlicka, *Physiological and Medical Observations*, Bureau of American Ethnology, Bull. XXXIV, 1908, p. 171.

[2] L. Spier, *Havasupai Ethnography*, Anthropological Papers of the American Bureau of Natural History, Vol. XXIX, 1928, p. 343.

[3] E. W. Voegelin, 'Suicide in Northeastern California', *American Anthropologist*, Vol. XXXIX (New Series), p. 456.

[4] C. Osgood, 'Tanaina Culture', *American Anthropologist*, Vol. XXXV (New Series), p. 714.

[5] G. Devereux, 'Mohave Soul Concepts', *American Anthropologist*, Vol. XXXIX (New Series), p. 422.

deserted them at middle age; children resented restraint, and men sought to avoid physical suffering, either martyrdom or blood revenge; some cases involve loss of status . . . Avoidance remains the dominating motive of Iroquois suicide.'[1]

Suicide among the Trobriand Islanders, says Malinowski, 'is certainly not a means of administering justice, but it affords the accused and oppressed one—whether he be guilty or innocent—a means of escape and rehabilitation. It looms large in the psychology of the natives, is a permanent damper on any violence of language or behaviour, on any deviation from custom or tradition, which might hurt or offend another. Thus suicide, like sorcery, is a means of keeping the native to the strict observance of the law, a means of preventing people from extreme and unusual types of behaviour. Both are pronounced conservative influences and as such are strong supports of law and order'.[2]

This is a little too emphatic for the situation in Bastar, but duly modified might apply there also. But whatever primitive suicide may be, it is not trivial. Nor is it altogether dishonourable. The man insulted escapes, it is true, but he restores his honour. The girl forced into an unwelcome marriage runs away from it, but she preserves her dignity and prestige.

[1] W. N. Fenton, *Iroquois Suicide*, Bureau of American Ethnology; Anthropological Papers, Washington, 1941, p. 134.

[2] B. Malinowski, *Crime and Custom in Savage Society* (London, 1932), p. 98.

CHAPTER FIVE

THE CAUSES OF CRIME: WITCHCRAFT AND MAGIC

I

THE ORIGIN OF MAGIC

THE origin of black magic has been described by the Maria in a number of villages and the reports generally agree. 'The first man in the world to practise magic was Nandraj Guru. All the gods [1] and the Dead went to him to learn the art. At one time seven gods were being taught by him daily. One day a Maria of the Maja clan was digging roots in the jungle when he heard voices and went stealthily to see what was happening. From behind a tree he saw Nandraj Guru teaching the seven gods. Every day the Maria went to the place and overheard everything that was said. On the last day the pupils brought offerings of pigs and chickens for their Guru. He sacrificed them and divided the meat into seven equal shares. But to his surprise after a few moments he noticed that the number of shares had grown to eight. He called his disciples and said, "Search the jungle around, for there must surely be a ghost or an animal hiding near". The search revealed the presence of the Maria on the branch of a tree, and he was brought before the Guru.

'Nandraj said, "Listen, everyone here is a god and you are the only human being who has learned our magic. Unless you give an offering as the gods have done, your son will die". "What offering should I give?" asked the Maria. "In your house", said the Guru, "there is a pigeon. Offer that to me." Now by the word "pigeon" the Guru meant the Maria's only son and the reason why he demanded him was that his knowledge could only be imparted to immortal beings who would use it in the proper way. But the Guru feared that now that a human being had discovered the secret, he would make use of the magic at all times. There would be no deaths. Pain would be banished, and the gods would have

[1] God, spelt without a capital, represents the Hindi *deo*. The Gondi *pen* is translated 'clan-god'. A *deo* is little more than what the Middle Ages called a 'demon'.

no Dead to people their kingdom. But if this human being were to eat a bit of the liver of his own son, then there would be deaths in the world and the Maria himself would have learned the knowledge of evil and death and would become a magician.

'The Maria, little knowing that when Nandraj Guru said "pigeon", he meant his son, asked one of the gods to go to his

A typical Anga Pen, a clan-god. Carried by four men, it is sometimes used to detect witches.

house and fetch the bird. The god killed the boy, removed the liver, and the Maria and the seven gods ate it together. As the Maria unwittingly ate the liver of his own son, he was filled with the knowledge of death and evil, and became the first sorcerer. Before he died, he taught his own disciples the art and today many men know how to harm and kill their enemies. But in every case the liver must be obtained, for the liver is the *jiwa* (soul) of all beings.'

In Khutepal the Maria said that they began learning magic in the month of June. The young disciples must go to the jungle and set up a small stone which represents an uraskal menhir. To the left of the pillar they place another stone flat on the ground to represent a danyakal. Then between the uraskal and the danyakal a number of small stones are placed in line from right to left. This line of stones represents one kind of magic, say the magic for curing the sick. Parallel to this they place a second line of small stones. This represents another kind of magic, say doing injury to an enemy.

A third line is put for making women barren, a fourth line for destroying crops and cattle, and so on.

Then the Guru begins to teach the young men in the name of Nandraj, Bodhraj, Kirkod, Markod, Indor and Bandor. He holds a bamboo stick in his hand and as he recites his mantra he beats the stones in turn, beginning with the uraskal and striking each stone from left to right. He must not, however, touch the danyakal with his stick. The disciples chant the mantra after him, and then one by one they stand up and strike the stones with the stick. By December the whole art of black magic is acquired.

At the beginning of the course of study, the disciples subscribe to buy a pig and chicken for their Guru. At the end they also bring offerings and a pot of rice-beer. On the last day a little rice is placed on the danyakal stone and the chicken brought by the disciples is made to eat it. Then it is killed and the boys feast with their Guru.

One homicide not in our list, which occurred at Dhurli, was connected with such a school of magic. A youth named Telami Dhurwa used to go daily to Dogi Para to learn magic from an older man of the same name. The rule here was that from time to time the students should subscribe for a pig and that each should take their instructor a pot of rice-beer. One day Dhurwa and his fellow-students took the required pig and rice-beer, and after their class was finished they feasted with their Guru. On their way home the boys began to quarrel, and Dhurwa and another boy killed a third boy named Hunga. The people at Dhurli said that Hunga's soul was not mingled with the dead because he was learning black magic, and a memorial stone was not erected for the same reason. Hunga in fact became a very dangerous ghost, a Rau Bhut. The two boys were sentenced to short terms of imprisonment as no intention to murder was proved. When Dhurwa was released he had to offer, in addition to the usual ceremonies, a special and expensive sacrifice to his clan-god.

II

THE SORCERER'S METHODS

The Maria sorcerer goes about his business in much the same way as elsewhere in India or the world. He may attack his enemy directly by blowing something at him, by putting a charm into his food, by performing certain rites or by the evil eye. He may turn into an animal and attack his foe in wild and bestial guise. He may obtain the services of a ghost or a godling to do his work for him.

Stories illustrating all these methods are common in the Maria villages. At Khutepal I was told that there was once a man there who could transform himself into a tiger. He would then lie hid in the jungle and when any human being or cow came by, he used to kill and devour him. He then took his human form again and came home and lay with his wife. After he had killed five or six people in this way, the villagers finally summoned up courage to track down the 'tiger' and kill it. A watch was kept and one day to their surprise and horror they saw the man actually changing into a tiger and then back to human form. They rushed at him and killed him instantly. Similar stories were told me in Dhurli, but here they said that it was most common for such things to happen in the great Zamindari of Jeypore. It is generally believed that if a were-tiger is injured, similar marks will appear on the human body of the man who has possessed it.

Sometimes, instead of turning into an animal, the sorcerer sends an animal to do his business for him. There are many stories of how people have been attacked by bears and tigers on this account. Indeed many Maria believe that no animal or snake will ever attack a human being unless it is incited to do so by magic. Once on the way from Pordem to Rewali I saw the funeral pyre of a snake. A little while previously a very long snake marked with alternate black and yellow bands had been sent to Rewali by a magician to kill one of his enemies, Nupo Bira. Bira, however, was able to kill the snake in time, and its body was then carried out of the village and cremated beyond the boundary-line. Four pegs of ebony wood were driven into the ground at the four corners of the pyre, and the people claimed that the ritual cremation together with the pegs would effectively protect Bira from any further attack.[1]

[1] An extraordinary case occurred at Bhandara in 1929. A Kunbin (Hindu) woman was bitten by a snake and to avoid further trouble installed the image of Nagoba (the cobra god) in her house. This deity used to possess her and she gained a wide reputation as a healer. One day a fisherwoman, haunted by evil spirits, came for treatment.

(*a*) Youth with Hill Maria dancing dress

(*b*) Markami Marka wearing head-dress

PLATE XI

(*c*) Boys preparing their head-dress for a dance (p. 19)

Detail of Muchaki Hunga's pillar at Dilmilli (p. 32)

(*b*) Newly erected pillar near Chitrakot (p. 33)

PLATE XII

Witches seem to prefer the direct attack. At Mokhpal I was given a vivid description of how a witch performed her hideous rites. 'She goes out of her house at night and finds an ant-hill. She takes off all her clothes and removes even the waist-band. Seven times she goes round the hill. She appears more like a ghost than a human being. Anyone who looks at her goes blind at the sight. She goes to her victim's house, places a bit of grass on his breast and sucks his blood through it. She takes it back to the ant-hill and mixes the blood with milk. Then she can tell by looking at it whether that man will be lucky or unlucky. If the milk is red, he will die, but if it is white wealth will come to his house. If a man dies the witch goes to the grave, revives him and cuts off his head.'

At Tikanpal I was given another account. 'A witch sees a youth and desires him, but she is not content to lie with him as a lover. She must devour his whole body. She goes to him at night and turns his liver over inside his body. After he has been buried, she takes the body out of the grave. She eats the flesh and drinks the blood and puts the bones back into the grave. Sometimes when she robs a man of his blood, she puts it in a bit of broken pot and cooks it on a fire which must be made of a single piece of wood.'

Thirdly, and most sinister, a sorcerer is able to employ the services of a ghost or an evil spirit. Here the danger to the intended victim is, of course, twofold, for he has to face not only the malice of the magician but also the power of a supernatural being who has become his ally. It is notable that the ghosts of executed murderers are specially liable to be used by the magicians in this way.

Witches also have the power of affecting the domestic life of their victims. At Samgiri the Maria described how the witch could destroy a man's seed and, even though he were not impotent, he would never be able to have a child. This happened at Kuchepal where a man was in love with a widow who was a witch. After a time he left her, and in revenge she destroyed his seed. When after a long time he found

The Kunbin stripped herself and her patient and then, overwhelmed with frenzy, thrust a burning log into the unfortunate victim's belly and killed her. She removed all the internal organs of the thorax and abdomen and offered them to Nagoba, claiming that in this way the hostile spirits had been destroyed.

that his wife did not bear him a child, he went to the Waddai who discovered the real reason and performed the proper rites. Before long, I was told, be found himself with a large family.

Witches can injure women by prolonging their menstrual periods. The Siraha can counter this by offering sacrifices to the Dead and to the Mirchuk. In Kameli a woman who was suffering from menorrhagia was cured by this means. But sometimes the Siraha can do nothing, and in despair the unhappy woman may hang herself.

At Borgum I was told that only widows can perform black magic and that they usually call on the ghosts of the dead to help them in their wicked deeds. Here too I was given an interesting account of how a witch can take precautions against discovery. She takes her familiar, say the ghost of a murderer or suicide, with her to an ant-hill and there she 'binds its mouth' by removing some of the earth from the hill and uttering charms. She says to the ghost, 'When the Siraha questions you, do not disclose my name'. Then she replaces the earth. It is believed that, just as any earth that is removed from an ant-hill is automatically filled up the next day, so misfortune will enter the house of the ghost she has bound if it betrays her.

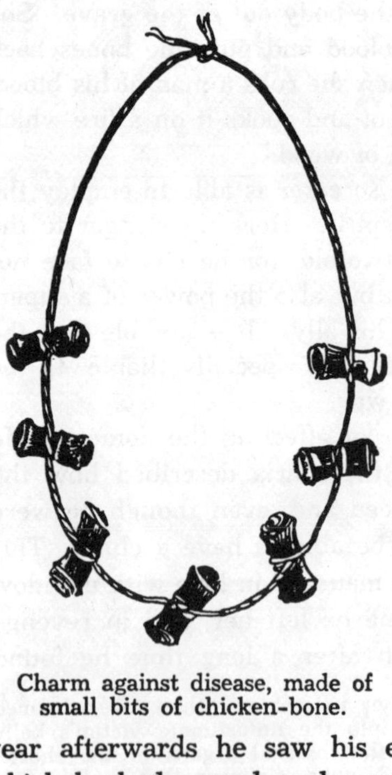

Charm against disease, made of small bits of chicken-bone.

Dread of this witchcraft or enchantment is a very powerful factor driving men to violence, for the fear is still a live one and the dangers are supposed to be great. Guma Hunga left his home and village because he believed that his family was being bewitched by a man called Burgi. A year afterwards he saw his enemy in the new village to which he had moved, and murdered him in a sudden access of fear. Sori Bhima killed a neighbour, one Kosa, who suffered from yaws, believing him to be a wizard and responsible for the death of his children.

Vedta Sukra murdered his uncle Kola, the headman of Surguda, for being a wizard. Three years before, Sukra's three-year-old daughter had died, and the death was attributed to Kola's magic. Immediately before the tragedy, Sukra's little son died after a month's illness, and members of the family went to a Siraha at Sarjiguda to find out why. The Siraha invoked the deity Madin Deo onto his person, and the deity declared through him that this death also was the result of Kola's magic. The next day Sukra went with a number of villagers to the place where his child had been cremated. Heaps of rice were placed in front of the ashes, in the names of Mirchuk (which kills children), the Village Mother, the Departed, Bhagavan and the suspect Kola. A chicken was allowed to make its choice among the heaps, and it pecked up rice from those of Mirchuk and Kola. From this the people deduced that Kola had killed the child with the help of Mirchuk Deo.

The following day Kola was found lying dead in a pool of blood on his own thrashing-floor. Sukra admitted his crime and no doubt considered that his action was justified and indeed laudable.

One day the sago palm belonging to Hunga of Gudse village ceased to give the usual juice. Hunga went to the village Siraha, a young man called Kosa, to find out what was the matter, and received the reply that it was due to the magic of Pandru, one of the neighbours. Sometime later, Pandru and Kosa met in the local liquor shop and had a drink together, and presently Kosa accused Pandru to his face of doing magic against Hunga's tree. Pandru became very angry at this, and abused Kosa and his gods. Expressing himself in typical Maria fashion, he pulled out a few of his pubic hairs and threw them on Kosa's head. Kosa slapped Pandru's face twice and went away.

Nothing happened for five months. But then on the evening of 14 April 1922, Kosa went out to look for a straying cow. His way took him near Pandru's house who, when he saw his enemy, got out his bow and arrow and shot him in the stomach.[1]

III

THE POWER OF BLOOD

The belief in the magical power of blood is world-wide, and has been so fully studied that I need only briefly refer to it here. Its virtues are imparted by the blood-covenant, by drinking, by bathing in it and by being baptized in it. Charms against sickness are sometimes written in blood in China. The blood bath was believed to be a cure for leprosy down to the Middle Ages ; the idea even occurs in Grimm's fairy-tales where leprosy is treated by a bath of the blood of innocent maidens. Constantine the Great was advised to bathe in the blood of virgin children to cure an illness, but the parents' cries dissuaded him and he was miraculously healed instead.

'In the past', says Haikerwal, 'the custom of human sacrifice was common in India chiefly amongst the Dravidians. One of its forms was Purusamedha, which was celebrated for the attainment of supremacy over all created beings and at which eleven human beings and eleven barren cows were offered up. The Puranas and Tantras also contain frequent references to Narabali or human sacrifice to the goddess Chandika. These Tantrik sacrifices to Kali or Chandika were formerly common. People were freely offered in the days of Maharatta rule, and in Western India there are many temples existing even today at which such sacrifices were common only a century ago. In the North-East of India also human sacrifice to Kali was very common.'[2]

Crooke gives a number of modern examples. 'In 1870, a

[1] This fear of witchcraft is by no means confined to the aboriginals. In 1931, a Gwara schoolmaster in the Central Provinces lost several of his cattle and his children fell ill. He traced the cause to a Powar sorcerer. He dressed up in a green skirt, green shirt, green cap, and put bells on his feet to make himself appear like his goddess and killed the sorcerer with a trident from the village temple. In 1935, some Hindus killed a Gond medicine-man in the Amraoti District because he threw a charmed lemon (believed to be infected with disease) into their compound. In Mandla District in 1935, a Mohammedan Sub-Inspector of Police, believing a Panka woman had 'overlooked' his child, sent his constables to force her to remove the charm. She was beaten with castor plants, made to drink water from a Chamar's shoe and subjected to other indignities.

[2] Haikerwal, op. cit., p. 66.

Mohammedan butcher losing his child was told by a Hindu conjuror that if he washed his wife in the blood of a boy, his next infant would be healthy. To ensure this result a child was murdered. A similar case occurred in Muzaffarnagar, where a child was killed and the blood drunk by a barren woman'. Later, in the same locality, 'a childless Jat woman was told that she would attain her desire if she bathed in water mixed with the blood of a Brahman child. A Hindu coolie at Mauritius bathed in and drank the blood of a girl, thinking that thereby he would be gifted with supernatural powers.'[1] More recently three cases of the murder of children in order to obtain offspring occurred in the Punjab in 1921, and in one of these a barren woman bathed in the child's blood.

In a small village in Chanda District in 1935, a Maria and a Marar planned to sacrifice a boy or girl at the Holi festival to improve the crops. The other villagers objected, but on the night of the festival, as the Holi fire was dying down, they forced an elderly Marar to stand before the fire, stripped him naked and threw him into the flames. In the following year a little Kurmi girl was killed by two women on behalf of the priest of a Mahadeo temple on the bank of the Narbada River in Hoshangabad District. They cut out a little of the left lobe of the liver while the child was still alive—the liver was needed for the treatment of a merchant.

In the *Katha Sarit Sagara* of Somadeva a pregnant queen asked her husband to gratify her craving by making a tank full of blood for her to bathe in. In order to avoid taking human life, he had a tank filled with the juice of lac, and the woman thinking it was blood was satisfied. In the tale of Devasmita in the same collection a king is told by the Brahmins that, if he wished to have a large number of children, he must kill his son and offer up his flesh in the fire. When his wives smelt the smell of the sacrifice, each bore the king a son.[2]

Here blood is effective for the fertilization of the human body, but among the aboriginals (as in the Meriah sacrifice of the Kond) it is chiefly valued for its enrichment of the soil.

[1] Crooke, op. cit., Vol. II, pp. 172 f. See Halliday, *Folk-Lore*, Vol. XXXV (1934), p. 404.

[2] Penzer, op. cit., Vol. I, p. 98.

This belief is probably still very widely held in Bastar, and Grigson quotes an interesting example reported by the police from Madder in the Bhopalpatnam Zamindari. On the night of 13 June 1937, a Mohammedan woman asleep in her courtyard was slightly wounded with a sharp instrument, and woke to see what she believed to be two Maria running away. 'The police enquiry elicited information that many Maria in Kutru Zamindari before sowing try to get some human blood, especially of women, to mix with their seed. Their usual method is to go to distant villages by night and inflict slight wounds on sleeping women with a knife or arrow. They then take the blood-stained weapon home, and wash it with water, in which they steep their rice seed before sowing, confident of securing thereby a bumper crop. Before wounding their victim they offer near her cot a little rice and turmeric; such an offering was found near the Madder woman's cot.'[1]

Cases of human sacrifice are not common, and in the whole of Bastar only 3 have been proved in the last 10 years, though there is reasonable ground to suppose that in 2 other cases, which did not proceed to a conviction, such sacrifice was the real motive of the crime.[2]

The most notorious example of human sacrifice occurred in 1940. The Raj Gond Zamindar of Bhopalpatnam had been removed from office because he was insane, and his nephew wanted to succeed him. He made a number of representations to the Darbar which were rejected. As a last resort, he decided to offer a sacrifice to the family deity, Bhumsaria Deo, whose temple is situated in a remote part of the Zamindari. A fatherless child about five years old was kidnapped and taken to the shrine. The usual worship was performed and red powder applied to the image of the god. A chicken was killed. The boy's hands and feet were washed, and the Zamindar's nephew himself applied red powder to the child's forehead and put into his mouth rice that had been offered to the deity. He prayed with folded hands that he should be given the Zamindari. He then, with the help

[1] Grigson, op. cit., p. 221.

[2] The memory of the Meriah sacrifices is preserved in a game played by the Maria and Muria of North Bastar. In the Meriah Karsana, a gang of boys kidnap their victims and 'sacrifice' them to an imaginary goddess.

of his assistants, laid the child on the ground before the image, and with a long sharp knife cut his throat until the head was completely severed from the body. This is the normal method of sacrificing a pig or chicken. The crime was discovered and the would-be Zamindar and two of his assistants were hanged.

The second case, which occurred among the Bison-horn Maria, I will describe immediately. The third example was in 1934 when a Muria of the north, who had not been getting good harvests, was accused of vowing to the goddess of his irrigation tank that, if the winter crops were good, he would offer her a child. That year he had unusually good crops, and in fulfilment of his vow he is said to have killed his nephew, an orphan boy of fourteen years, whom he had reared from infancy. The accused was sentenced to death by the Sessions Judge, but was acquitted by the Appellate Court, and the murder went undiscovered.

A very mysterious crime occurred in Jhoriabadhan in 1923. A little boy named Sukra about two-and-a-half years old disappeared and was never seen again. An elderly Maria of the village was accused of his murder, but was acquitted for lack of evidence. I have little doubt that this was a case of human sacrifice. It was proved in Court that about a month before the child's disappearance the accused told some friends while they were crossing over his embankment that he had promised to sacrifice a male child if the dam did not burst. He warned them that they should not allow their children to pass that way for fear they should fall in. At this stage he was probably thinking that the deity of the tank would herself push a child into the water. But later when this did not happen, he himself probably drowned the child.

IV

THE HUMAN SACRIFICE AT MARDUM

Kuhrami Guddi of Mardum near Katakalian had built a tank for the irrigation of his fields. Unfortunately this did not result in the expected improvement of the harvest and he plotted to find a pregnant woman [1] and sacrifice her to the

[1] Crimes against pregnant women are probably always motivated by superstition. Some extraordinary examples are found in *A Hang-*

spirits presiding over the tank, Mirchuk Deo and the Yer Kanyang or Water Maiden.

On Wednesday, 20 April 1938, the usual ceremonies for the newly-born daughter of Guddi's nephew, Hirma, were being celebrated at Guddi's house. About midday a Mahara woman named Bote, who was four months pregnant, came to the house and joined the party. It was suggested later that Guddi had met the woman that morning while he had been engaged on repairs to the village Rest-house. She too had been working there and when she left with her axe and crowbar, Guddi followed her and persuaded her to come home with him. Whether it happened just like this or not, it certainly seems probable that Guddi had already determined that Bote was to be his victim. He made her drink rice-beer and when the other visitors prepared to leave, persuaded her to stay on and take some food. The food (since, as a Mahara, Bote would not have eaten from the Maria's hands) was probably more rice-beer and it looks as though Guddi succeeded in making the woman more or less fuddled, for she stayed on in the house till nightfall and Guddi persuaded her not to go away by promising presents for her children.

Early in the evening Guddi left the house and found his brother Nari, who was joint owner with him of the tank, and his nephew Hirma sitting in a small open shed outside. He told them that he had decided to make a sacrifice of a foetal child, and that Bote was to provide it. It will be noted that the important part of the sacrifice was not the mother but

man's Diary, edited by Albrecht Keller (London, 1928).

In 1577 at Bamberg (Germany) Nicklauss Stuller of Aydtsfeld was drawn out on a sledge and his body was torn thrice with red-hot tongs before he was executed on the wheel. He and two associates had committed eight murders. First he shot a horse-soldier, secondly he cut open a pregnant woman in whom was a dead child; thirdly he cut open a pregnant woman in whom was a female child; fourthly he cut open a pregnant woman in whom were two male children. One of his associates said they had committed a great sin and that he would take the infants to a priest for baptism but the other associate, saying that he would act as priest and baptise them, took them by the legs and dashed them to the ground.

In 1580 at Nuremberg Hans Muller aged 60 was executed on the wheel for the murder of his sister who was pregnant. After the murder he 'dealt lustfully' with her and buried the body in a field.

In 1601 at Nuremberg Bastian Griibl, a thief, was executed. He confessed to twenty murders and among his victims were five pregnant women. These he had caused to live in debauchery with his companions, then cut them open and cut off the hands of the infants and made candles of the hands to be used in burglaries.

the unborn child. Nari later claimed that he tried to dissuade Guddi from this plan, but Guddi, who was the head of the family, said that he would take all responsibility and that he had already prepared the woman by making her drunk.

When it became dark Bote picked up her axe and crowbar, and at last insisted on going home. Guddi said that, as it was dark, he would go with her for part of the way. He took a knife and an axe and persuaded Nari to accompany them. After they had gone some two hundred and fifty yards, Guddi caught hold of the woman and when she began to scream, pressed her throat to silence her. The two men then dragged her about half a mile to the tank. They took her into the water and Guddi pushed her head under and held her there until she was drowned. He then cut open her belly with his knife, half removed the foetus and slit its throat. Nari's nerve seems to have failed him at this point and he ran away home.

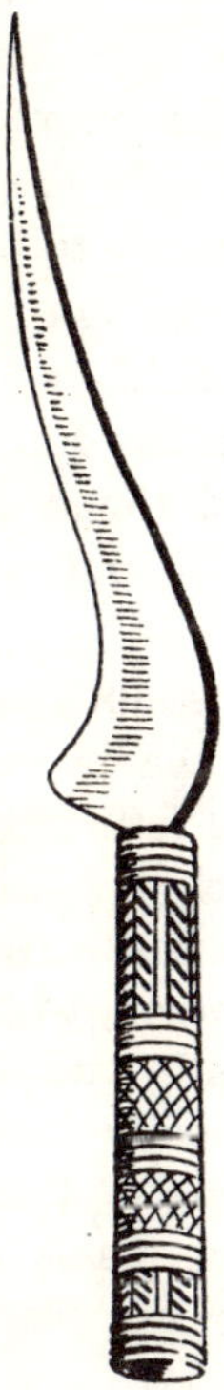

Maria knife (*Length of blade* 10″)

Shortly after Nari's return Bote's husband came with a party of neighbours searching for his wife. He asked Nari if she had been there, and he said she had not. Very late at night Guddi returned. His wife asked him where he had been, and he beat her for being inquisitive. In spite of his late night, however, he got up very early before dawn, and abused his nephews Hirma and Rainu for over-sleeping. He told them to get up quickly and plough the field by the tank. He went ahead with his bullocks, and the two boys and Nari followed. After ploughing for a little while, Guddi left his bullocks and took the others to the tank. There he showed them the body of Bote floating in the water, and told them that he had killed her as a sacrifice. He pulled the corpse to the bank, and the others saw how the belly had been cut and the foetus partly pulled out and its throat slit. Guddi then persuaded the others to help him carry the corpse to a place nearby called Ital

Lata where there was thick undergrowth. That night the four men went again and took the corpse to a hillside in the Koder forest some miles away, dragging it along so that it should appear as if a tiger had killed it.

The search for Bote continued. The husband went to everyone in authority in the neighbourhood, and called the villagers to help him, continuing distractedly to search all Friday and Saturday. A Sub-Inspector of Police was touring nearby and his aid was also enlisted. For three days more they searched. On 27 April, a week after the murder, Hirma and Rainu went to the Koder jungle ostensibly to get bamboos, probably really to see what had happened to the corpse. When they returned they said that it had not yet decomposed, and Guddi suggested that they should report that they had noticed a very unpleasant smell in the forest. The next day the villagers went to the place and found the body. It was, however, considerably decomposed and was only identified by the ornaments and combs.

By 1 May the police were in full charge. It is not quite clear what happened, but it seems to me probable that Nari immediately gave his brother away. In the first fright and confusion, Guddi also lost his head. He took the Sub-Inspector to the place where he had hidden Bote's basket, axe and crowbar. He brought from his house some thread, which the woman had given him on the day of her death, and the knife that he had used to kill her. The Sub-Inspector found stains on his loin-cloth and on Nari's cloth, and seized them. The Imperial Serologist later established that the stains on Guddi's clothes were of human blood; those on Nari's could not be determined owing to disintegration.

After his first fright, however, Guddi denied everything, but Nari, who all along seems to have been an unwilling participant in the crime, turned approver. At the trial Guddi declared that on the day of the birth ceremony he had drunk so much rice-beer that he had become unconscious and had slept till morning. He denied that he went out at dawn; denied that he ever ploughed the land or made the sacrifice. He claimed that the stains on his loin-cloth were due to the red earth of his field, and declared that he showed the Sub-Inspector the woman's possessions, the knife and the thread, only because he was beaten and forced to make a false confession.

There can be no doubt whatever of Guddi's guilt. The evidence of Nari alone would have hardly been sufficient, but Guddi's two nephews corroborated it and Hirma was present when Guddi declared his decision to sacrifice his unfortunate victim.

All the circumstantial evidence was against Guddi. There was the blood on his loin-cloth; the condition of the corpse was consistent with death by drowning; none of the bones were fractured and there were no signs that the woman had been killed by a wild animal. Unless Guddi had been concerned in the matter, how did he know where Bote's axe and crowbar were hidden? It may well be that he was forced by the police to reveal their hiding-place, but it is equally clear that what he showed was true. Evidence was led to show that on the day of her death Bote took some thread which she had spun to Guddi's house.

This crime is notable for two things. First the motive is a very deep and ancient one. Nari described at the trial how, as Guddi was drowning the woman, he called on the Mirchuk and the Yer Kanyang by name, telling them that he was fulfilling his vow by sacrificing a pregnant woman, and praying to them to bless his fields and give them increase. Some of the blood was scattered on the ground, and this blood-stained land was ploughed before dawn the following morning in order to ensure its fertility.

The second remarkable point about the case is the extraordinary stupidity of Guddi which cost him his life. He had a whole week in which to wash his loin-cloth, yet he left it marked with the most damaging evidence against him. He could not leave the body alone, but sent his nephews off to inspect it and then told them to make a report. Had he said nothing, it would have been comparatively easy to dispose of the bones so that they would never have been discovered. When the police arrived, he immediately went to pieces and implicated himself so thoroughly that his later protestations of innocence were of no avail. He was sentenced to death and hanged on 5 September 1938.

Westermarck suggests that the ultimate reason of human sacrifice is to effect a sort of life-insurance.

> A comparative study of the practice of human sacrifice shows that human victims are frequently offered in war, before a battle, or during a siege; for the purpose of stopping or preventing an epidemic; in order to put an end to a devastating famine; when the earth fails to supply the people with water; with a view to averting perils arising from the sea or from rivers; and in order to prevent the death of some particular person, especially a chief or a king. From these facts I have thought it justifiable to draw the conclusion that human sacrifice is, largely at least, a method of life-insurance, based upon the idea of substitution; and though the human sacrifice offered as a means of putting an end to or averting a ravaging famine and securing an abundant crop has been explained as serving as a magical manure, it may be asked why this particular gruesome kind of manure was chosen if not because human life was in danger.[1]

But in the Bastar cases, there was no danger to life: the sacrifices seem to have been motived by a straightforward desire of gain and to have depended for their efficacy on the power of blood which as the source of life is also a cause of fertility. The connexion with irrigation tanks is noteworthy.

V

THE SIRAHA AND HOMICIDE

It is a curious fact that the leaders of the powers of good against the forces of black magic, especially the Siraha and Gunia, seem to cause quite as many murders as the witch or sorcerer.

The Siraha with his magic winnowing-fan and lamp and broomsticks appears in case after case, not always, of course, as the criminal or victim, but as an influential force in the background.

For example, it is the Siraha who diagnoses the cause of death or disease and who, by naming some living person as the author, directly incites to crime. Equally, by his failure to treat a sick person who believes that he is suffering from witchcraft, he may drive him to despair and suicide.

The Siraha is proud of his position and his connexion

[1] E. Westermarck, 'Methods in Social Anthropology', *J.R.A.I.*, Vol. LXVI (1936), p. 232, and *The Origin and Development of the Moral Ideas* (London, 1912), Vol. I, p. 440. See also R. Karsten, *The Civilization of the South American Indians* (London, 1926), p. 408.

with the gods. He is extremely touchy, and immediately resents the least hint of criticism. When Markami Ganga abused his brother who had recently taken up his sacred duties, criticizing him as an economic liability to the family, the latter seized the trident in the village temple and killed his critic with it.

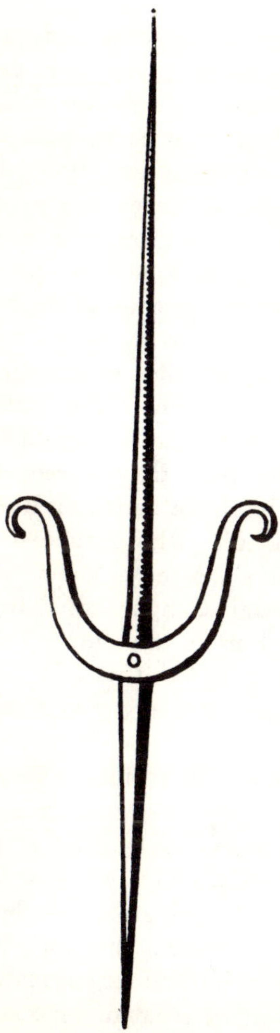

Iron trident

Another incident of the same kind occurred in Kosalnar. An old man Hemla Mukka had a leprous wife. He used to call the Siraha, Jhoria Hunga, to his house to treat her. One day when she was feeling specially ill, she asked her husband to go and fetch him. He went for him, but found him asleep. He woke him up and told him what he wanted. But Jhoria, who was tired after watching his fields, was annoyed at being woken, and got up and hit the old man saying he was not going to give up his own work in order to treat other people. Mukka went away, but just outside the house he said loudly that his wife could be cured without the help of any Siraha. This Siraha, he said, was a *chor mailotia* (a thief who lies with his mother). When Hunga heard this insult to his profession, he came out of the house with a heavy bamboo stick and beat Mukka till he died.

One of the features of any Siraha's house is the little hut for 'in-patients' built a short distance away in the garden or under trees. Especially when a Siraha gets some kind of reputation for diagnosis and cure, he is visited by patients from many different villages. These come laden with dark and unknown infections and must not be admitted into his house. Little huts of leaves and branches are made for them outside, where they live in some discomfort and under unnatural and strained conditions. These abnormal strains have resulted, more than once, in murder being committed.

Barse Chappe was a polygamous invalid. After suffering for some time from giddiness and trouble with his heart and eyes, he went to the village Siraha named Pocha for treatment. He became an 'in-patient' and was accommodated in a little hut. After Chappe had spent three days there, he felt better and went to Jagdalpur to give evidence in a police case. Here again he got ill and fell to the ground in a fit, and the Public Prosecutor was compelled to give him up. He returned to his own house, but when he reached it he had to spend the night outside on the veranda, as his wives told him that he would have to offer certain sacrifices in gratitude for his previous recovery before he could enter the house. The following day he again went to the Siraha for treatment and camped under a mango tree nearby. He was accompanied by his senior wife Sukhi and his little daughter Bode. From time to time his junior wife Chule, who remained in charge of the home, came to see him. After a week, one afternoon when Chule had brought food, Chappe asked both his wives to have intercourse with him in the hut. They refused saying that the place was too open, for it was daytime and everyone would see them. Chappe got angry and beat them.

A few days later, at about 5 o'clock in the evening, Chappe again asked his senior wife to have intercourse with him in the hut. But Bode and two women were sitting only a few paces away on the veranda of the Siraha's hut—whence the hut was in full view—and they were able to overhear Chappe's conversation. Sukhi again refused and told her husband that he ought to be ashamed of himself for suggesting such a thing in the hearing of three other women, especially when one of them was his own daughter.

At this Chappe lost his temper. He picked up a heavy bamboo stick and beat his wife so heavily that she died.

In his defence Chappe gave evidence of delusions. He denied that his reason for beating Sukhi was that she refused to have intercourse with him. He said that for the past week she had been giving him contaminated food. He had asked her not to cook in the Siraha's house where anybody might infect the food magically, but in a special place where only she herself would have access to it. This she refused to do.[1] She was also trying, he said, to have him outcasted for some moral offence. But the nature of this was not made clear in evidence.

The Court decided that Chappe was undoubtedly at the time of the murder a sick and unbalanced person. Although on that very day every able-bodied man in the village had gone out on a ceremonial hunt, Chappe did not feel well enough to do so, a clear sign that he considered himself in a serious condition. It is probable that a number of factors combined to bring about the tragedy. The very fact of being unable to attend the great occasion of the hunt must have been depressing. His wife had refused him access to her for several days. It is more than likely that he attributed his illness to someone's tampering with his food. At last the accumulated frustration and anxiety exploded within him, and murder was the result.

VI

MAGIC AND SUICIDE

In some cases, the torment of disease, the fear of the sinister and hostile magic causing it, and the failure of the magicians to effect a cure, led—not to the murder of the sorcerer or of the doctor—but to the suicide of the patient. The reason why all this misery resulted in suicide rather than murder is generally evident: the suicides were so wretched and so weak that it was impossible for them either to protect themselves against their supernormal enemies or to revenge themselves upon the human representatives of an unhappy fate.

For example, Markami Hunga suffered from yaws. She was old and covered with ulcers, unable to eat for pain and misery. One night, when all were asleep, she hanged herself from a rafter of her house.

Atami Kosa, a Maria of Poyali, was driven to suicide by the

[1] A similar delusion drove a Dhurwa of Darbha to commit suicide in 1939. He believed that his wife was poisoning his food, and he used to wait till she went to work in the fields when he would stealthily go into the house and get what food he could.

pain of a septic ulcer on his left calf. Sori Hirma of Korra got very drunk at a harvest festival and dislocated his hip. For eighteen months he lay in his house, pulling himself up by a rope tied to the roof. But at last he could bear it no longer and managed to hang himself with the very rope that had been so long his friend.

Menstrual troubles are always due to the magic of a jealous woman, usually a frustrated and malicious widow. The catamenial period in any case is regarded as a time of contagious danger and taboo, and any irregularity is sufficient to cause a strong psychotic disturbance.[1] Karti Sukri, a young girl of only fifteen years, apparently suffered from menorrhagia; she bore it for six months and then hanged herself with her own cloth from a mahua tree near her home. Markami Kosi had been married for twenty years, but she suffered acutely during menstruation—'the pain was so great she behaved as if she was mad'—and she too committed suicide. As is often the case when a woman suffers from menstrual troubles, the husband had married a second wife and I have little doubt that the jealousy and annoyance inevitable in a polygynous household played its part in hastening Markami Kosi's death. The younger wife, however, did her best to save the other woman; she cut her down while still breathing and tried to revive her.

In all these cases, matters were made worse by the failure of the magicians to effect a cure. This naturally added fear and depression to the physical suffering of the patient. Whenever the Siraha is found helpless, an atmosphere of deep gloom and apprehension is created: the supernatural powers arrayed against the sufferer take on a new majesty and horror.

VII

CRIME AND SUPERSTITION

I have not found many superstitions about crime, probably because there are so few professional criminals among the Maria. We have already seen how valuable blood is as a fertilizer. In one case I heard of women throwing their

[1] Havelock Ellis goes so far as to say that 'whenever a woman commits a deed of criminal violence it is extremely probable that she is at her monthly periods', but Stanley Hall assembles evidence to show that this view is over-stated. Hall, op. cit., Vol. I, p. 500.

(*a*) Apparatus for distilling mahua spirit (pp. 132ff.)

(*b*) Detail of memorial pillar Kopa Dhurwa at Massenar, showing people serving rice beer (p. 33)

(*c*) Woman making rice-beer

PLATE XIII

Plate XIV. Maria climbing toddy tree to extract the juice

rings on a murdered man's memorial stone as it was being carried to the grave. Afterwards they picked up these rings and wore them believing them to be extremely lucky. But I am not sure that a ring associated with any kind of death is not equally useful.

The Maria magicians believe themselves able to foretell a child's destiny by certain signs at birth. If, at the place where the placenta is buried, there appear the footprints of a tiger or the marks of a snake, they declare that the child will be either killed by a tiger or bitten by a snake. If the water in the pot that is placed above the placenta-pit runs out of its own accord, it means that the child will be drowned. If a baby is born with a strangulating cord, it means that, when it grows up, it will either be hanged or will commit suicide by hanging.

But there is nothing to compare with the superstitions in Europe; the belief, for example, that the heart of a still-born child eaten while yet warm renders the eater invisible, thus aiding him to steal. Adam gives a number of beliefs from the Western world that equal the most bizarre of those recorded in Asia. He describes the soporiferous candles made of the fat of virgin children and used to see whether anyone was still awake in a house about to be burgled. The left thumb of a corpse nine weeks in the grave enables a thief to enter a house at night without rousing the occupants. In Poland the right hand of the corpse of a suicide may be used to discover stolen goods. In Italy, especially in Sicily, it is still believed that treasure can be unearthed with the assistance of the blood of innocent children.[1]

[1] Adam, op. cit., pp. 261 ff. In Mandla District I have met Gond who believe that when a man is hanged a few drops of *jiv-tel*, or 'life-oil', fall from his body. If this oil can be obtained and applied to a dying man, he will be restored to life. At one time Shamrao Hivale was believed to possess a few drops of this precious liquid. The 'Hand of Glory' idea has its parallel in India. In Chittagong it was at one time customary for dacoits (mostly Mohammedan) to spread a shroud stolen from a corpse over the roof of a house to prevent the inhabitants from waking. See E. O. Sherborne, *Man*, Feb. 1934.

CHAPTER SIX

THE CAUSES OF CRIME: MARITAL INFIDELITY

I

THE Maria allow their women a great deal of freedom in their pre-nuptial period, but for matrimonial relationships they have a strict regard. They are jealous and possessive by temperament, passionate as lovers,[1] suspicious and

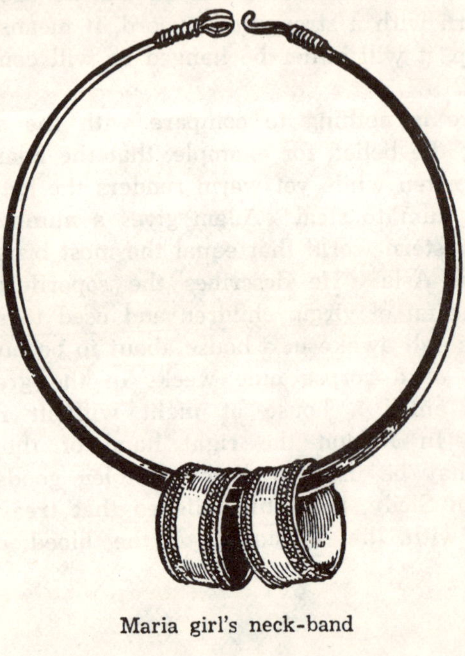

Maria girl's neck-band

exacting husbands. Divorce is rare; adultery is dangerous, a crime the end of which cannot be foreseen.

Adultery is dangerous, for unless proper precautions are taken the ancestors of the household and the clan-god may

[1] But as elsewhere in India 'lust-murder' does not occur. 'True lust-murder, as one of the phenomena of *psychopathia sexualis*, appears to be better known in the more highly cultured countries of the West than in the East, where capital offences have their basis in less recondite mental processes.'—S. M. Edwardes, *Crime in India* (Oxford, 1924), p. 28.

get offended, and in their anger kill the cattle and other livestock. When an animal dies for this cause, its tongue protrudes and a watery discharge issues from its mouth. In Dhurli the Maria said that the guilty person might go blind, and in Mathadi we were told how an old woman did actually become blind as a result of betraying her husband. If a wife commits adultery when her husband is absent on a hunting expedition, her act will 'defile the earth' and the hunt will be ruined. The arrows will fly crookedly, and the husband himself may trip over a stump. He may be bitten by a snake or hit with an arrow. If the deceived husband is a magician, his vision will be clouded. If the proper ceremonies are not performed, he may be afflicted with a watery swelling that may cause death.

If a murder is committed on account of adultery, the families of both the murderer and his victim may suffer from this swelling. To prevent the danger, the elders of each house gather together; they mix milk and water in a leaf-cup of mahua leaves and say, 'These sinned; but let not their sin be on us'. Then a representative of each house drinks a little. The family of the murdered man gives a present (which is called in Halbi *bhul-karcha*) to the family of the murderer. A measure of rice is put under the eaves of the victim's house. In the rice there is placed some thread, a ring and an arrow. The two families feast together on pork and rice, and swear friendship with each other. The arrow remains as witness to their oath. Then the murderer's family take the *bhul-karcha* home, and offer it to the Departed in their own house.

Quarrels are always dangerous, for they disturb tribal solidarity and may earn the vengeance of the Departed. Indeed it is dangerous even to dream of a quarrel; if you do, you should sacrifice to the Earth the next morning. If husband and wife are known to be constantly at odds with one another, a panchayat is held and one or both may be fined.

When Oyami Anda of Harmamunda carried off and married a girl for whom another youth was serving as Lamhada, he not only had to pay compensation for the work done by the other boy, but a ceremony was performed to purify both parties of enmity. Anda stood with the Lamhada under the thatch by the door of his house. The palm of his right hand was placed below the Lamhada's right hand. On the ground, below their hands, a pile of rice was made, and an arrow placed in it. Then the Waddai climbed on to the roof and poured down water which fell through the thatch on to their hands, and thence to the rice. After this a pig and two chickens were given to the Lamhada to be offered to his ancestors. The Waddai as clan-priest officiated since the Dead of the clan were to be appeased.

A curious story related by Oyami Harma of the same village illustrates the manner in which the Maria expect supernatural punishment to fall upon the criminal. 'Long ago,' said Oyami Harma, 'my ancestors, who were a family of seven brothers and one sister, were living beyond Bailadila. A youth of the Uika clan came as Lamhada for the girl, and in due time she was married to him. Twin boys were born, but after a few days one of them died. During Dassara the husband went to Jagdalpur at the invitation of the eldest brother and while he was away his wife together with the wives of the seven brothers went to reap the harvest, taking their two hunting-dogs. The surviving twin was taken with them, and as they were working, he was put to sleep in a swing. While the women were busy in the field, a hare jumped out of a bush and ran towards the baby. The two hunting-dogs chased it, and mistaking the baby for the hare bit him and killed him.

'When the husband returned he asked for his baby, and his wife said, "He has been taken out by our neighbour. First eat your food and then you can play with the child." The husband sat down and ate, and his wife told him what had happened. In the meantime the other brothers told their eldest brother of the child's death, and he was afraid that the bereaved father would revenge himself on him, because it was at his invitation that he had gone to Jagdalpur. So they all decided to run away. The father pursued them saying that it was they who were responsible for the death of his child. They went to Gadapal closely pursued by the angry father. In Gadapal there was a shrine for Kas Pona Pen which was in the form of a bird. This god hid the eldest brother under its wings, and when the father arrived at the shrine, he could find no trace of him. But as he had seen him entering, he knew that he was hiding somewhere and so he set fire to the building and went away. The fire did not harm the man, but some of the bird's feathers were burnt. The soul of the clan-god in Gadapal is in that bird, and to this day the bird can be seen, though now it is made of iron, and on its body the marks made by the burns remain.

'The eldest brother then went to Mailawada and lived there. He consulted the Waddai about the death of his sister's child, and it was revealed to him that the girl had been committing adultery with another man, and that on the very day she had bathed after her menstrual period, she had had intercourse both with her husband and her lover. The result of this was twins. But the Departed were offended at her conduct, and as a result one of the twins died after a few days and the second was killed by the Departed who first took the form of a hare and excited the dogs, and then possessed the dogs and killed the child in the swing.'

Such stories are not mere fairy-tales. They are part of the actual life of the people, vividly believed and actually experienced. To aboriginals who live in such an atmosphere and depend so entirely on the supernatural, the cumbersome and vulgar machinery of human courts of justice seems comparatively unimportant. It is said that many murderers find a sort of relief in going to jail, since they believe that this earthly punishment may save them from the vengeance of the Departed.

But, as often in the aboriginal world, there are regular methods of evading these dangers. If a man wishes to commit adultery he makes offerings to the Departed and prays, 'Let me not swell with water. Let the sin be on the husband of the girl and not on me', and then he addresses his ancestors, 'Away with you. Go to water and to wind. Go beyond the boundary-line. Do not trouble me whatever happens'.

There is no doubt, however, that many Maria are not satisfied with such ceremonies, and that they consider themselves entirely justified in killing a wife who is disloyal. In particular, the discovery of a woman actually in the arms of her lover appears to have so overwhelming an emotional effect that the husband is almost bound to strike and kill.[1] A few young husbands keep careful guard over their wives and when they see them going to an assignation, do not stop them then, but follow, watch and at the critical moment intervene.

Poyami Masa had two wives, Gadme and Dome. One day Dome found her elder co-wife in conversation with a Dhobi who was trying to seduce her. In order to get him to go away Gadme told him to come at night to the house and promised to meet him. When Masa came home from his work, the younger wife told him everything, probably only too glad to make trouble. He became very angry and beat Gadme and took her immediately to confront the Dhobi, but was unable to find him. Then he went to the headman to ask him to take action against the Dhobi. All day long he was in a passion of rage, clenching his teeth and continually talking about his wife's scandalous behaviour. When she tried to give him food, he refused to take it. After supper Gadme and her three children went to bed, but Masa lay awake in the dark brooding until he could contain himself no longer. Just before dawn he got up and stabbed Gadme with an arrow. He was probably intending by this to make it look as though Gadme had committed suicide out of remorse for her behaviour. But he did not do his work properly, and the woman lived long enough to say what had happened to her. In this case the Court took into consideration the fact not only that Masa had been wronged, but that he believed himself to have been wronged by a member of a caste which the Maria despise.

In Chhindgaon a man of about thirty-five years, Burka by name, began to suspect his wife of deceiving him with Hirma, a neighbour who lived opposite his house. One afternoon—it was Tuesday, 16 December 1924—the woman told her husband that she was going to catch fish in a tank. Burka was suspicious and watched her secretly.

[1] By the Kanikar of Travancore, 'adultery is viewed with great abhorrence, and punishment for this offence varies in different localities. At Kulathupula the punishment inflicted on the adulterer is this. His legs are tied to the branch of a tree with the head hanging down. Straw stewn with chillies is spread on the ground and burned. The body of the culprit is swung to and fro and he is in the meanwhile given twenty-five lashes with a cane on the buttocks. The guilty woman is given fifteen lashes by a man who marries her, even though he may have already been married'. L. A. Krishna Iyer and N. Kunjan Pillai in *Census of India, 1931*, Vol. I, Part III-B, p. 224.

He saw her go across the road to where Hirma was winnowing grain, and after a word with him proceed towards the tank. After a little while, Burka went over to Hirma's house to see if he was there, but did not find him. So he got his axe and went off in pursuit. Below the tank he saw Hirma and his wife going into the jungle together. He crept quietly to the place, and there discovered the two lovers in the act of sexual congress. He struck Hirma on the back with his axe and rolled him over, and then gave him four blows on the head and left him for dead. His wife sprang up, but he gave her a heavy blow with the back of his axe behind the left ear. She fell to the ground and he gave her a second blow just above the first, and she died.

Burka then went and told the Kotwar of the village what he had done, and with the Kotwar went to the Manjhi. When they went to see the bodies, they found Hirma still alive and Burka tried to get his axe in order to finish him off. But he was prevented.

Poriami Podiya was a young man of about twenty years who had been married only for a year. He either suspected or (as he himself claimed) actually discovered that his wife was having intercourse with another man. He beat her with his fists and dragged her to the jungle in spite of several remonstrances from the neighbours, and went on beating her there till she fell to the ground. Even then, as he himself admitted, when he found she still had some life in her, he determined to make an end of her and her intrigues with her lover. He twisted a creeper-thong round her neck, but finding it was not long enough for the purpose, tied a cloth round her neck and to a tree. Probably he first strangled her, and then tied her up to give the impression of suicide. During his trial Podiya showed no sign of appreciating the enormity of his crime, which he seems to have regarded as a just retribution for his wife's unchastity.

Marvi Deva killed his little daughter about four years old and tried to kill his wife, because he suspected her of betraying him. He declared that he had twice caught her in the arms of men whom he was unable to identify, and that on the night of the murder he had seen her talking to a man in a neighbour's compound. The man had run away before he could catch him. He took his wife home and tried to force her to give him the name of her lover. When she refused, he took his axe and struck his little daughter who was standing by and crying with fright, and killed her instantly. He then tried to kill his wife who was carrying her baby in a cloth passed round her shoulder, but she managed to escape. Deva picked up the body of his dead child and carried it into the jungle where he left it under a tree covered with a cloth. The Court was sceptical about Deva's accusations of his wife's unchastity, particularly because he could not give the names of her lovers. But this seems to me entirely in keeping with a Maria's pride, particularly if Deva knew that the seducer was someone in a forbidden relationship or someone whom he disliked. Although some aboriginals have no shame in these matters, others are very reluctant to admit the actual names of men who have seduced their wives.

There is the curious point that, according to one version of the incident, Deva asked his wife to give him tobacco or, in other words, to have sexual intercourse with him, and her refusal to do so was the final spark that caused the explosion. This again is, I think, in line with primitive psychology. The husband would have been powerfully excited sexually by the thought of his wife being possessed by another man; he would desire to reassert his rights over her and perhaps to test her. Her refusal to do what he wanted proved to him that his suspicions were well founded.

A very influential man named Nanda, who was the Siraha of Killepal, met his death on the night of the festival of the Village Mother in April 1932. Nanda and Poyami Panda had married two sisters and both families lived in one compound with the old father-in-law. For some time past Panda had suspected Nanda of an intrigue with his wife Hirme. He had been foolish enough to go to the Tea Gardens leaving her behind in too close an association with the exciting and important personality of the Siraha. When he returned he displayed many of the symptoms of pathological jealousy. He was continually asking his wife whether she had had intercourse with Nanda, and he tried hard to get her to leave the village, where she lived in such an undesirable proximity to her lover, and go to live elsewhere. This, however, she refused to do.

It is very difficult to discover what really happened on the night of the festival, for everybody was drunk on rice-beer. Several different versions of the incident were given. It seems probable that early in the evening Panda found his wife standing in the courtyard and slapped her; perhaps he suspected that she was looking for her lover. Nanda saw what happened and told Panda not to hit his wife, for the child she was holding in her arms might fall down and be injured. A little later, Panda wanted to get a bamboo tube to keep his tobacco in. He started to cut a bit from a pole on which bunches of maize were hanging. Nanda again interfered and told him not to cut it, for the maize would fall down. Panda took no notice and went on cutting the bamboo. Nanda then lost his temper, and told him that he was a very quarrelsome person and no one could live with him. He suggested that he should go away to another village and live with his brother. At this Panda retorted that the real reason why Nanda wanted him to go away was because he was in love with Hirme.

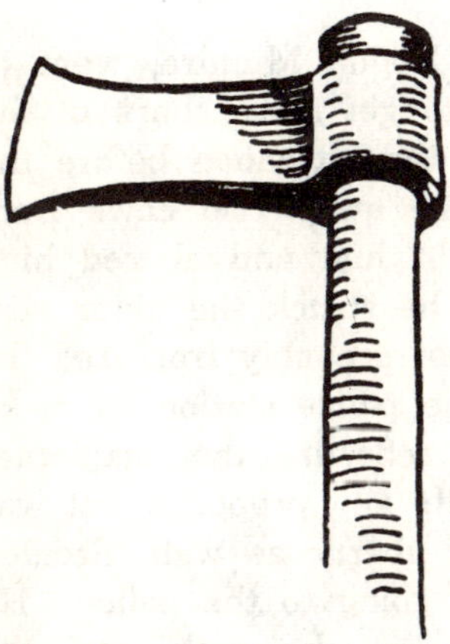
Godel axe

There was no violence in the quarrel at this point, and Nanda went away to his own house in the same compound. Hirme was making leaf-cups in her father's house, and later—it was dark and everyone was drunk—Nanda took the opportunity of slipping into the room and embracing her. Suddenly Panda entered, and finding his wife and her lover together—he claims that they were actually enjoying sexual intercourse—he lost all control of himself, picked up an axe and killed his rival.

Hemla Gunda was the Dhurwa or clan-priest of the Hemla clan-god. He was also a well-known medicine-man and, although he was excommunicated for reasons that will appear immediately, was a person of great influence among the Maria of Bijapur Tahsil.

He was, however, a cruel and unnatural man. About a year before his murder, he seduced the wives of each of his two sons, and not content merely to seduce them drove out of his house his own wife and his two sons, and lived there openly with the two young girls. He refused to do anything to maintain his wife and would not give his sons any share in the family property, although by tribal custom he should have allowed its partition, since he was doing nothing to support his family.

When the sons applied to the panchayat for justice, that body met, but so great was Gunda's influence that they were afraid to take any strong line against him. But they did excommunicate him for his relations with the wives of his own sons and for the even more serious offence of keeping a Ghasia woman.

In May 1928, one of the sons, Hemla Mundra, went to his father's house and attempted to get some share of the property. He failed then, but on the afternoon before the murder, returned and tried to take away two cows from the family herd. His father caught him and abused him, and the boy was so annoyed that he struck the older man on the face with a lathi, a blow that probably fractured the jaw. Gunda prepared to go to the police station to make a report against his son. Mundra, reflecting that his father had not only robbed him of his wife and property, but was now going to deprive him of his liberty as well, decided to kill him and prevent him from going to the police. He managed to get ahead of Gunda on the path, and the moment he appeared broke his skull with several blows of a heavy stick.

The murder was regarded by the other Maria as justified, and they hushed up the whole affair, reporting to the police that Gunda had died of smallpox. Indeed the case would never have come to light, had it not been that a prisoner in jail in the vain hope of getting his own sentence mitigated reported the matter. Grigson, who tried the case, sentenced the accused to one month's imprisonment.[1]

[1] A similar case was reported from the north of the State in 1940. Kande, a Muria boy, killed his father near Pupgaon. The father had

Murders committed on account of an unwelcome and unexpected pregnancy are not common, because of the high standard of domestic morals among the Maria and because if an unmarried girl is found pregnant, she is immediately married and the child is thus legitimized. But there is one authentic case in which a man was driven to kill his lover, though it may be said that it was her stupidity rather than her pregnancy that caused the tragedy. Mase was the wife of a man who deserted her for the Tea Gardens, leaving her alone and unsupported with three little children. She used to make some sort of living as a coolie. But presently Poriami Hirma fell in love with her and used constantly to visit her in her house, although he never officially kept her as his wife. In time she became pregnant and a panchayat was called to consider the matter. The elders decided to send information to Mase's husband's elder brother, an ex-convict and a harsh violent man, of whom the girl was greatly afraid.

Early in the morning of Tuesday, 21 February 1933, Mase left her three children in the house and went to tell Hirma what had happened. She expected that her husband's elder brother would come that day and beat her and she suggested that Hirma should run away with her and hide. Hirma agreed and they went some way into the jungle and sat down under a tamarind tree. The weather was cold and they lit a fire, beside which they sat and talked. Mase was very frightened and depressed. She wept and threatened to kill herself. Hirma very properly asked her to come and live with him as his wife, and promised to look after her and the children. But the girl, who was obviously in

seduced Kande's first wife, and the proper ceremonies of purification had been conducted. But when Kande took another wife, the father again attempted or, as some say, succeeded in seducing her, and this time there was a violent quarrel between father and son while they were catching birds in the jungle. The father actually complained to his son that the girl did not respond properly to his advances. Kande was assaulted by his father and killed him in return. When I saw this boy in jail a year later, the extraordinary sadness of his face contrasted strikingly with the expression of many of the more regular criminals. The villagers concealed the crime and when it was by chance discovered five months later, were very backward in co-operating with the police. Obviously as in the Mundra case, they considered it a very proper murder. But Kande was not so fortunate as Mundra and was sentenced not to a month, but to five years' imprisonment. This was later reduced to three years, and he was released in 1943.

a hysterical condition, rebuked him and said that she would not go to his house or to any other, accusing him of having brought the trouble on her. Hirma got annoyed and kicked her violently in the stomach and the vagina. Mase was three months pregnant, and it is probable that the kick which was simply intended to bring her to her senses was the real cause of her death.

II

Only rarely do the complications of infidelity lead to suicide. A girl called Kare of Kosalnar came one day to Kadti Pandu as a Paitu wife. This means that she forcibly entered his house of her own accord, and he had to agree to accept her as his wife. They lived together for five months. Then there was a quarrel, and Kare went off to another village, Pharaspal, where she repeated the same trick with another man. Pandu ordered her to come home and she refused. So he beat her and brought her back by force. The following day the girl disappeared, and a search discovered her hanging from a mahua tree.

The reaction of Barse Konda to unchastity in his family circle was remarkable. He had one daughter named Jabbo. This girl was that very rare thing, a Maria girl of promiscuous habits. She was first married to a man of Samgiri. Then she went to a man at Gongpal. From him she went to a man at Molasnar. From him she went to a man at Palnar. Some time in 1937 she left her Palnar husband and went to live with Kawasi Kosa of Rewali. For the Korta Pandum, the harvest festival of the new cucumbers and gourds, Jabbo went to her home at Nakulnar, and after three days her father Konda took her back to Rewali. Rewali is a notoriously ill-tempered village, and when Konda arrived he was badly received and abused by several of the people for his daughter's behaviour. He went home, angry and depressed, told his wife what had happened, and got very drunk. At supper he caught his wife by the hair and beat her. She ran away to a neighbour's house. Then Konda got out his drum and danced with it all night long. As the first cocks crew, he went into his house and hanged himself from the central beam of the roof.

CHAPTER SEVEN

THE CAUSES OF CRIME: THE DESIRE TO ELIMINATE

I

THE murder for elimination is described by Tennyson Jesse. 'The range is wide—from the lovers who plot to remove an inconvenient spouse, as did Jeanne Weiss and her lover, Roques, at Ain Fezza, to the removal of an inconvenient lover or a blackmailer. The case of a husband or wife who kills a rival comes under the heading of jealousy, since that would be the dominating motive—as the dominating motive behind the removal of someone who stands in the way of an inheritance comes under that of murder for gain. The dominating motive of a pure murder for elimination is to remove someone who is inconveniencing the potential murderer by his presence and conduct, as L'Angelier certainly inconvenienced Madeleine Smith. Indeed, the killing of a blackmailer is a pure murder for elimination; and so is the killing of a householder who chances to disturb burglars at their work. A classic murder for elimination is that of Harriet Lane by Wainwright, whose mistress she had been. He cherished his respectability, and it became impossible to retain both that and Harriet, therefore he eliminated the woman.' [1]

This type of crime is not very common in Bastar. But a few cases have occurred. Two murders were inspired by fear, when the threat to the murderer's security could only be eliminated by death. Six Maria were involved in a robbery during a famine year, and when two of them were caught, they were murdered by the others to prevent them turning approver.[2] In another case two men were on their way to make a report at the Kuakonda police station about the theft of a cow, and in order to avoid arrest and imprisonment the thieves followed and murdered them. Here there was probably a strong feeling that a matter of this kind ought to be settled by the tribal elders, and not

[1] Tennyson Jesse, op. cit., pp. 14 f.

[2] Case No. 30.

to go to the police. There was then the murder of Markami Handa by a young Maria Lohar in 1923. Handa had two wives and the younger, Bandi, fell in love with the young and attractive Masa who was employed as a farm labourer in a neighbour's house, and one day they eloped together. Some time previously Handa had warned the girl that, if she continued her friendship with the boy, he would kill them both. Indeed he took the intrigue so seriously that he moved his entire household to another village, but to no avail. Bandi seems to have been terrified for her lover's safety and when she heard how Handa was searching everywhere for her, she told Masa of the danger they were in, and Masa made up his mind to remove the dangerous husband so that he would be able to live freely with his girl. For four days and nights they enjoyed a sort of happiness in the jungle, then they went together under cover of darkness to Handa's house and climbed a tree outside the compound. Here they sat for a long time until they were sure that everyone was asleep. About midnight Masa went to the house, opened the bamboo door and shot Handa who was lying asleep on the ground near the entrance. Masa probably hoped to get away without being noticed, but unfortunately for him Handa's elder wife woke up and saw him clearly in the moonlight. He was arrested by the villagers the following day, and in due course was hanged. But Bandi, who was a young girl only eighteen years old, was acquitted.

This is, as far as I can see, a pure example of the murder for elimination. The only motive was fear of Bandi's husband. The difference between this and many European crimes is simply that it is more usual for civilized people to eliminate the inconvenient husband or wife first. Masa in true Maria fashion first got the girl, and then set to work to deal with the husband.

II

THE SIRISGUDA POISONING

Marvi Boti and his lover Mase, his elder 'brother's' wife, set about eliminating her inconvenient and rather useless husband, Marvi Bododi, in a more civilized fashion. Mase and Bododi married each other rather late in life, and both had been married before. Mase's first husband died leaving her with five children, and one of her daughters Dallo had been married three years at the time of the tragedy. Bododi also was a widower and had five children by his former wife, the youngest of whom, a boy named Hunga, was about twelve years old and lived with his father. The two lonely people met and married. They lived for some months in Mase's house at Maolibata, and then moved to Sirisguda in April 1940, where they were entertained by Bododi's younger 'brother' Boti. After a time they built a hut of their own close to Boti's house and went to live there.

Bododi's profession was that of a Siraha, but he seems to have been as poor a magician as he was a husband. Mase was a large vigorous woman, who expected much of life, and already by this time was getting tired of her elderly husband who produced so little money to run the household. Boti, as Bododi's younger 'brother', stood in a privileged relationship to Mase. Tribal custom regards an intrigue between those who stand to each other in this relationship very lightly and readily forgives it. Mase soon found herself fascinated by the young Boti, though when I saw him he was unattractive enough, with a broad stupid face and a very large flat nose.

Bododi's duties as Siraha always kept him on the move, and he was continually going from place to place treating his patients. In his absence Mase and Boti were naturally free to develop their friendship. One night Bododi came home unexpectedly and found his wife absent. Mase's son-in-law Gagru, the husband of Dallo, had come there for a First Fruits festival, and Bododi asked him where Mase was. He said she had gone to drink rice-beer somewhere. Bododi went to look for her, but failing to find her came back and sent Gagru in search instead. Gagru found Mase and Boti coming together out of a field of maize. Mase begged Gagru not to say anything about it, and went straight to Boti's house. Gagru went and told Bododi where his wife was hiding, and there was a violent quarrel.

Patients who came to Bododi's house for treatment reported other quarrels between Bododi and his wife. One day Mase accused her husband of doing nothing to earn his living, and he slapped her. She took up a piece of burning wood and tried to hit him with it, and Bododi took refuge in Boti's house. About a week after this quarrel, during a festival, Mase again abused Bododi for wandering about doing the work of a Siraha, and urged him to do something more profitable for the support of the children. Bododi again beat her, and she went away to stay for a time with her daughter Dallo at Kurenga. During this visit she confided in her daughter how miserable she was with Bododi, and told her that Boti had promised to give her poison so that they could get rid of him. Boti, she said, had promised to marry her and care for the children. Dallo begged her to do nothing of the kind. Mase returned home and a few days later her daughter, perhaps anxious about the situation that was developing, came to Sirisguda. Bododi was away and Dallo slept with her mother in the same room. During the night the older woman had a visitor and when the daughter asked who it was, she admitted it was Boti. During this week's visit, Boti visited his lover three times.

A few days later Boti gave some oleander seeds to Mase, and told her to pound them up, mix the powder with vegetables and give them to her husband. It was typical of the carelessness with which the whole affair was planned, that he did this in the presence of Mase's little daughter who was about six years old. Mase pounded the seeds on a stone with a big wooden spoon, and hid the powder in a leaf-packet in the roof of the house. Boti said that he knew that pigs died when they ate these seeds, but he did not know whether they would be fatal to human beings. As the taste was bitter, it was decided to cook the powder with the bitter vegetable called karela.

Accordingly on Saturday, 28 September 1940, Mase cooked rice in one pot and karela and mushrooms together in another. When Bododi came in for supper, Mase served rice to him, his son Hunga and her own little girl. She poured the cooked vegetables into three leaf-cups mixing the powdered seeds in one of them. She gave the poisoned cup to Bododi and the other two cups to his son and her own daughter. Bododi remarked on the bitterness of the vegetable, and gave some of it to his son. A little

(*a*) Girl cleaning grain at Tikan-pal before a decorated door

(*b*) Hinge, a Maria girl of Rewali

PLATE XV

(*a*) Quarrying memorial stones at Dugeli

(*b*) Row of uraskal stones (p. 30)

PLATE XVI

while afterwards they both began to vomit and purge, and cried out that they felt as though their livers were being cut to pieces. One of the patients was staying in the house, and Bododi called him and told him that he had been poisoned and was going to die. He staggered over to Boti's house and told him the same thing. All night the two unhappy men were in agony, rolling on the ground and tearing at themselves with their hands. Bododi died the following morning at about 8 o'clock and Hunga at midday.

The Kotwar was informed, and taking specimens of the vomited matter went at once with Boti and others to the police station at Jagdalpur. Boti's behaviour then was extraordinary. He reported that Bododi had come to him in the night vomiting and in pain and had told him that his wife had cooked karela and mushrooms, that he had found them bitter in taste, and that immediately after eating them he had begun to vomit. The police went at once to Sirisguda. As usual the nerve of the criminals broke under examination, and they both confessed. The Sub-Inspector seized the cooking utensils, the stone, the leaf-cup and the spoon with which the poison had been prepared, and arrested Boti and Mase.

Traces of oleander powder were found in the organs of the dead men, as well as on the stone, the wooden spoon and the leaf-packet in which it had been kept. In their first confessions before the Tahsildar at Jagdalpur both Boti and Mase admitted everything, but later in Court Boti denied having given his lover any seeds, and said that he had been forced by the police to make his previous confession. Mase, however, stuck to her story that Boti had been her lover, that he had made her pregnant, that Bododi had ill-treated her for that reason and that Boti had given her the seeds and promised to keep her as his wife after her husband's death. In Court evidence was given by Dallo, Mase's own daughter, and by her husband Gagru; even Mase's little daughter Nande described how she had seen Boti giving the seeds to her mother. It is remarkable that these close relatives should have been willing to testify against the woman. It is probable that they were frightened into believing that, if they did not do so, they also would be arrested.

Mase denied that she had any intention of giving poison to the boy Hunga. There is indeed no evidence that she had. She had nothing to gain from his death, and she herself said that she put the poison in only one leaf-cup and then Bododi himself, finding the vegetable bitter, gave some of it to his son to eat with the result that he unwittingly killed him.

Here is another futile crime. Mase and Boti did not take even the most elementary precautions. Boti told Mase what she was to do in the presence of a witness, a very stupid act even though he may have thought that the little girl would never testify against them. Mase had plenty of time to burn the leaf-packet in which the powder had been kept, and to clean the stone and spoon with which it had been prepared. The actual deed was performed at a time when other people were staying in the house. There was no need for Boti to have gone to the police station at all, nor for him to have made an incriminating report against his own lover at the very outset. With all their attempts, therefore, to eliminate the inconvenient husband, the murderers only succeeded in eliminating themselves.

CHAPTER EIGHT

THE CAUSES OF CRIME: DISPUTES ABOUT PROPERTY

I

In Europe, and indeed wherever modern civilization has made its way, the great majority of murders are murders for gain. Among the Maria also many acts of violence arise in sequel to disputes about property. But there is a great difference.

How few are the possessions of the Maria! There are some little huts of mud and thatch, some weedy cattle, land which is ultimately the property of the State, a few knives and axes, some pots, perhaps a store of grain and a handful of rupees hidden somewhere. When a man dies, questions of inheritance only rarely arise, for after a few valuables have been buried in the grave there is hardly anything left to distribute. Rules of inheritance do, however, exist. After the death of a father his fields are jointly owned by his sons, his brothers and his brothers' sons. Widows and daughters do not usually inherit, though there are a few examples where there is either no obvious rival claimant or the widow is of strong character and has refused to hand over the property of her dead husband to anyone else.

Quarrels more often arise over the partition of the family goods while the head of the household is alive. The traditional idea was clearly not to partition the family property during the father's lifetime. But nowadays elder sons often desire a share of land or cattle when they set up a separate establishment. Brothers who, after the death of their father, have shared his possessions sometimes quarrel with one another, and desire a formal separation and partition. Where such partition is permitted in the father's lifetime the youngest son, who often remains at home when the older boys go away to live elsewhere, has a special claim over his father's remaining goods.

Murders connected with property are not generally committed for gain in the ordinary sense. They rather arise out of disputes about rights and privileges, and the actual murder is the result of anger and resentment rather than a desire for possession. In several cases indeed murder has been a form of self-defence against someone who tries to take away land or other property that the murderer believes to be his by right. Thus Marvi Buti was the elder brother of Marvi Chule, and for some time they lived in separate villages. Two years before the tragedy, Chule came to live next-door to his elder brother at Bara Gudra and got two of his fields and two tanks for irrigation. Chule cultivated them and paid two rupees as rent. Buti spent the money and when the time for the next payment came round, demanded and recovered four rupees from his younger brother. The following year Buti refused to give Chule any land at all. But Chule, claiming that he had already paid in advance for that year since he had actually paid six rupees and had only cultivated for one year, ploughed up the fields in spite of Buti's protests, and sowed grain in one of them. Buti countered this by giving the fields and the tanks to another brother who used the tanks, but was unable to get possession of the land. Then Buti threatened that he would drive the village cattle into the fields where Chule had sown his crop and would thus destroy it. Chule seems to have felt that it was no use carrying on the unequal struggle any longer, and he decided to leave the village and go elsewhere. He actually built a house in another village, and at the beginning of the rains went to move his possessions. When he reached his old house, he found one of his plantain trees cut down; he was told that Buti had been there and had cut the tree saying that he would cut down Chule in the same way. As he was removing his mahua seed from the building, someone came running to say that Buti was approaching with a knife in his hand. Chule got his axe and faced his enemy. Apparently Buti tried to run away, but Chule followed him and killed him.

Now here, although the tragedy arose out of a question about property, it is evident that Chule was not moved by the desire of gain. Indeed he had abandoned his claim to the fields in dispute, for he had already moved to another village where he would get new land. I think it is probable that he never intended to kill Buti. But when he reached his old house and found his tree cut down, and when on top of this he saw his enemy approaching with a knife in his hand, the double passions of revenge and fear so moved him that he lost all control and went out to kill his adversary. It is said indeed that, as he pursued him, he shouted that they would both die together.

Another incident developed on similar lines. Dudhi Bhima and his uncle Marvi Deva lived on opposite sides of a field at Pordem, and cultivated it jointly. The real owner of the land had abandoned the field on the death of his father some eight years previously. Four years later Deva's father also died, and when Deva himself fell ill, he decided that whatever good or evil spirit was in occupation there was dangerous and he too abandoned the land and moved to another village. For four years Bhima cultivated the land as a sub-tenant of the original owner, Sori Masa. According to the State Law Masa forfeited his right to his land by sub-letting it for a period longer than three years, and Bhima actually had, by virtue of long residence, become the real owner, though in typical aboriginal fashion he never thought of getting this officially recorded. All went well, however, until in the middle of 1929 Marvi Deva, apparently persuaded that the supernatural danger from the field was not as great as he had feared, or perhaps as a result of performing the necessary prophylactic sacrifices, returned to the village and claimed the land. Bhima refused to surrender it, and in the summer and rains of 1930 he ploughed it and sowed and reaped his crop. After the field was cleared Marvi Deva decided on forcible measures, and one morning he started ploughing the field with the idea of sowing rape seed on it. His nephew did nothing at the moment, but that evening he went to his uncle's house and killed him while he was sitting by the fire after supper.

In this case it might conceivably be said that Bhima's crime was a crime for gain, because once the uncle was out of the way, he would be left in undisturbed possession of the field. But it is much more likely that the crime was one of sheer anger and revenge. In the first place, as we have seen, the land belonged legally to Bhima and he could easily have asserted his right to it by preferring a claim to any State official. Secondly he must have known that after killing his uncle so openly—he made confession immediately to the Zamindar of Sukma—he would not be able to enjoy the fruit of his crime. Bhima's action was indeed judicial and an expression of his indignation against the anti-social conduct of his uncle. Unhappily he chose far too drastic a means of indicating his displeasure.

The case of Marvi Khotla arose out of a dispute about the partition of property. After the death of Manjhi Wijja, his sons Bande and Khotla inherited his property and continued to share the land and cattle. At the time of the murder Bande was about sixty years old and had succeeded his father as headman or Peda of the village. All the family cattle, though actually the joint property of the two brothers, were in his hands. The younger brother was anxious to have his own share separate. But since he and Bande were married to two sisters and were practically one family of which Bande regarded himself as the patriarchal head, the villagers and Bande himself did not consider that there was a sufficient case for partition. Khotla, however, was continually badgering his elder brother, and one day at the beginning of the monsoon he went at sunset to Bande's house and standing before it demanded his share. Bande as usual put him off on some pretext, and there was the usual quarrel. Khotla went home and had his supper. During supper his wife, who was, it will be remembered, the sister of Bande's wife, urged him not to quarrel about the cattle. But directly after supper Khotla again went back to Bande's house and abused him violently. He sat down by the fire, and continued for some time shouting at him. Bande was gradually getting more and more annoyed, and it is said that he exclaimed that he would kill Khotla if he did not keep quiet. A little later he declared, 'I am the Peda of this village, and I will have to beat you if you abuse me like this'. Presently Khotla's own wife came and begged her husband to stop quarrelling and come home to bed. But the man took no notice, and continued shouting every sort of foul abuse until at last Bande came quietly out of his house and knocked him senseless to the ground. The next day shortly after noon he died, and his wife beat a drum in order to give the alarm.

It is not easy to say whether Bande's motive here was primarily to keep control of the family property or not. His feelings were probably very mixed. He was an elderly man and the Peda of the village. Division of his herd of cattle might do something to lower his prestige. As Peda he was accustomed to give abuse, not to receive it. He believed, and in this he had the support of the villagers, that his brother's claim was unreasonable. Outraged dignity, wounded pride and sheer exasperation probably played as strong a part in his catastrophic revenge as any other motive.

Sometimes the quarrels arise about what may seem to the outsider quite trivial matters, though we should never fall into the error of judging the value of things to an aboriginal by our own standards. For example, two murders were committed on account of cocks, one a cock that was needed at a feast in honour of a brother-in-law and the other a fighting-cock.[1] In another case the quarrel arose between two brothers about the possession of a drum which was sold for two rupees ten annas, out of which the real owner only got a rupee.[2] In yet another case a youth murdered his own father as a result of a dispute over a tobacco crop. The son had a debt of four rupees to pay, and he asked his father to give him the tobacco so that he could sell it and pay off his debt. The father wanted the proceeds to buy clothes for himself. Tempers rose quickly and soon the father was saying that his son could sell the children to pay off his debt, but he would never part with his tobacco, a remark that cost him his life.[3]

II

Suicides from economic causes are extremely rare. This remarkable fact has been noticed also for the Bantu in South Africa. 'Conditions of starvation, prolonged droughts and disease among live-stock', says Laubscher, 'are common, and still no cases of suicides are known to magistrates of as much as thirty years' experience which can be considered as the result of despair in the face of economic difficulties'.[4] Only one Bison-horn Maria, Veko Lakhma, killed himself as the

[1] See Cases No. 52 and 16.
[2] Case No. 40.
[3] Case No. 86.
[4] Laubscher, op. cit., p. 290.

result of the burden of a debt. Yet his debt was not especially heavy. He had engaged himself to work for a Thakur as a Kabari against a loan of seventeen khandi-measures of paddy. He worked for a year, and then wearied of it. The Thakur beat him for his slackness, and Lakhma hanged himself in his employer's field—probably as much from a desire for revenge as from despair.

The story of Alami Mata throws some light on the attachment of the Bison-horn Maria to their cherished institutions. This youth, about twenty years of age, was devoted to dancing and used to preserve his magnificent hereditary bison-horn head-dress with the greatest care. In a neighbouring village lived a beautiful girl, unmarried and in love with him, whom he used to meet during the dances. One day he found his splendid horns and feathers stolen. He would not go to dance without his finery; he could not meet his girl; on top of it all his father abused him for not working hard enough. Life without music, rhythm and love was not worth living, and he ended it.

Another young Maria, Poyami Kosa, hanged himself after a dispute about clothes. He went with a group of other boys to cut grass; they all put their clothes together, but when the time came for recovering them, Kosa's cloth was claimed by another boy. In spite of everything Kosa could say the other boy went off with it. This may seem a trivial enough matter, but to people as poor as the Maria the loss of a cloth is serious and during the dispute Kosa was greatly insulted. The combination of loss and insult was too much for him, and he hanged himself.

CHAPTER NINE

CRIME IN THE RELATIONSHIPS OF FAMILY LIFE

I

NOT only to the aboriginals, but to all the inhabitants of India family relationships mean far more than to the dispersed and individualistic peoples of the West. People live together and share things; they control one another and interfere with each other; they are connected by rules of jest or taboo; proximity sometimes leads on to disaster. The following Table illustrates the murders resulting from such relationships.

TABLE EIGHTEEN

ILLUSTRATING THE RELATIONSHIPS OF 107 VICTIMS IN 100 CASES

Wives killed by husbands	18
Husbands killed by wives	3
Fathers-in-law killed by sons-in-law	5
Mothers-in-law killed by sons-in-law	3
Young children killed by parents	6
Brothers killed by brothers	9
Fathers killed by sons	3
Mother killed by son	1
Sisters-in-law killed by brothers-in-law	3
Son killed by father	1
Other murders where the parties were related	10

To a Maria youth and his wife marriage is a real partnership in living and not merely an association for the production of children. Husband and wife share far more of life together than is common in the ordinary Indian village. They work together in the fields. They go to the jungle for wood. They eat in company. They sit together to drink rice-beer. Women even attend funerals with the men and help them to erect memorial pillars. Their life together is happy and united, and woe to the man who disturbs it.

Man and wife generally settle down at first in a small hut of their own. But there is a sort of joint family system with the father or elder brother as the patriarchal head, and sometimes a large family occupies an entire hamlet of its own in one part of the village territory. The institution of the cross-cousin marriage tends to unite families very closely.

This happy and united family life is disturbed by several factors. One, as we have seen, is the commonplace invasion of the happiness of two people by a third. Another is the presence of the husband's younger brother in the house, and the privileged relationship which he has with the elder brother's wife. Another is the custom that allows a married girl to visit her mother's house. Yet another is man's insatiable passion for domestic experiment which leads to the complicated and dubious joys of plural marriage.

It will be of interest to compare with this the situation in ordinary Hindu families, where the common disparity of age between husband and wife creates stresses from which the Maria are free. 'There are tendencies at work within the family institution itself which sometimes lead to criminal action. The joint family rests upon the mutual toleration and sacrifice of the different members of the household. While forbearance is the outcome of long discipline in joint family life, it is put to a severe test as a result of the growth of individualism. Again, the disparity between the ages of husband and wife, of parents-in-law and girl-wife, offers opportunities of exploitation and even cruelty. The custom of infant marriage is apt to promote oppression, especially where there is a striking difference in age between the husband and the wife. Cases of cruelty to young wives are often brought to the courts in India.

'In 1929 a Hindu weaver in Hyderabad, who had married a young girl, chained her like an animal to a big mill-stone to prevent her making frequent attempts to run away. She subsequently died.

'In another case in the same year a young girl-wife who was being forcibly taken to her husband's house managed to free herself, jumped into a wayside well, and was drowned.' [1]

[1] Haikerwal, op. cit., p. 35.

II

HUSBAND AND WIFE

The murder by Veko Chamru of his wife and two children and his subsequent execution which thus removed a whole family from the world, makes a strange and sombre tale. Chamru and his wife Hirme had two young children, a daughter of ten called Lakhmi and son of six named Hando. Apparently for some time they had not been getting on very well. One day Chamru asked his wife to husk rice, as he had to give his share of the Maharaja's tribute at Dassara, but she refused. He brought some sweets for his children and dried fish from the Alnar bazaar. But when he gave them to his daughter, Hirme snatched them out of her hand and threw them away. The woman was evidently suffering from an extreme attack of sulks. She refused to husk rice for supper and she did not cook food that evening or the next morning. The husband went to bathe in the river taking his little daughter with him, but she fetched the child back, and when he returned to the house he found that Hirme had gone away with the two children. She went to a friend's house and told her that she was frightened of her husband, and stayed there two days. She then went to another friend and again stayed two days and went away in the night. At last she went to the house of Chamru's uncle, and he advised her not to quarrel with her husband and told her to go home. The woman came back, but sat at a distance of about a hundred yards from the house and shouted to Chamru that she was going to leave him. He had to go out to get his cattle, and on his return found that his wife had disappeared. After a few days he left his house in charge of a boy, and went to the Alnar bazaar. He met a friend, drank some liquor with him and the two men did not start home till evening. On the way they met Hirme with the two children. Chamru scolded her asking her where she had been and saying he would kill her. When they came to the cross-roads near their village, Chamru went home with his wife and children and his friend turned off by another path. When they got home the boy, who had been left in charge of the house, was there and in his presence Chamru twice struck his wife on the back with the handle of his axe.

That night one of the neighbours was watching his crops as usual and as he was going home after making a round of the fields, he heard a noise in Chamru's house. He went there and found the man sitting near the door supporting his dead wife in his arms and weeping loudly. Chamru declared that he had killed her. The neighbour went away and brought his friends, and before them Chamru declared that he had hanged his wife and children because they had run away. He said that he would get another wife the next morning, and tried to borrow rice and bullocks for her bride-price.

The people then went to the house, and found the dead body of Hirme lying near the door and the little boy and girl hanging from a rafter. The next day they went to the police station and reported that Hirme had hanged herself, and the two children had followed her example, during Chamru's absence at the Alnar bazaar.

It is evident that Chamru intended to make a deal with the villagers. He supposed that, if he frankly admitted what he had done and paid suitable compensation, they would agree to hush the matter up, and indeed it is obvious that they did agree to do so. What they did not realize was that a police investigation was bound to discover the weak points in their story. Directly the police came to investigate the alleged suicides, they found suspicious inconsistencies. For example, the knot by which the rope round the boy's neck was tied was not a slip-knot, and it would have been difficult for him to have died by strangulation under the circumstances. The girl's neck was tied with a cloth which was hardly adapted to kill her, and her feet were hanging close to a heap of rice on which she could easily have supported herself. The medical evidence immediately disposed of any idea that the three victims had met their deaths by hanging. The usual marks of such a death—constriction of the neck, ligature mark in the neck interrupted at one side, open eyes, protruding tongue, clenched hands, dislocation of the second vertebra from the first—were absent. Medical opinion was that the cause of death in all three cases was congestion of the chest due to shock, but it was certainly not due to hanging.

When these facts were put to the villagers and they saw that the matter was known, they changed their attitude; and three different lots of people, none of whom apparently had any kind of enmity towards Chamru in spite of his allegations to that effect, described how on the night of the murder he had admitted killing his wife and children. Chamru, however, insisted that he had not met his wife and children on the way back from the bazaar as the witnesses described, but that on reaching home late at night he had, as he entered, collided against the naked corpse of his wife hanging from the roof. He had taken a blazing piece of wood and had discovered his son and daughter in a similar plight. He had cut down his wife's naked body and wrapped it in the cloth with which she had hanged herself, and had sat there weeping and wondering whether he himself should not commit suicide.

There was abundant evidence, however, that Chamru had met his wife and children on the way home from the Alnar bazaar and had gone with them to the house. He was seen in their company by the boy who had been left to guard the building. Nobody saw what happened from sunset until late at night when his perhaps not wholly hypocritical cries of distress attracted the attention of a neighbour. But it is obvious that he was present in the house, and that no other person could have come in and killed his wife and children. Frustrated sexual desire, injured pride, jealousy at the children's affection for their mother, hunger and fatigue (for Hirme's absence meant there was no one to cook or do the house-work) drove the distracted man to a shocking vengeance and his own death on the scaffold in the end.

Marvi Paklu and his wife Dallo had been married for about three years, and had two children who died. They got on fairly well together for some time. But particularly after the death of the children disagreements arose; Dallo appears to have been that rather unusual type among aboriginals, a frigid woman who refused full sexual privileges to her husband and yet at the same time was jealous of him and possessive. Two years after their marriage she went to an uncle at Dilmilli without any proper clothes and only wearing a small bit of cloth for decency. She declared that she had been beaten by her husband and turned out of the house. According to one version of what happened, she stayed at Dilmilli for a whole year. According to Paklu's own story, he went for her after a week and brought her home. This is, I think, more likely. But it is quite possible that Dallo then for a whole year refused to live with him as his wife.

Paklu's home was at Muskonta, a little hamlet of only three houses among rocks and woods near Mutanpal. One of the houses belonged to an old widow called Wage, whose widowed daughter Jimme had come to live with her. Jimme was an attractive girl, and she and Dallo became great friends; they used to go out together to get leaves, fruit and mushrooms. As Dallo got more and more frigid towards her husband, she used to go every night to sleep in Jimme's house. The result was what perhaps might be expected. Paklu, rejected by his wife, fell in love with his wife's friend. One afternoon in July 1939 Paklu and Jimme arranged to meet in a cave among the rocks of a hill about half a mile from the hamlet. That afternoon, as one of the neighbours was sitting on his verandah, he saw Paklu going to the place and a little afterwards Jimme following him. But then to his dismay he observed Dallo going in the same direction with a basket in her hand.

The prosecution story was that Paklu and Jimme were together in the cave and were in the act of intercourse when Dallo discovered them. She asked her husband what he was doing there and struck Jimme with a thin bamboo stick. Paklu, naturally enraged at the interruption, got up and pulled off his wife's cloth, trying to shame her by making her naked. He struck her on the head twice with the blunt side of his axe. She fell down, and then Paklu knelt on her chest and twisted her neck till she died. He dragged her out into the forest and left her body there. Her combs and ornaments and the basket were hidden by Jimme. Paklu went to get some bamboos and returned home. When the body was found, he declared that his wife had been killed by a tiger.

But later Paklu first declared that he had caught his wife having intercourse with another man, who ran away as he approached, and that in a fit of rage at his wife's infidelity he had killed her; and then later admitted that he had gone to the cave, but denied that he ever approached Jimme sexually. He said that he had been sitting on the rocks above when his wife threw a stone at him. He slapped her, and she fell accidentally from the rocks and was killed.

There can be little doubt, however, that the prosecution story was true. When the police searched the cave, they found on the dust of the floor the clear signs of a woman lying on her back and a pair of footprints on either side of the marks made by the woman's buttocks. This clearly shows that intercourse practised according to the normal aboriginal technique had been in progress, and Jimme confirmed the fact.

Paklu, when I saw him in jail, was still young, a man of fine physique and good-looking. He has behaved well in jail, for he has been made a Lambardar and wears the tall yellow cap which indicates his office.

Nine cases of suicide were due to disputes between wife and husband. Thus Kome is said to have been quick-tempered, a person who always exaggerated things. She was a young wife, only twenty years old, and when her husband came in one day tired and wet from the fields, and found no food ready, and abused her, she took a rope and slipped out of the house. Her husband, also young, found some stale food and took it back to the field. When he came home in the evening his wife was dead.

Mate had a row with her husband over lighting the fire. He was drunk and beat her, and she attacked him. But her husband's elder brother, to whom she was strictly taboo and who had no business to touch her, intervened and beat her also. During the night, she left the house and tried to get across the Indrawati River in order to reach her mother's house. But there was no ferry and she hanged herself with her clothes. It is worthy of note that although there was a deep river at hand, the girl preferred to end her life by hanging.

An unusually tragic incident occurred at Metapal in February 1937. Kuhrami Hurra returned one day from the bazaar and found that one of his calves had been killed by a panther. Rightly or wrongly he considered that this was the fault of his wife and daughter, who had not tied the calf up properly in the evening. Hurra's wife was well known for her quick temper; she was continually quarrelling, especially if her husband ventured to interfere with household matters, and it is said that the daughter had learnt to take her mother's side. After the quarrel about the calf, the older woman set fire to their house and took her daughter away to the field-house out in their clearing. Here she first hanged her daughter and then herself.

Yet another wife from the same area, Galle, was obviously a bad housewife; she used to tell her husband that she would throw their child on the ground if he ordered her to do any work. On the day of her death she had been asked to prepare leaf-cups and food for the whole family—a large one. This seems to have been the immediate cause of disturbance, and she hanged herself. But there was undoubtedly a long and miserable tale of domestic unhappiness behind it.

In three remarkable cases it was the husband who committed suicide from remorse and sorrow. Barse Chewa asked his wife, a sick and miserable woman, to light the fire early in the morning. She was rather slow about it and Chewa beat and kicked her, knocking her unconscious. He was so ashamed and frightened that he killed himself. Sori Deva, angry at the loss of two of his cows, miserable because he had beaten his wife, did the same. So did Marvi Dhodsa who beat his wife, who was suffering from sore eyes, for not keeping the baby quiet. That night Dhodsa felt very miserable; he realized that his wife was ill, that he had no right to beat her, and that the child too had sore eyes and was bound to cry. He crept out of the house and hanged himself on a mahua tree with his own cloth.

III

THE POLYGAMOUS HOME

The strains and stresses of a polygamous household do not appear to result in tragedy so often as we might expect. Polygamy is not perhaps very common among the Maria, for the simple reason that there are not enough women to make it often possible. Those men who do keep more than one

(*b*) Detail of Marvi Masa's memorial pillar, showing him as a Siraha sitting on his swing.

PLATE XVII

(*a*) A murderer's memorial. Wooden pillar in memory of Oyami Marvi Masa at Jabeli (pp. 202f.)

(*a*) Oyami Masa with family on the scene of the death of the younger wife (p. 113)

(*b*) Officials investigating a suspicious death at Pondem

PLATE XVIII

wife at a time are generally the sort of people who would make a success of anything, even of so complicated a matrimonial adventure as this. The rough, dominating Goge, for example, was exactly the sort of person who would have had three wives.[1] Oyami Masa, who killed his younger wife at Khutepal, was again a strong, powerful, interesting character, a typical polygamist. And indeed provided the husband treats his wives with more or less equal consideration, and provided he is sufficiently potent to satisfy them all, there is a chance that such a domestic arrangement may succeed.

The failures that come to light are not many, but they are interesting. Sometimes the jealousies and quarrels lead to murder, sometimes to suicide. At Khutepal I visited the family of Oyami Masa, and met the charming old lady who was his senior wife. He was just out of jail after a year's imprisonment for killing his younger wife, Tokki. Tokki was a widow and by no means young, for her son by her previous husband had been old enough to go to the Tea Gardens of Assam. At the beginning of 1940, when Tokki had been living with Masa for about six months, the son returned from the Tea Gardens bringing three bits of cloth with him as a present for his mother. Masa, as one would expect, took possession of the cloth and this naturally upset Tokki very much. She declared that the older wife had persuaded him to keep the cloth simply in order to be vexatious. Masa replied that, since he was the head of the house and was feeding her and her son and everyone else, it did not matter whether he kept the cloth or she did. The quarrel—as such quarrels do—went on and on and at last during supper one evening Masa got so angry at the woman's nagging on the subject that he picked up a stick and beat her. It is not known how hard he beat her or whether he intended to kill her or not, since he had the body cremated immediately. For the woman died. No report was made to the police for three weeks, by which time all the evidence had disappeared, and it was impossible for the court to do more than to sentence Masa to a year's imprisonment under Section 323, I.P.C. for what he admitted, voluntarily causing hurt to his wife.

[1] See Case No. 71.

At Dugeli I met Bugori and his senior wife Jimme. Bugori, a most attractive young man, had been able to win the affection of two women both of whom appear to have loved him devotedly. Unfortunately Jimme's jealousy knew no bounds, and one day, when the two women were out together working in the jungle, Jimme, who was robust and powerful, tried to kill the younger girl with her axe. But she survived, and Jimme went to jail for three years. During her absence the younger wife remained with Bugori. But when Jimme was due for release, the village held a panchayat and decided that the younger wife must go to live at her mother's house for fear that Jimme might try to kill her again. When Jimme came home, therefore, after Bugori had given the usual feast to the villagers and had purified her of jail defilement, he took her to his house where she has lived very happily and borne him children. He visits his younger wife in her mother's village from time to time, but does not allow her to come to his house for fear of another tragedy.

Markami Handa had two wives, but does not seem to have been able to keep the affection of the younger, an attractive girl about twenty-four years old. She fell in love with another man and he killed the husband to prevent him taking revenge. Marvi Kesa had three wives, and ill-treated the youngest. One day, after he had beaten her, she ran away to her father's house. There was a quarrel there, and Kesa killed his father-in-law. Poyami Masa had two wives, and a Dhobi tried to seduce the elder. The younger discovered the intrigue, and probably thought it was an excellent opportunity to get rid of her rival. She told her husband, and he was so angry that he stabbed the older woman with an arrow and was himself sentenced to life imprisonment.

Tati Harma had three wives. At the time of the tragedy which brings his name into this record, only two were living. The younger wife had borne him four children, but Harma used to beat her constantly saying that she did not work properly and ate too much. So serious were the disputes in the home that a panchayat fined husband and wife four annas each for not living happily together. One morning the elder wife went to fetch Harma from the field-hut where he had been sleeping, and found him dead, killed by the younger woman who could not endure his ill-treatment longer.

The complications and petty miseries of a polygamous home are illustrated in the story of how Sori Dome murdered her elder co-wife, Chule. Even while their husband was alive, the two women were always quarrelling. Three years before his death Dome beat Chule over the head with a bit of a broken plough, and Chule took a whole month to recover from the blow. Dome used continually to threaten the older woman that one day she would kill her. After the husband's death matters got even worse. Chule was old and feeble and suffered from yaws, which made her irritable and exacting. But the two women continued to live together, along with their husband's elder brother, in their husband's house. Just before the tragedy, Chule made peevish complaints that Dome had been extravagant in using up the rice, to which the other replied that, since she had eaten it, it was not wasted. One evening, after they had been working in the fields and quarrelling all the time, they set out to go home. Dome had an axe in her hand and her two children were with her. Chule was carrying a bamboo basket. Dome urged the old woman to hurry up, but she replied that her feet were hurting her and she would follow later. Exasperated, Dome pushed Chule by the back of her neck and then struck her a blow with the axe. The old woman fell down, and Dome hit her again and she seems to have died on the spot. Medical examination, however, showed that there was no fracture and no dislocation either in the head or ribs where the blows had fallen. Dome did not use the sharp edge of the axe, and it is possible that she did not intend to kill the woman, but only wanted to teach her a lesson. On the other hand, of course, it was greatly to her advantage that Chule should be eliminated.

It is perhaps rather surprising that there is not more suicide in polygamous households. But it does, of course, occur. Bandi, headman of Khutepal, had two wives. They quarrelled and the elder woman hanged herself. Masa of Samgiri also had two wives, and the younger girl quarrelled with him saying that he did not give her proper clothing or ornaments and that he did not sleep with her often enough. Jealous and frustrated, she hanged herself in a fit of despair. Poyami Gupe of Bastanar, a girl of about eighteen years, was widowed at sixteen and remarried two years later as the junior wife of Guddi. One day, about seven months after the new marriage, Gupe went to collect young bamboo shoots—a great delicacy to the aboriginal—and came home rather late in the evening. For this she was scolded by her co-wife and no doubt accused of every crime that jealousy could suggest. She left the house and went to stay with her maternal uncle. Guddi went to bring her back, but rather than go with him she hanged herself.

Kawasi Dulga's reaction was unusual. He appears to have been one of those husbands who should never have tried such an experiment; a man of weak character who could not keep his two wives in order. The women were always quarrelling and made his home and life a misery. One day he went with the younger to the bazaar and, as they were coming home, they quarrelled and Dulga slapped her. Presently he told her to go ahead as he wanted to relieve himself. She walked on a little way, but he did not appear and when she went back to look for him she found him hanging from a tree.

IV

The relationship between the wives of brothers is carefully regulated. Between an elder brother and his younger brother's wife there is an absolute taboo: there is no stronger rule of avoidance in all primitive society. But the younger brother stands in a special and privileged relationship to his elder brother's wife: he can flirt with her; he can make indecent jokes; he can become her lover; after her husband's death he has the first claim on her person and if she marries anyone else he has a right to compensation.[1]

It is obvious that among a people where brothers often live together, sharing house and lands, where jealousy is strong and sexual desire passionate and keen, such a tradition may

[1] For a detailed study, see Shamrao Hivale, 'The Dewar-Bhauji Relationship', *Man in India*, Vol. XXIII (1943), pp. 157-67.

sometimes lead to trouble. To the younger man, his elder brother's wife is delightful because she is accessible and does not burden his conscience. To the elder man, the younger girl is doubly attractive because she is forbidden. The word 'brother', of course, under the classificatory system of relationship, includes also male relations who are more usually called cousins.

A youth Hemla Bakka killed his wife Jimme for having betrayed him with his elder cousin Hemla Dhurwa. During the season when the mangoes ripen, Jimme had gone with Dhurwa to collect and eat the fruit, and the husband suspecting them followed and watched them secretly. Dhurwa climbed the tree and shook it; the woman collected the fallen mangoes, and they ate them together. Then Dhurwa took her behind some bushes and was about to have intercourse with her, when Bakka appeared and separated them. Some time later Bakka returned suddenly from his field to drink water and discovered Dhurwa coming out of his house. He said that he would report the matter to the village elders. When he scolded his wife for her behaviour, she retorted that she would live with the man she loved and that nothing could prevent her. There was then a regular family quarrel, in which Bakka's father was beaten, and this so enraged the boy that he struck his wife a heavy blow on the head and killed her. There can be no doubt that in this case Bakka's feelings were outraged not only because his wife was unfaithful, but because she was unfaithful with a forbidden person, an act which might bring all manner of supernatural vengeance upon him—cattle might die and he himself might be afflicted with a psycho-dropsical swelling.

Another case of the same kind is that of Marvi Boti of Telam. Boti and his younger brother Kosa were living with their father, and were both married. Boti's wife died and he fell in love with his younger brother's wife, though the villagers said that it was really the girl who made overtures to Boti and threatened to commit suicide if he did not marry her. Kosa suspected his wife and beat her, and this seems to have decided Boti, for a week later he ran away with the girl to the Jeypore Zamindari. After about three weeks Boti decided to go to his father's house to get his children by his former wife. The girl insisted on going with him. As they were approaching Telam they had the misfortune to meet Kosa coming along the same path. Apparently some people returning from a bazaar had told him that Boti had returned, and he had set out to seek vengeance armed with a *gagra*. When the boy saw his elder brother, he said, 'My fate is good, for it has sent you to me, since you have run away with my wife'. And so saying he struck Boti across the face. At that Boti seized his brother by his arms, and there was a struggle in the course of which Kosa was killed.

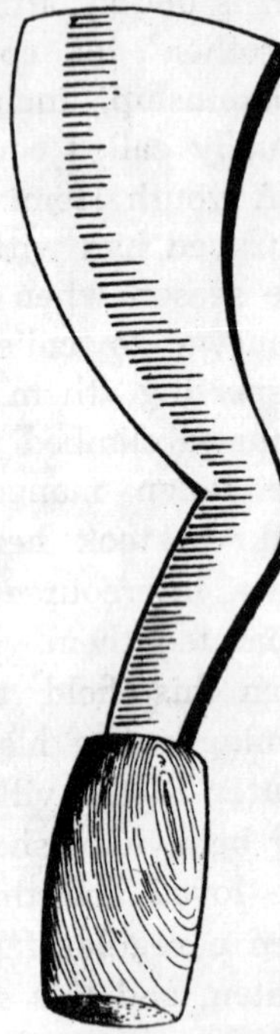

Gagra knife
(*Length* 18")

When Boti returned from jail, he had to make special offerings in addition to undergoing the usual ceremony of purification. Since he had kept his younger brother's wife, he had to sacrifice to the Departed of his house, and to his clan-god. If he had not done this, his body would have swollen and he would have died. As it was, he was impotent for a whole year after he was released from jail.

V

It is perhaps surprising that there are not more murders as a result of the liberties allowed a youth with his elder brother's wife. Boti stood in this pleasant relation to Mase and as a result they poisoned Mase's husband in order that they could be regularly married. The murder of Tati Hirme was due to her rejection of her dead husband's younger brother when he came to claim her.

It is possible that the remarkable forbearance shown by Ujji Poda towards Kopa, his younger cousin, who was in love with his wife, Ragho, was due to his realization that Kopa was not breaking any tribal or social conventions:

he was only outraging his personal marital feelings. Kopa was working as Poda's Kabari or farm-servant at Kaurgaon on the banks of the Indrawati River. Five years before the murder Poda discovered that the boy was enjoying a love affair with his wife, taking advantage of the privileged relationship in which he stood to her. A ceremony of purification and appeasement was performed and Kopa left Ragho alone for a time. But they were evidently really in love with one another, and soon their intimacy began again. In July 1933, Poda discovered this and turned Kopa out of his house and service. Kopa went to live with another cousin in the same village.

On the night of Sunday, 30 July, Kopa crept into Poda's house in the middle of the night in order to lie with Ragho. But while they were together, her hand accidentally knocked against her husband who was sleeping by her side and woke him. Kopa ran for his life, but not before he had been recognized.

The following day news came that a member of the family in another village, Chota Karka, had died, and Poda with Ragho, Kopa and other relatives went to the place for the funeral ceremonies. On the Wednesday there was an open quarrel there between the two men, and Poda told the elders of the village of Kopa's behaviour and beat him publicly. Kopa ran away and hid in the forest. Then on the Thursday everyone went home.

That afternoon three of Poda's servants were working in his field, weeding the kosra crop. In the field there was the usual field-hut in which the cultivators rest and guard the crops. It was raining that day, and at about 4-30 in the afternoon Kopa arrived there carrying a bamboo umbrella and sat down by the fire in the field-hut to dry himself. A little later Poda came and when he saw who was sitting there he fell into a great rage. He beat Kopa several times with his bare fists, knocked him on his back, sat on his chest and throttled him with both hands. The three servants did not dare to interfere, but stood watching.

Then Poda had the body taken to another hut in someone else's field, tied a rope round the neck of the corpse, and strung it up to the roof to give the impression that the dead man had committed suicide. He bribed the witnesses and told everyone who knew anything about the matter to make a report of suicide, and since he was a man of great influence this was done.

The remarkable thing about this case is not the violence with which the murder was committed, but the very great forbearance shown by Poda. After forgiving Kopa the first time, he himself went to the expense of marrying him to a young girl, perhaps with the idea that this would divert his attention. Even on the second occasion he refrained from physical violence, and contented himself with turning the boy out of his house. Few Maria would have failed to kill Kopa immediately after discovering him in the house at night. But all Poda did was to put the matter before the village elders. It seems to have been Kopa's impertinence in going to the hut and sitting there as if nothing had happened that suddenly deprived Poda of his self-control. The Court, taking these matters into consideration, sentenced him to only five years' imprisonment.

VI

THE MOTHER'S HOUSE

Another very common source of domestic friction is the custom that allows a girl to visit her mother's house. These visits are an exciting and important part in the life of every aboriginal girl. During her marriage ceremony many of the songs deal with the happiness of her childhood home, and the misery of a life with a husband under the domination of her parents-in-law. After marriage the mother's house acquires a sweet and romantic memory. Its hardships and quarrels are easily forgotten, and the love of one's own parents appears tender and kind compared to the constant friction of the new home. It is generally considered correct for girls to go to their parents' house for important domestic events such as the ceremonies for the birth of children, marriages and funerals, for some of the chief festivals and to help in the more urgent work of the fields. Husbands, especially young husbands, resent this, for it means one pair of hands the less to work in their own house. Girls are not always very tactful in the enthusiasm they show at returning to their old homes, and some girls make a regular habit of going there, far too often for the comfort of their husbands.

There have been several suicides arising out of this situation, but only one of our hundred murders. This was the tragedy of Habka Masa who, when I saw him in jail, was a sad gaunt man utterly crushed by the tragedy that had befallen him. He had been married to his wife Pakli for some three years, and was living with his old blind parents at Hallur in the Kutru Zamindari. In June his wife went home to Gangalur for the Pen Karsita festival. Masa insisted on going with her. Two days after the festival, Masa told his father-in-law that he wanted to go back to his house, for it was the beginning of the rains and there was a lot to do. The older man was agreeable, and gave him the customary clothes and a basket of oil-seed, which is the usual present to a son-in-law when he leaves the house. But Pakli refused to go. Her parents were on the point of going to work as coolies, and she wanted to go with them. Masa, fearing that he might lose his wife altogether, decided to accompany her. The party set out and went to Gidam, a prosperous little country town on the main road, and again Masa tried to get his wife to go home. From Gidam they went to Tirthum and worked at the construction of a bridge for the P.W.D. When the bridge was ready, they all went on to Silakjhori where they got work as farm-servants. The parents-in-law built a little hut for themselves, and Masa and Pakli occupied a deserted hut belonging to sawyers. From the day of their arrival there were constant quarrels between Masa and his wife, for Masa was anxious about his cultivation—he was the only able-bodied man in the family. Pakli used to put forward every possible excuse for not going back. One day it was raining heavily. The next the rivers were flooded and she was afraid to cross them. A third day she promised to go when the rains were over.

On the night of 10 July 1939, there was heavy rain and a strong wind. After supper with the family Masa and Pakli struggled through the wind to their little hut. They then began to quarrel violently. Masa again asked Pakli to go home and she refused. Then he asked her to give him some tobacco, or, in other words, to have intercourse with him, and this also she refused. She abused him saying, '*Puk nak*, lick my privates ', and told him to go home without her. This, he said, was impossible and she again abused him. He got so angry that he hit her on the head with a heavy piece of wood and she died immediately.

More frequently these disputes have ended in suicide. The wife of Markami Pide was in love with another man, and frequently used to leave her husband and go to stay at her mother's house where it was possible for her to meet her lover. Pide as frequently would go and bring her back and beat her. At last she killed herself in despair. Mundri, the wife of the headman of Kaklur, frequently quarrelled with her husband over the question of visiting her parents, and one day when she wished to go and her husband stopped her, she became so miserable that she hanged herself from a mango tree.

Wooden tobacco box
(*Length* 3¾″)

In two cases it was the husband who committed suicide. Marvi Gutami, a young man of twenty-two years, married a girl to whom he was much attached. Indeed it is said that he loved her so much that he was quite unable to control her, and she got on the nerves of the older women in the house, who lost no opportunity of venting their spite upon her. As a result she often used to go away to her mother's house, and Gutami would have to go and bring her back. One day when this happened, the youth found that she had gone into hiding elsewhere. Despairing of happiness, he returned home and hanged himself behind his house. Kawasi Hurra's wife Lakhmi did not care for him and was always slipping away to her parents' house. He brought her back five or six times, but she would run away again after staying with him for a few days. Hurra seems to have been very fond of the girl, and her constant absence made him so miserable that he ended his life.

A situation where the roles of the characters were reversed, and it was the mother who wished to visit the daughter's house, led to an even more pathetic tragedy.

In November 1939, a mother at Killepal was rebuked by her son and daughter-in-law for not helping them with the reaping of the kosra crop. She had been a widow for ten years and seems to have got a certain amount of pleasure and relaxation from paying visits to her married daughter at Dilmilli. This was resented by the son and brother with whom she lived. When she found that she was to be robbed even of this happiness, she killed herself.

VII

PARENTS-IN-LAW

The relationship between a man and his parents-in-law is always difficult. But the general tradition in Maria, as in Hindu society, is that the older people should treat a son-in-law with respect and consideration. Neglect of this rule is apt to arouse very strong feelings in a man's mind. Marvi Keṣa had three wives, the youngest of whom ran away to her parents' house after a beating. This is a common practice of aboriginal wives, and causes great annoyance to their husbands especially if the parents take their daughters' side. On this occasion Kesa followed his wife to the house and found her enjoying a drink of rice-beer with the neighbours. He went to his father-in-law and asked him why he had not sent his wife back. The older man replied casually that she had only arrived that morning, and this answer so annoyed Kesa that he struck him on the head with his axe and killed him.

In another case it was the mother-in-law who was the victim. Marvi Hinga took his wife Hirme, who was suffering from fever, to a neighbouring village to a Siraha for treatment. He stayed with her during the night and the next morning returned to his house. There his mother-in-law saw him. She jumped to the conclusion that he had left her daughter uncared-for and had come to the village in search of amorous adventure and she abused him, saying that he was an eater of excreta and urine, and that though he had married her daughter he did not take the least care of her. Hinga, who was apparently a very good husband, was so annoyed at receiving this insult from a woman who should have treated him with respect, especially as the words were shouted at him in the hearing of the village from a distance of about twenty-five paces, that he rushed at her and battered her to death with his axe.

The relationship between a son-in-law and the father of a wife who had betrayed him, was at the bottom of the Aranpur murder of 1941. In 1937 Barse Chewa took Bandi, daughter of Tati Pandu, a Maria blacksmith, as his wife. For the bride-price he paid a cow with a calf and a basketful of rice. About a year later Chewa's house caught fire, and his elder brother who was then living with them lodged a complaint with the police that Bandi herself had set fire to the building. She was prosecuted, but acquitted. After the disposal of the case against her, Chewa sent the girl back to her parents, and some time afterwards she married a man at Kondasauli. Chewa now went to his original father-in-law Pandu, and demanded a refund of the expense he had incurred in marrying his daughter. Pandu refused to pay anything on the ground that Chewa had turned her out of his house, and that he himself had had to maintain her for two years. He further claimed that any money that could be extracted from the new husband must come to him and not to Chewa. The quarrel went on for some time until at last Chewa grew so exasperated that he went at night to Pandu's house and shot him in the stomach. All Chewa's attempts to exonerate himself and implicate other people were frustrated by the fact that when the blacksmith removed the arrow from his stomach, he was able to recognize it as one which he himself had made for Chewa in his own smithy.

In this case tribal opinion was divided about the question in dispute. The normal rule is that if a woman leaves a husband for another man, he must repay the bride-price (possibly with certain reductions) to the original husband, and that the father of the girl is only entitled to receive money or goods from the first husband and not from his successors. But in this case the question was complicated by the fact that Chewa had himself turned the girl out and that between her first and second marriages she had spent two years in her father's house. The matter was thus a difficult one, and was still further complicated by Pandu being a blacksmith who probably did not anticipate fair treatment from the tribal panchayat.

There was a very curious and tragic murder when young sixteen-year-old Marvi Hunga killed Hirma, a boy three years younger than himself. These two boys were related as uncle and nephew; Hunga's mother was married to the uncle of Hirma's father. This relationship is a privileged one. Just as a grandson may joke with his grandmother, so an uncle may abuse his nephew and even threaten to sleep with his mother, and neither uncle nor nephew is supposed to take any notice of it.

But on this occasion when Hunga met his young nephew Hirma in a field and asked him where he was going, the younger boy abused his uncle's mother and wife saying that he would keep them both as his wives; this annoyed Hunga and he drew his bow and shot the boy with an arrow. The incident apparently had nothing whatever behind it. The boys were not drunk and were on good terms. Hunga seems to have been suddenly, but quite improperly, excited by the abuse given by his nephew, and in a few moments two lives were ruined.

VIII

THE LAMHADA

Among the Maria, as in many other parts of tribal India, there is an arrangement whereby youths from poor families who cannot afford the price of a bride can serve for her for three, five or seven years. In Bastar such a youth is known as Lamhada, Lamanai, Lamsena or Gharjamai. The relations between the Lamhada and his future parents-in-law is not always a happy one, and it is complicated by the intimate proximity in which he has to live with the girl to whom he is not yet married. Sometimes, however, especially if the Lamhada happens to make the girl pregnant, the marriage is celebrated before the end of his term of service.

Only two cases of murder have arisen out of a Lamhada

situation. The first reproduced incidents that are constantly happening all over India. Kalmumi Masa was living as a Lamhada in the house of his mother-in-law, a widow named Hungi. He was already married to the girl, Kohale, though he was still fulfilling his contract of service. The two women, as often happens when they deal with a youth of this kind (for the Lamhada as a poor boy and often without relatives is generally despised), were careless in their treatment of him, and did not bother to cook his meals properly. A few days before the tragedy they went out for a funeral ceremony, and Hungi only sent Kohale home very late in the evening to see to her husband's food. When he found that nothing had been prepared, he was very angry and for fear of being beaten the girl ran away and spent the night in a fig tree.

The next day a panchayat was called to consider the relations of Masa and his wife. Masa objected to his affairs being discussed in public, and probably suspected that his mother-in-law had too much influence with the panchayat. He had to be forcibly brought to the meeting which decided that the women were not cooking properly for the boy, and ordered them to behave better in future. But Masa was also reproved. He was slapped by the Gaita (priest) and ordered not to beat his wife who was six months with child. Masa was very angry at this, and removed his things from Hungi's house. He no longer took his meals there, but only went there to sleep. He did not go away immediately to another village, because he wanted to take his wife with him, get his share of the rice crop and make arrangements for removing his cattle.

Hungi, of course, did not want to lose Masa's services. As a widow she was entirely dependent on him for the cultivation of her land. She persuaded her daughter to refuse to go away with him, and did everything she could to stop him removing his rice. On the eve of the tragedy the boy filled three baskets with the grain, and put them ready for removal the following morning. Hungi said that she would on no account let him take the rice, and spent the night sleeping in front of it, on guard with her two children. Early in the morning Masa went to get his property. The old woman tried to prevent him; Masa flew into a rage, struck her heavily and killed her. Kohale tried to intervene, and he so injured her also that she died a fortnight later.

Marvi Risami was the Maria blacksmith of Bastanar. Towards the end of 1934 he brought a youth, Markami Wango, to serve as a Lamhada for his young daughter Paike. The boy worked in the house for about a year and a half, and Risami intended to celebrate the marriage in 1936.

All went well at first. But there was living in the house a youth of about Wango's age, Marvi Kuma, a son of Risami's elder brother, whose parents had died when he was a child and who had been, for all practical purposes, adopted by the Bastanar household. This boy was thus, according to the classificatory system of relationship, Paike's brother and, of course, belonged to the same clan. Any relationship between the two would be regarded by tribal custom as extremely serious, as a form of incest. In spite of this, however, Kuma and Paike were greatly attracted by each other and Paike soon found that she had little time to give to her betrothed Wango. One day at the end of the hot weather, Wango and Paike went with Kuma and another youth, Kosa, to the hill near Lakhapal to get ore for smelting in the smithy. When they arrived there, Kosa went to the village on some business of his own and Wango accompanied him to get a drink of water. It is possible that he deliberately left Kuma and Paike together with the idea of spying on them and catching them *in flagrante*. He returned quietly and claims that he caught them actually in the act of intercourse. He threw a stone at his rival but missed him, and then chased him with a knife. Kuma ran away, and when Kosa rejoined the party, he found Wango quarrelling with Paike and throwing stones at her. Wango declared that he would kill all the people of the Marvi clan, and would either be hanged or run away to the Tea Gardens.

About a month later, the whole family with a number of other relatives and neighbours went to Handa Khodra to fetch grass for the thatching of their houses at the beginning of the rains (it was 2 June 1936), and when they got home late in the afternoon they found Risami with a pot of rice-beer and everyone had a little. Apparently no one was actually intoxicated, but they were at least revived after their long day's work. That night at supper Wango accused Kuma of allowing Paike to flirt with him and of distracting her affections from himself. The boy seems to have been

Necklace in Muria style, part of a dancing outfit

genuinely upset at his betrothed's lack of interest in him and her frigid attitude. He threatened to shoot her with an arrow. Kuma told his uncle Risami about this, and the old man got angry and declared that it was disgraceful of Wango to accuse a girl betrothed to him of so serious a crime as incest, and hit the boy twice. Wango caught hold of his future father-in-law, but the others separated them. So Wango walked out of the house. Risami followed to bring

(a) Wife and sons at Doriras await the return of their father Borga from life imprisonment (p. 198)

(b) Kawasi Borga in jail

PLATE XIX

Iarvi Boti who, for love of
is elder 'brother's' wife,
assisted her to murder
(Case No. 48 and
pp. 94ff.)

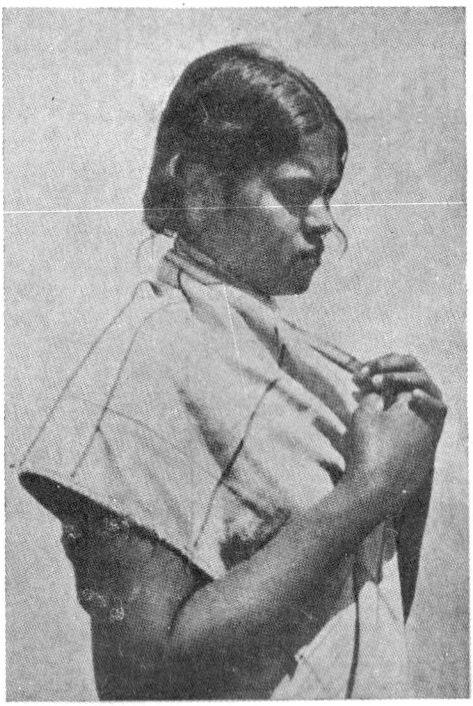

(b) Mase who, helped by her husband's younger 'brother', poisoned her husband (Case No. 48 and pp. 94ff.)

) Tati Doga, who killed his
elder brother's wife (Case
No. 90 and p. xxvii)

PLATE XX

him back, for he had no desire to lose such a useful person as a Lamhada. But Wango threw a stone at him, hitting him on the back of the head and making it bleed. Risami then went to the village headman and reported the matter, and they arranged with the Kotwar to hold an inquiry the next morning.

While Risami and the others were at the headman's house, Wango returned home to fetch his dancing kit. This was not the usual bison-horn outfit, but a collection of small and big bells, waist-band and necklaces. It looks as though he had decided to leave the house and abandon his duties as Lamhada out of disgust with the family that seemed allied against him. While he was removing the dancing things, Paike came out of the house and stopped him, saying that they belonged to her and had been given her by her parents. Paike's mother, who was eight months pregnant and was lying in the house, also seems to have shouted to the boy abusively to return the things. Wango, already in a towering rage, drew his bow and shot the girl just below the left breast. She lived till the following morning but then died of an acute generalized peritonitis.

In Court Wango declared that on the night of the quarrel he had again caught Kuma having intercourse with Paike, and that this had so enraged him that he had gone to remove his possessions from the house. But when Paike and her mother tried to stop him he shot the girl. This part of the story was doubted, since the other members of the party declared that Kuma had gone with Risami to make a report to the headman. But obviously everybody was concerned to hush up the matter of Paike's intimacy with her cousin, and it is possible that Wango, who appears to have had something of the voyeur's temperament, may have again been hanging about to catch them together and may have again succeeded.

It is interesting that the immediate cause of this murder, like the last, was the attempt by the women of the house to prevent a Lamhada from going away and removing his property. It is not easy to say whether Wango found the loss of his property, or the sight of his betrothed in the arms of another man the more provocative. I think probably it was the struggle over the dancing outfit that really provoked the murder.

With these cases we may compare the tragic destiny of Dome, a young unmarried Dhurwa girl aged about seventeen. A youth called Joga had been living as her Lamhada for the past five years, and their marriage had been arranged to take place at the next harvest. Dome did not care for Joga, but like any other Maria girl she was prepared to follow her parents' wishes in regard to her marriage and become his wife.

One night the girl found herself alone in her house. Joga was not supposed to sleep indoors, but outside in the courtyard. The girl went to bed and shut the door of her room. Late that night Joga went to her and asked her to have sexual intercourse with him. She refused, saying that, if she did, the gods would be angry with her and her cattle would die, and Joga went away. Fearing that the boy might ravish her, she got her axe and kept it by her side. Presently she fell asleep and again Joga came into the house and caught hold of her. She started up and struck him a violent blow with her axe, making a deep wound from which he died in a few minutes.

The Court held that Dome had acted according to her right of self-defence when she was unprotected in the house at dead of night. It is not known why Dome rejected her future husband, for it is not really a very common habit among girls for whom Lamhada are serving. It is possible that she was in her menstrual period, a thought that is suggested by her saying that the gods would be angry and the cattle die if she had intercourse. On the other hand, it may merely be that she disliked the boy and did not wish to have anything to do with him until she had to after marriage.

Another Lamhada, who in 1942 was serving a sentence of life imprisonment in Jagdalpur, is Khuja, a Muria boy from Esalnar. He is a cheerful and rather stupid youth who, when he described his crime to me, laughed heartily at what he considered the amusing bits. Khuja was living with his father-in-law and though the girl was very young had already been married to her. One day a Ghasia beggar woman came to the house and said to him, 'Come along, boy'. He asked her what she wanted him for, and she replied, ' For your wife's head '. A fortnight later she came again and complained to the father-in-law that Khuja had abused her, repeating the words that he had used. This annoyed Khuja so much that he followed her home, and when they came to the boundary of the village, threw her down and beat her to death. Khuja's anger may have been due to the fact that he was sensitive about being a Lamhada, particularly as he had married a very young wife.

In two cases conflict between a Lamhada and his father-in-law led to suicide. Ghasia went to dance with the other boys and girls of the village when he should have been working at home. Akali Modi had served three years for his wife, to whom he was married four months before his death. As is often the case he was continuing to serve his father-in-law until the payment of the bride-price was completed. On the night before his suicide, two cows broke their tethering cords and damaged the crops. On such occasions it is almost routine to blame the Lamhada, and the father-in-law doubtless bewailed his mistake in giving his daughter to such a fool and made offensive remarks about the boy's mother. Modi, who is said to have been a sensitive, quick-tempered youth, waited till the rest of the family went into the fields and then hanged himself from a tree outside the village.

CHAPTEN TEN

THE CAUSES OF CRIME: ALCOHOL

I

THE special and characteristic drink of the Bison-horn Maria is rice-beer. Mahua spirit and the *surem* that is made from mahua[1] flowers, and the fermented sap of the toddy,[2] sago[3] and date[4] palms is also drunk. But landa rice-beer is not only obligatory on most festival occasions; it is also the favourite drink of boon companions. The Maria regards it both as an intoxicant and as a food—which indeed it is. It accompanies him from birth to death. It is drunk first at the ceremonies when he is named, again at his betrothal, again in large quantities at his marriage, and it is finally poured over his memorial stone after he is dead. At every great festival and at every point of the agricultural year, this nourishing and potent drink is made and enjoyed.

Mahua spirit, which is the ceremonial drink of the northern Gond, is also offered by the Bison-horn Maria at the time of sacrifice, and in small quantities on most ceremonial and domestic occasions. The juice of the toddy and sago palms is used almost entirely for happiness—as a stimulant and for recreation—though gourds full of the refreshing juice are often supplied at weddings and funerals to supplement the supply of rice-beer. A poor man who cannot provide sufficient beer or spirits for his son's betrothal or marriage may provide toddy instead. When Muka went to ask for the hand of the beautiful Kume in marriage, he took with him a gourdful of this juice. Surem, which is made by boiling the mahua flowers, is sometimes taken as a substitute for the properly distilled spirit.

All these drinks are gifts of the gods. Liquor comes from heaven, and who could resist so gracious a blessing? Mahua was discovered much as in Muria and Baiga tradition. An ancient hero went out to find some means of entertaining his guests. He came to a mahua tree with a hole full of water beneath it, into which many of the flowers had fallen.

[1] *Bassia latifolia*, Roxb.
[2] *Borassus flabellifer*, Linn.
[3] *Caryota urens*, Linn.
[4] *Phoenix sylvestris*, Roxb.

All round the little pond were sitting rame birds singing, wagging their heads to and fro and flapping their wings in great excitement. The hero tasted the water and soon he too was singing, dancing and flapping his arms in company with the birds.

The recipe for rice-beer was given to the Maria by the Supreme Being for no other purpose apparently but to cheer them up.

The origin of sago and toddy juice is more elaborately described.

> Long ago there was a Maria called Iro Kawachi who had two beautiful daughters, Ilo and Palo. He made a seat of mahua wood and covered it with the skins of lice. He proclaimed that anyone who could first lift it up and put it where he could bathe upon it, and who could say what kind of wood it was made of, and what skin covered it, would get his daughters. All the boys of the neighbourhood came to try but none could tell what the seat was and none could lift it up. At last came a lame boy called Mad Moda from the Irma Raj with an open sore upon his leg. He too was unable to guess what the seat was made of until a fly came and said, 'Let me sit on your sore and eat it and then I will tell you what the wood is'. The boy let the fly settle upon him and after it had taken its fill it told him that the seat was of mahua wood and covered with the skins of lice. Then the boy was able to lift up the seat and put it where Iro Kawachi could bathe.
>
> Now Mad Moda was lame and ugly and covered with hideous sores. When the two girls Ilo and Palo saw him, they ran away in terror, but the boy went stumbling along after them and dropped his dancing-stick. He went on and at last caught the girls by the strings with which they tied their hair into a bun. He pulled the cloth off their shoulders and tore out some of their hair. Then he threw them down in the bed of the Indaltom River and enjoyed them. Afterwards the river divided and flowed onwards in two streams.
>
> The boy's bell-stick turned into a toddy tree; the strings from the girls' hair became sago palms; the hair itself grew up as a date palm; the cloth became the broad-leaved plantain tree. Because on that day the girls' cloth fell from their shoulders, they now do not cover their breasts.

This is the story as it was told in Garmiri village. It is known in its main outlines in many other places, though with small variations. In Dualkarka it was Ira Dhurwa who made the seat and its covering was of cloth. In Muskel it was Gaja Bhimul who made it and the end of the story is that Ilo and Palo jumped into the river at Dantewara and were drowned.

A few stories resemble the tales of the northern Muria. The Pen Kaina come down to bathe in the Godaveri river; they come singing to eat jamun fruit; or they simply come to dance. They sing, 'Whoever can tell what our names are, we will go with him'. When the village boys find they cannot tell their names they get angry and try to catch them. As the girls run away their bell-sticks fall and become toddy trees. The boys throw their sticks at them and these become sago palms. As the girls run away the kardan-belts round their waists break and turn into the date palm. The knots on these belts are its fruit. The god cuts off the testicles of the boys and sticks them on to the end of the dancing-sticks and these become toddy fruit. That is why, the Maria say, their women beat the sticks so vigorously as they dance. This version of the story is from Bara Harmamunda. In Palnar the situation is reversed. When the boys begin to flirt with the girls, the girls beat them with their bell-sticks and it is the boys who run away. Here they add that the toddy trees said, 'We won't stay here', and went down below the hills. But the sago palms remained on the Dantewara plateau.

Another completely different type of story is told in the neighbourhood of Bailadila. Long ago a group of Maria were hunting on the Bailadila Hills. They grew very thirsty and went searching for water. A rat had nibbled at the peduncle of a sago palm and a jungle cock had scratched a hole in the ground at its foot. The juice dropped into this hole and filled it. When the hunters came to the place they found a hole full of refreshing juice and drank it and thus learnt to tap the tree.

The comparative strength of these drinks is given in Bedford's *Technical Excise Manual*. The alcoholic strength of toddy varies according to the nature of the palm tapped, the season of the year, the time for which it has been drawn and other circumstances. The average results of a number of tests made with toddy from all parts of the Madras Presidency were:

		Percentage by volume
Coconut	85·7° U.P.	8·1
Palmyra	90·8° U.P.	5·2
Date	91·4° U.P.	4·9
Sago	89·6° U.P.	5·9

Toddy exposed for sale in Bengal in 1909 was found generally to range in alcoholic strength from about 93° to 94° U.P. When reasonably fresh it is said to have a food value somewhat comparable with that of well-made malt beer.

The strength of country beers (which include landa) made generally from rice or millet varies from about 75° U.P. to 93° U.P. (14·3 to 4·0 per cent by volume) and the average may be taken at about 85° U.P. (8·6 per cent by volume). *Rasi* liquor made of mahua is permitted to be sold between the strengths of 50° to 70° U.P. and *phuli* liquor between 15° to 35° U.P., and although the strength of liquor offered for sale at shops in the south of Bastar is stronger than that in the north, the average strength of *rasi* liquor may be taken as 60° U.P. (22·8 per cent by volume) and that of *phuli* as 25° U.P. (42·8 per cent by volume).

The Maria themselves say that it is the mixture of drinks that is most dangerous. I have everywhere heard it said that they do not consider the rice-beer to be the most intoxicating. Mahua spirit is that. Rice-beer is a food which fills the stomach.[1] But when a man drinks first rice-beer, then a little mahua spirit and finishes off with a gourd or two of sago or toddy juice, he will get drunk on a grand scale. It is also said that it is when the juice of male and female toddy palms is mixed together that it becomes very intoxicating. It apparently makes no difference to the potency of rice-beer whether it is made with rice or with the smaller millets. Indeed it is generally a mixture of several grains.

Excise Sub-Inspectors whom I have consulted support the Maria in their opinion that mahua spirit is more intoxicating

[1] Dalton was impressed by the way Uraon boys and girls could go to work after a night's dancing 'as cheerfully and vigorously as if their night had been passed in sound sleep. This says much for the wholesomeness of the beverage (rice-beer) that supplies them with the *staying* power'.—*Descriptive Ethnology*, p. 249.

than rice-beer or the fermented palm juices. They have added that the mahua liquor is much more rapid in its effect ; rice-beer must be taken in large quantities and acts slowly ; men do not usually become violent unless they take some liquor as well. A seer of rice-beer is considered equivalent to a bottle of liquor at 70° U.P. Intoxication from rice-beer lasts longer and has a much less deleterious effect. Since it has a high food value, the beer-drinker does not weaken like the mahua-addict. The Sub-Inspectors were unanimously of opinion that Maria did not drink to excess and did not consider that intoxication was a major cause of homicide.

The making of rice-beer is to some extent a ceremonial act. It should be done by a woman in the relation of daughter-in-law to the head of the household or the priest of the village, and she should work on 'a hungry belly'. It is made of a mixture of rice or kosra,[1] and mandia.[2] The mandia is pounded, soaked in water and put in a basket covered with a leaf which is kept in place with a stone. After two or three days in the basket the grain begins to sprout. It is then washed and dried and ground. In the meantime the kosra or rice, or kosra and rice mixed together, are husked and cleaned, and then husked or ground in an ordinary mill. The flour is mixed with hot water into a paste. A very large earthenware pot of water is kept boiling, and into the mouth of this pot is placed a bamboo funnel called the *jib*, and the paste is put into this and steamed. Now the pot of water is removed from the fire, and the mandia flour is put into another pot. The steamed rice or kosra paste is put above this and then above it again more mandia flour. The pot is filled to the top with cold water, the lid is closed with leaves, and it is put aside to ferment. After three or four days it begins to bubble and when, as Grigson says, 'there is a smell like a fowl-house that badly needs cleaning, they know that it is ready'.

There are many rules and superstitions about the use of sago and toddy juice. Women must not take it when a tree is first tapped. It should not be drunk when it is too sweet, and so on. Careful precautions are taken to guard the trees against theft. Sometimes a large bamboo mat is tied round

[1] *Panicum miliaceum.* [2] *Eleusine coracana.*

the trunk; sometimes bundles of thorns are placed to deter the thief. The owners sometimes live in little leaf-huts built below the trees in order to guard them. The tree is climbed by a long bamboo pole which hooks on to a branch at the summit. The side-shoots of the pole are not removed and these serve as the steps of the ladder. When not in use it is removed and kept in a house or in some hiding-place in the jungle. Sometimes a large loop is made at the end of the ladder and it fixes on to a bamboo hook which is tied to the tree. Once in Gogonda I saw a Maria getting up a very tall sago palm with great ingenuity. At the foot there was a pole eight feet high fixed in the ground. The climber had to get to the top of this and then, supporting himself upon it with his legs, had to catch the hook twenty feet above him with a long double bamboo pole with a loop at its end. This was no mean feat, and when it was done he had to tie the end of the swinging stick to the pole on which he had been standing and climb up to where he was able to hoist himself to the top of the tree by the branches.

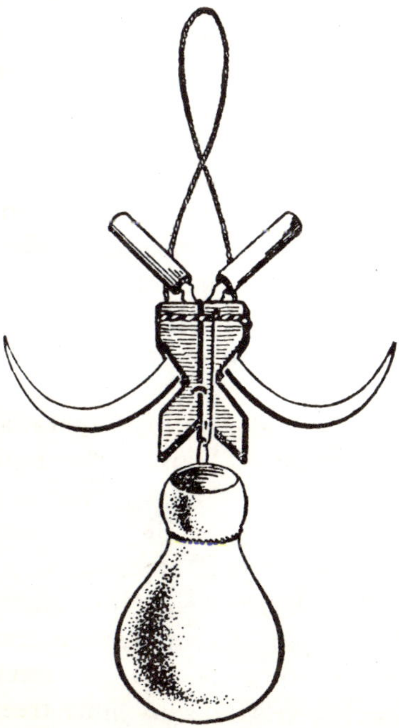

Kach-pirik apparatus for extracting toddy-juice

In the Konta Tahsil the method of climbing is the same as that recorded for the Kadir, which again compares with that of the Dyak of Borneo. Long lengths of bamboo are tied to the trunk. The climber ties round his waist an ingenious gadget, called *kach pirik,* holding two knives and a gourd, and he then climbs straight up the tree. In other villages the *mohukum* is used. This is a beautifully made arrangement of ropes by which the climber's body is attached to the trunk, and can be slipped up it. Between his feet is tied another rope which holds them against the tree. He is thus able to get up the tree like a humping caterpillar. A Maria told me that in the evening the people go up the trees 'like a company of monkeys'. When villagers go to drink sago or toddy, they often take with them little leaf-bundles containing dry fish, roasted crabs, red ants or mahua paste.

It is impossible to say how much alcohol is drunk by the Maria. According to the Excise figures in the Dantewara Tahsil and Sukma Zamindari where the population is overwhelmingly Maria, the consumption per 100 in proof gallons is 46·48 and 50·51 respectively. In the Muria Tahsil to the north it is 32·43 in Kondagaon and 58·90 in Narayanpur. Narayanpur, it must be remembered, has a large population of Hill Maria who do not drink rice-beer, which may explain why there is a higher consumption of mahua spirit. In the Bison-horn Maria area, there are —according to the Settlement records—about 75,000 toddy trees. The number of sago palms is not known, but is—I believe—considerably smaller.

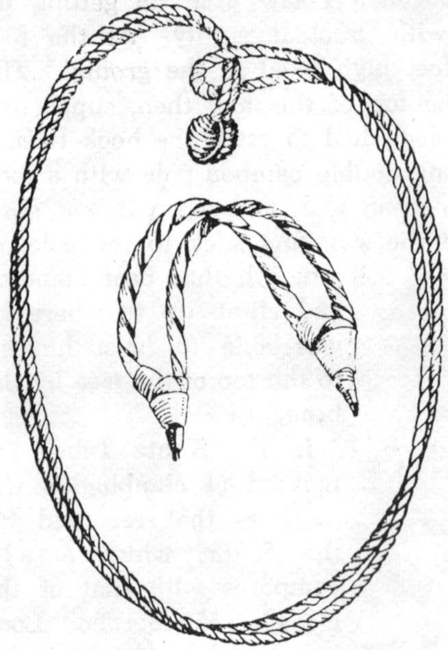

Mohukum ropes for climbing toddy trees

Illicit distillation was a feature of two at least of the murders. In the years 1938-42, 143 cases were detected in the Dantewara Tahsil, 91 in Bijapur, 65 in Jagdalpur as against only 11 in Kondagaon and 18 in Narayanpur. This certainly suggests that the Bison-horn Maria are much more given to illicit distillation than their brethren of the north. But, of course, these figures may only reflect greater energy on the part of the Excise staff in certain areas, or greater willingness of informers to come forward with their tale of what is going on.

Although drunkenness usually is a marked feature of festivals, marriages and funerals, habitual drunkenness is never common among the aboriginals. For one thing they are too poor for it; for another it is too much trouble. A certain proportion of the people are teetotal, and others never touch mahua spirit and do not drink at any times except on privileged and ceremonial occasions.

II

How far does this drinking of alcohol explain the heavy incidence of homicide among the Bison-horn Maria? It is commonly said that drinking, and especially the drinking of landa rice-beer, is the main cause. It is true that a plea of drunkenness is frequently put forward by accused persons in the Court. But there is reason to suppose that frequently this is suggested to them by their counsel. In many cases the excuse of intoxication was not made by the accused in his confession to the police, or before the lower Court. It was introduced as an afterthought before the Sessions Judge. In the 100 cases the Court only accepted as true a plea of drunkenness in 19 instances. Of these 19, 13 cases of intoxication were due to rice-beer, 4 to mahua spirit and 2 to palm juice. Landa intoxication usually occurred during festivals, but there is no record of any murder at a marriage or funeral, the other occasions when this drink is consumed in large quantities.

Table Nineteen

SHOWING THE OCCASIONS OF HOMICIDE COMMITTED THROUGH INTOXICATION

At festivals	12
At marriages	None
At funerals	None
After visiting a liquor shop	4

TABLE TWENTY

ILLUSTRATING THE INFLUENCE OF LIQUOR ON HOMICIDE IN 100 CASES

Due to drinking landa beer	13
„ „ mahua spirit	4
„ „ sago juice	1
„ „ toddy juice	1
Due to other causes	81

The question of alcoholism as a cause of crime has been discussed in an important article by Dr Norwood East, a former Commissioner of Prisons in England. He describes how he examined a series of 100 unselected cases of men and youths, who had been tried for murder in post-war years and had been examined by him. Alcohol was a predominant or contributing cause of homicide in 19 cases. Dr East concludes from this and from a study of other investigations that there appears to be no reason at the present time to consider alcohol as 'more than an occasional factor in the causation of crime in England'.

'Every practical criminologist', he says, 'will attach some importance to the association of alcoholism and crime. It is, however, very easy to over-emphasize the connexion.'[1]

Another investigation into the influence of alcohol on crime was made recently by Dr J. C. M. Matheson, Governor of Holloway Prison for Women. In an analysis of all the women received into the prison charged with homicide from 1935 to 1939, he found that in only 3 out of 55 cases did alcohol appear as a direct factor, and in one of them the accused was acquitted. The youngest of these women was 39 years old. In 3 there was a family history of alcoholism, but no history of alcoholic habit in the person herself.[2]

Kinberg gives an even more impressive judgement:

> Many see in the use of alcoholic liquors perhaps the worst social cancer, if not the root of all social evils, and are therefore inclined to consider drink one of the main causes of criminality too. It is most unlikely that such a

[1] W. Norwood East, 'The Problem of Alcohol in Relation to Crime', *The British Journal of Inebriety*, Vol. XXXVII (1939), pp. 55 ff.

[2] J. C. M. Matheson, 'Alcohol and Female Homicides', *The British Journal of Inebriety*, Vol. XXXVII (1939), pp. 87 ff.

schematic and uncomplicated view is correct. Social problems are usually very intricate and very simple solutions have so far always been found wanting.

It cannot be denied, however, that alcoholic liquor is liable to change an individual's mode of reaction, and therefore plays an important part as a crimino-etiological factor. The most prominent psychological effects of alcohol are: emotional changes, usually in the direction of euphoria and increased irritability, but occasionally towards dysphoria (especially in the later stages of intoxication); reduced inhibition of drive impulses, particularly of a sexual nature; more optimistically coloured judgements; a reckless disposition; reduced control of actions; increased physical mobility, with a tendency to impulsive and thoughtless actions; a general lowering of the moral level. These effects indicate that intoxication is conducive to certain kinds of criminality, such as acts of violence—assault, manslaughter, rape and other sexual crimes, defamation and resistance to the police. Alcohol is, as a matter of fact, a more or less important contributory cause in many such crimes.[1]

Typical crimes of drunkenness among the Maria may be briefly illustrated. A man and his wife were illegally distilling mahua liquor in a field. They both got very drunk on the fresh spirit and, as they went staggering home, the woman fell and broke the pot, and her husband beat and killed her in a drunken fury.[2] One day a party of men met to gamble. One of them (as is generally the case, since gambling is not an aboriginal vice) was a Mahara. The party drank a lot of palm wine, and perhaps some mahua spirit as well. There was a quarrel and the Mahara beat one of the Maria, a serious matter involving the latter's excommunication. The Maria in his drunken rage killed the Mahara and then gave himself up to the police.[3]

Twelve out of the thirteen cases where murder was due to drinking rice-beer occurred at festivals. For example, at one festival a man abused his elder brother's wife for not tethering the cattle properly or clearing away the cow-dung. She abused him in return, and in his drunken fit he stabbed her with an arrow.[4] At another festival party, one of the revellers got hungry and asked his mother for food. She

[1] Kinberg, op. cit., p. 211.
[2] Case No. 35.
[3] Case No. 36.
[4] Case No. 43.

told him to ask his wife, and his wife said she was too busy. The man picked up a hoe and killed his mother.[1] Sori Pandu of Mokhpal was notorious for the fits of rage to which he was subject when he was drunk. One day he went to play his sarangi-fiddle at a beer party. There was a drunken quarrel, and Pandu tried to kill his uncle with an axe, but the others intervened. So he went home and got out his bow and arrow and shot him.

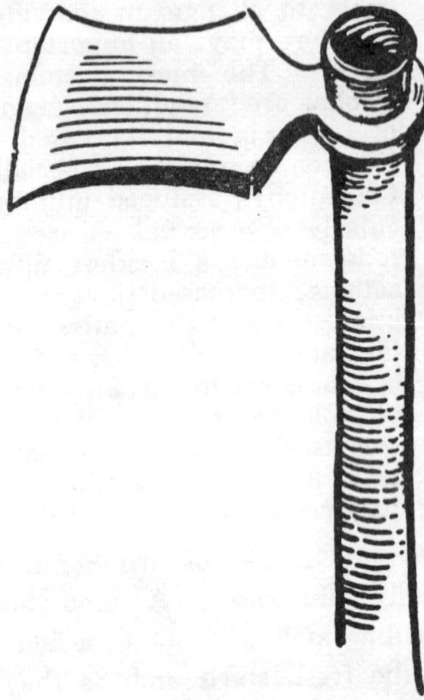

Korki hoe

In most of these cases intoxication was the immediate cause of the murder. There does not seem to have been any long-standing enmity between the parties, and most of the incidents should really be regarded as tragic accidents. It is only occasionally that the Maria uses rice-beer deliberately to free himself from his inhibitions. Poyami Panda had suspected his wife of intimacy with the village Siraha, Nanda, for months past, but he had not taken any serious action about it until on the night of a festival, after he had drunk a lot of beer, he caught Nanda and his wife together and, his inhibitions and fears of punishment having been removed by the alcohol he had taken, he killed his wife's seducer.

Toddy was responsible for only one homicide and that a very tragic one. Father and son were living together amicably. One evening the father tapped his toddy tree and brought home a gourdful of the juice. They drank it together. Over supper the son asked his father for a loan, and when the old man refused, the youth fell into a drunken rage and killed his father while he was still eating.

[1] Case No. 72.

Remorse for drunkenness was the rather unusual cause of a suicide at Dualkarka. Sori Hura was a heavy and reckless drinker. One day as he was indulging himself as usual, a friend, the Kandki of Kuakonda, a rather influential man, happened to visit him and gave him a little lecture on the evils of alcoholism. Hura expressed himself as greatly moved by his advice, and arranged for him to be rewarded with a feast. But directly the Kandki went away, Hura set to work to drink again. By midnight he was in a sorry condition of intoxication and remorse, and went into an inner room and hanged himself. It was about midnight, and his wife was husking grain in the next room for a festival on the morrow. Hearing a suspicious sound, she went to see what had happened and found her husband dead.

CHAPTER ELEVEN

THE CAUSES OF CRIME: FATIGUE

An important individual and mesological cause of crime which is largely overlooked in discussions of the subject in India is fatigue. This is so relevant that I make no apology for quoting Kinberg at length upon the subject. Fatigue is the result of environmental conditions, work, or other circumstances that strain the working capacity and willingness of the individual and may in its turn produce serious psychical changes, sometimes of a pathological kind.

> Great exhaustion will occasionally produce actual psychoses of a confusive type. A disturbed consciousness of externals, the presence of hallucinations and delusional ideas, may then naturally enough produce criminal actions. But even in cases where fatigue does not give rise to such pronounced mental disorders, it may produce a change of personality which, under certain circumstances, may result in criminal actions.
>
> The psychological fatigue-phenomena that are of special importance as crime factors are a strong feeling of dysphoria, dejection and irritability, worry, desperation, and an unreflecting, vague wish to escape from a situation which seems intolerable. Any intensification of the complicated emotional condition may cause a tendency to obnubilation, which weakens further the automatic action control.
>
> In recent years I have seen many cases by which my attention has been drawn to the crimino-etiological significance of fatigue. Most of these belonged to the agricultural classes—daughters or wives of small farmers. As a rule, small farmers in Sweden, whether freehold or tenant, cannot afford to hire sufficient labour. All the members of the family, husband, wife and children, must therefore strain every nerve to keep the whole going. This labour is particularly hard on the married women, who, besides tending the cattle and working in the fields, must also do all the domestic work, and to whom, above all, pregnancy is an additional burden.[1]

I believe that this may explain some of the apparently inexplicable aboriginal crimes in Bastar where, for example,

[1] Kinberg, op. cit., p. 215.

(*a*) Poriami Hirma (Case No. 75 and pp. 91f.)

(*b*) Marvi Paklu, who killed a tiresome wife (Case No. 63 and pp. 109f.)

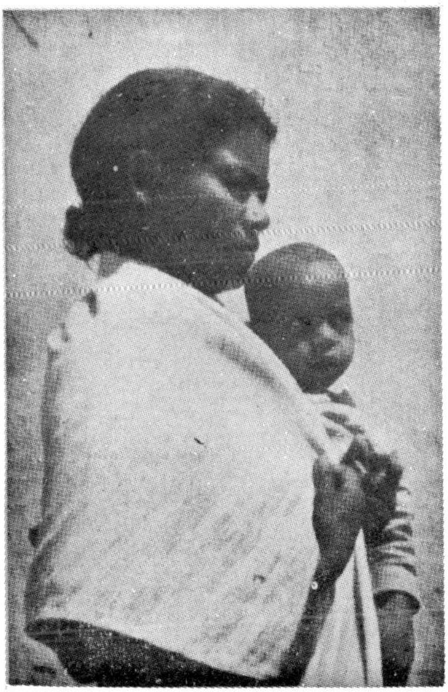

(*c*) Tati Mase, whose husband tormented her and drove her to despair (Case No. 91 and p. 164)

(*d*) Habka Mase, whose wife refused to obey him (Case No. 9 & p. 121)

PLATE XXI

(*a*) Kande Muria, whose father seduced his two wives (pp. 90f.)

(*b*) Marvi Kuma, who killed his son (Case No. 58 and p. 209)

(*c*) Punem Pidga, who killed his father (Case No. 86 and p. 103)

(*d*) Padami Guddi, who killed his father (Case No. 72 and p. 142)

PLATE XXII

a man kills a dearly-loved wife in a flash of temper simply because his dinner is not ready in time. Marvi Mundra and his wife came home very late one evening in October after working all day in the fields. When they reached the house, the girl at once began to cook their supper, and after a short time Mundra asked if it was ready. She said rather crossly that it was on the fire, and that directly it was ready she would give it to him. Mundra, exhausted by his long day in the fields and by the prospect of a still longer night watching the crops, lost his normal 'automatic control', picked up a stick from the fire and gave his wife three heavy blows which killed her.

Barse Kama, a man about thirty-five years old, earned his living by grazing the village cattle. His wife who was eight months with child had been out collecting young bamboo shoots for food. Kama came in at midday exhausted, and found that his food was not ready and his wife was lying down for a brief rest. She explained that she had only just returned from the jungle, and was very tired. He abused her and she replied that she could not prepare the meal any faster, and that if he wanted food more quickly he had better find another woman. Kama experienced a sudden explosion of rage, picked up his axe and struck his wife as she was lying on the mat. She died that night. Kama claimed that he was drunk at the time, but this was not accepted by the Court. In fact, he was intoxicated with fatigue.

Veko Dome, about twenty-five years old, was very busy gathering the kosra grain in his fields. On the eve of the tragedy, in the last week of November 1922, there was no rice in his house, and the family took gruel in the morning and in the evening drank a little of what was left. They all went to sleep without any proper food. Dome himself did not even get the stale gruel in the evening. Early next morning he went to his field again, and while he was away the rest of the family had some gruel. Then Dome's wife and his aunt Torka went to the fields to work. It had by now begun to drizzle. Dome asked his aunt if she had brought his food. She said as it was raining she had not brought any, and told him to go home and get it. At this he grumbled and the old woman was annoyed and said, 'What have you been doing in the field? Have you been eating excreta?' The women squatted down and began to reap the kosra. Dome quietly went and got his axe, walked up behind his aunt and struck her several times on the head, and she died without a sound. Dome went into the jungle for a time but returned home in the evening, drank some gruel and went to sleep in a hut behind the house. He had been working hard in the fields since the middle of the preceding day, and had had no food at all. His exhaustion drove him as surely as any alcoholic orgy to commit his crime.

Murders arising because a wife or other relation fails to give food in time may also be connected with the powerful oral needs of all aboriginals, which reflect the infantile nature of their culture. Laubscher has studied the underlying causes for the large number of stock thefts in South Africa. He finds that these are ultimately based on the people's craving for meat. The Tembu tribesman places a great value on meat as a food and whenever it is available he gorges himself to the utmost. 'There is something ravenously sadistic in his attitude towards meat. It is not only a great delicacy, but it is credited with great health-giving qualities. Elders have frequently remarked that the change of the times, the paucity of cattle, sheep and goats, have reduced to a minimum the meat supplies of the people. Once upon a time when cattle roamed in huge herds and they had plenty of meat to eat, their people were strong and healthy, but now they only have meat once or twice a month, and then not sufficient is available to make them feel they need not eat again for a few days.'[1]

Cattle theft is similarly very common among the Maria, and I have little doubt that a denial of oral needs that are commonly fulfilled without difficulty, throws them off their balance and drives them to violence. As among the Tembu, these oral activities are shown in the Maria's craving for bulk in food—their love of tobacco to smoke and chew and their delight in alcohol.

Oral needs are closely connected with the sexual impulse. It is remarkable that in no fewer than six cases, murder directly followed a wife's refusal to allow her husband sexual

[1] Laubscher, op. cit., p. 303.

congress. Habka Masa killed his wife Pakli in consequence of a long dispute, but immediately before the tragedy she refused to lie with him. Barse Chappe, a polygamous invalid, was first refused by both his wives and later by his senior wife because he desired to perform the act in a semi-public place. Marvi Deva saw his wife with a man and when, probably to test her, he asked her to give herself to him and she refused, he killed his baby daughter and tried to kill her. Kosa, an almost imbecile paralytic, asked his wife to have intercourse with him; she abused him and he stabbed her to death. Doga, rejected sexually by his elder brother's widow, was so affronted that he killed her. Mundra, who so brutally treated his wife Pande, asked her to have sexual congress with him and was refused only an hour before he met his death at her hands.

Decorated banda knife (*Length* 3')

Such a refusal may also drive a man to suicide. Marvi Joga, the Waddai of Mathadi, was always quarrelling with his wife and threatening to remarry. One day at the funeral ceremony of his brother's son, he drank a lot of surem, and when he came home he tried to have intercourse with his wife. But she refused saying, 'You are always talking about another wife. Why don't you go and get one?' and she went away to sleep in the Room of the Departed. Joga, intoxicated and desperate at his wife's refusal, hanged himself.

CHAPTER TWELVE

THE CRIME OF REVENGE

I

MOTIVES of revenge and implacable enmity operate in many cases. The Maria have various symbolic methods of expressing their hatred. One of these is to remove three handfuls of straw from an enemy's roof. This was done in a case where the murderer had a long-standing enmity with his victim, which came to a head over a quarrel about the cutting of an embankment. Another symbol is to pull out a few of the pubic hairs and to whistle loudly with one finger in the mouth. This was done by Muchaki Dasru shortly before he killed a man for not giving him the tribute that was due to him as Siraha of the village, and by Marvi Oyami Masa as he led his party to murder his cousin. Kartami Aitu dipped his hand in his victim's blood and made a mark on his own head. He cut the ground of the threshold with his axe in dramatic symbol of his triumph over the dead man's family.[1]

In some cases hostility between two Maria may continue for years before it breaks out into open conflict. Thus Vetti Hirma had been on bad terms for several years with Rawa Hirma, who was ultimately to be his victim. It began by a quarrel over land. Then when both were probably a little drunk at a First Fruits Festival, they tried to shoot each other with arrows, but missed their aim. It was only after three years that at last the theft of a pumpkin aroused Vetti Hirma to such a state of revengeful anger that he beat his enemy to death.

Outraged family pride that craved revenge, desire to eliminate a tiresome suitor, and a chivalrous sense of protectiveness towards a girl were combined in the murder of Muka, the young Siraha of Surnar. He was in love with Kume, the daughter of Poyami Irma, and one day in March 1935 he went to Ghatom with a pot of sago palm juice to ask

[1] In 1939, in a Telanga case, the murderer stabbed his victim with an arrow, disembowelled him with a knife, extracted the liver, and bit off a portion of it. But was this for revenge or magic?

for her in marriage. When he reached the house and Irma asked him his business, Muka said, 'I have started work in my fields and I have need of a cow. I hear you have a good one in your shed and I have come to buy it from you.'

'We have no cow here,' said Irma—who did not understand what Muka was talking about, for the Maria normally use the symbolism of a flower in their betrothal dialogues, saying 'I have come to pick a flower and put it in my hair' —'I am sorry you have troubled yourself unnecessarily. You must be tired and hungry. Take some rice and pulse, and cook your food and eat it.' For Muka being a Siraha could not eat from the hands of other people, but had to cook his own meals. He took the grain and gave Irma the palm juice which he had brought. Irma accepted it and took it into the house to drink. But then his wife told him that Muka had not come for a real cow, but to ask for their daughter in marriage. When he heard this, Irma was furious and abused Muka saying, '*Thu re mailotia*, I don't want your gift nor will I give you my daughter,' and he threw the juice away and turned the youth out of the house.

As Muka was going home, he saw Kume collecting mahua flowers in the forest. She was so beautiful that he could not restrain himself. He went to her and said, 'Come away with me' and took the basket of mahua flowers out of her hands. But the girl screamed, and some men who were working nearby ran to the place and abused Muka, asking him whether he was betrothed to the girl that he should take her away by force.

Two days later Muka again came to the village, and found Kume returning from the forest with a bundle of leaves. He caught her by the hand, and tried to carry her off. A neighbour saw the incident and rescued her. Muka hid himself in the village Rest-house. Presently Kume's brother Usodi came home and, hearing what had happened, went to Muka and killed him with his axe.

In a case at Michenar in 1939 when Poyami Kaner was accused of murdering his uncle but was acquitted, it is said that while he was asleep in his house someone came into the room and tried to throttle him. As the unfortunate man was struggling in agony he managed to catch hold of his wife, who was sleeping close by, and woke her. She got up and, catching hold of the assailant by the neck, dragged him outside. The would-be murderer shouted that he would apply his victim's blood to his forehead. From his voice they recognized who it was: it was a close relative, an uncle, who had sworn revenge after a dispute about partition of the family property. He again tried to attack, but Kaner managed to get hold of his bow and arrow and shot him. The Court held that Kaner was justified in protecting himself, and acquitted him. The interesting thing here is the assailant's declaration that he would place the blood of his victim on his own forehead in dramatic symbol of revenge.

II

Some of the murders for revenge were the result of the deliberate conspiracy of several people to eliminate the person who had offended them. We will consider two of these cases. The first occurred in 1930 at Jabeli at the time of the Wijja Pandum, the festival when, after a ceremonial hunt, the Maria consecrate the seed that is to be sown in the coming season.

Marvi Oyami Masa was a well-to-do and influential man and the Siraha of his village. He had a large family of whom Handa was his elder brother, Gutta his nephew, Doga his son-in-law, and Mundra and Tangra his sons. Oyami Masa was the leader of this family group, who were economically dependent upon him, and with whom he had joint cultivation. Elsewhere in the village was Oyami Masa's first cousin, Marvi Masa, who was the clan-uncle of Gutta, Mundra and Tangra, but lived with his own near relations separately; the two groups were not perhaps on very good terms with each other.

On the night of the festival, when as usual large quantities of rice-beer were being consumed everywhere, Gutta and Handa came to the village as the cattle were being driven in with loud shoutings and clouds of dust. They saw Masa in his house and demanded some rice-beer. But Masa said that he had not made any for the festival, and was not drinking that day. This annoyed the two youths who began to abuse the old man, calling him *mailotia* and thief. Masa did not mind the reflection on his relations with his mother who had been dead for many years. But he greatly objected to being called a thief, for this came nearer home and he replied hotly that it was Oyami Masa who was the real thief, since he had stolen seven cattle from a village in Sukma Zamindari. The boys were very angry at this—possibly the accusation was true and therefore dangerous—and went off threatening that they would tell Oyami Masa and take their revenge. Already drunk, the boys went to Oyami Masa's house and there the relatives gathered together and plotted to give Masa a good beating; they may even have decided to get rid of him altogether. At about 10 o'clock that night the six men armed with sticks came to Masa's house. Oyami Masa led the way in and began to beat his cousin. The stick he had was a rotten one and broke immediately. But as bad luck would have it, his eye fell on a heavy rice-pestle, and he picked this up and delivered several heavy blows which fractured Masa's skull in two places and would alone have been sufficient to kill him. Masa's son and brother tried to save him. But the other men knocked them down, and then belaboured Masa with their sticks until they were certain he was dead. When examined the body was a mass of injuries—there were nine fractures of the ribs, the left ear was torn and the spleen badly ruptured; there were bruises everywhere. When their work was done, the men departed doing the *sui* whistle which, indeed, one witness declared Oyami Masa whistled as he led the attack on his cousin.

Rice-pestle (*Length* 4′)

Perhaps the most notable thing about this incident was the way Oyami Masa tried to save his fellow-conspirators by taking all the blame upon himself. He said that, as he was going for the night worship in connexion with the festival, Masa shouted at him and accused him of instigating some Mahara weavers to report to the police that he had burnt their houses. He was slapped by Masa, lost his temper, picked up the pestle and hit his cousin over the head. He said that nobody else was present except Mundra and Doga who tried to intervene in the quarrel. There was no evidence at all, however, to support Oyami Masa's story, and he was sentenced to life-imprisonment along with the two older men, all three of whom died in jail. But the respect with which Marvi Oyami Masa was regarded, the respect which from his behaviour at the trial does not seem to have been altogether unjustified, is shown in the elaborate funeral arrangements that were made for him after his death. He was given a large danyakal stone, an earthen tomb was made above his clothes and ornaments and an elaborately carved pillar was erected to his memory. It was from seeing this pillar that the villagers of Massenar got the idea of erecting a similar pillar to the famous Kopa Dhurwa.

Another case of murder for revenge by a body of men was the Phulpar tragedy of 1931, a murder which is remarkable for the behaviour of the accused.

For a long time there had been ill-feeling between the landlord of Phulpar, a wealthy Maria, and Pandu, one of his tenants. At the beginning of May 1931, a cowherd in the village lost a goat and reported the fact to his landlord who called for the Kotwar and others and started an inquiry. They went to Pandu's house and questioned him about the missing animal, for apparently the goat used to wander into Pandu's garden, and Pandu was known as a cattle thief—he had previously been beaten by the landlord for this. There was a report too that a few days before Pandu had killed and eaten a goat. But Pandu said that it was his own goat that had died, and produced a white goatskin and some bits of meat threaded on a stick. When the cowherd saw the skin, he admitted that it was not his. But another member of the company claimed it instead. At this the landlord told Pandu that he was a thief and brought his village into disgrace. He further accused him of not paying his rent, and said that he would have him turned out of his house. Pandu replied that he could turn him out if he wanted to, but he would take care to have his revenge before he went.

A few days afterwards, a man called Nanda came with a friend to Pandu's house to borrow a rupee, bringing a pot of toddy juice with him. That evening, as they were sitting, drinking and talking, Pandu offered Nanda two rupees if he would kill the landlord. Nanda said this was not enough, but at last agreed to commit the murder for five rupees. Accordingly that night Pandu and Nanda went with a farm-servant, a youth of about nineteen called Bhima, to find their victim. Bhima was left in a field some distance away to keep watch, while Pandu and his helper tried to get into the house. But the dogs barked and they had to go home with their plan frustrated for that night.

The next day was bazaar day. Pandu collected Nanda and Bhima, and they decided to kill the landlord as he was going to the bazaar. Bhima's duty was to get the landlord's axe out of his hands; Nanda was to do the actual killing and was armed with a heavy stick for this purpose; Pandu came last to direct operations.

They found the landlord sitting in his field-hut, and Bhima and Nanda joined him there saying that they had come to settle the matter of the stolen goat amicably and that Pandu was on his way with a bottle of liquor. This was at about 8 o'clock in the morning. Bhima then said he wanted to skin some mangoes and on this pretext got possession of the landlord's axe. Just then a number of neighbours came by, and this seems to have suggested to the murderers that the place was too public. Nanda told the landlord that Pandu was bringing the liquor to a mahua tree some distance away. The three men, therefore, got up and proceeded towards the tree, where they sat down. At the same time Pandu approached cautiously by a different route. He stopped first under a kumi tree and then went on towards the mahua tree. Directly Pandu arrived, Nanda struck the landlord, as he was sitting down, on the left side of the head with his stick, and the unfortunate man fell over. Nanda struck him again, and then Bhima hit him behind the left ear with the blunt side of his axe. After delivering the blow the boy began to tremble, and got hold of a small jamun tree to support himself. It is said that he trembled so violently that the tree shook to and fro. At this moment Pandu pushed by saying, 'Beat him, beat him. This is not the time for trembling.' He took the axe out of Bhima's hand and struck the landlord two more blows with the sharp edge. Just then they caught sight of two men coming by. They hurriedly dropped their weapons and stood upright with their hands straight down round the landlord's body so that the passers-by could not see what was happening. These men were going to get some meat from a dead cow which was lying near a tank in the next village. They do not seem to have seen anything, and went on their way. Another witness came by and he saw Pandu look cautiously round and then rub the blade of his axe in the earth and throw it down beside the landlord's body. This witness was so frightened that he did not go to get meat from the dead cow as he originally intended, but went home and lay down.

This story shows on the one hand an unusual degree of premeditation and a careful adherence to plan, and on the other a rather unusual susceptibility on the part of some of those concerned in the affair. The youth Bhima, who was Pandu's bond-servant, evidently had no heart in the business and trembled so much after striking one blow that he could do no more. One witness was so frightened that he could hardly walk and had to go home and lie down. Without the urging of Pandu, who seems to have been an unusual type of criminal, the other men would certainly have never carried out the plan. For this reason Pandu was sentenced to death and was executed, and the other murderers went for life-imprisonment.

III

The subject of aboriginal abuse is obscure, and outsiders often find it hard to understand why expressions that are continually used in ordinary conversation should sometimes arouse the most passionate feelings of indignation. The most abusive terms are sometimes actually used in love-making, and a Maria employs the word *mailotia*, for example, which means 'cohabit with your mother', as freely as a British soldier uses the word 'bloody' and generally with as little meaning.

For abuse to be offensive everything depends on the

occasion, the tone of voice and the relationship of the people concerned. Word-magic is an important and dangerous element in Maria life. A witch can make a man impotent by giving him 'corpse-abuse'. It is possible for a man to use a normally inoffensive expression in a certain tone of voice, which under the circumstances is so dangerous and insulting as to lead to murder. A mother-in-law, for example, may abuse her son-in-law privately as much as she wishes. But if she shouts an insulting epithet at him in the presence of half the village, she has committed an unbearable insult.

Two types of abuse are not used in ordinary conversation. You do not call somebody a thief, unless you want trouble. You certainly do not call anyone a witch or a wizard. In a number of our cases the allegation that someone was a thief or a wizard led to murder.

Excreta-abuse is also not very common in daily life. In several cases it has led to murder. Thus the elder of two brothers told the younger that he was eating excreta. A son-in-law killed his father-in-law when he told him that he ate the excreta and drank the urine of his wife. A nephew killed his aunt for accusing him of eating excreta.

On two occasions fathers were killed by sons for insulting them. One father told his son to 'get out of the house' and was killed for it. Another father, who was asked by his son for a loan of money, replied that the boy might sell his own children for the money, but he would not get it from him. Such remarks were not to be endured.

Markami Turka killed his elder brother's wife Kosi for abusing him. He told her that if she did not do her work properly he would not give her cattle for cultivation, and she replied that 'her pubic hairs would not be pulled up' if she did not get them. This ought not to have greatly offended someone in that relationship, but it did: probably it was the way she said it.

Yet another case (not in our list) in which a father was murdered by his son was when a youth about nineteen years old, Poyami Lakhma, killed his father Linga in 1940. The two men had a drunken quarrel, and the father abused his son and told him to get out of his house. As before, this seems to have been regarded by the boy as an almost unbearable insult. He replied, 'Why did you not kill me and throw me away while I was a child, if you want to turn me out of your house now?' The father replied, 'I will kill you even now and throw you away'. He also called the boy *chor* (thief), *mailotia* (one who cohabits with his mother) and Dhed (a member of the despised Mahara caste). Finally he said, 'You are not my son, and whose son you are I cannot say'. At last the boy, driven to madness by these insults, struck his father with an axe and killed him.

The most common abuse in everyday life is based on straightforward natural sex—there are no words, as in Europe, associated with perversion—the words *mailotia* and *baplotia*, suggestions that somebody should lick the private parts or eat the pubic hairs, insinuations about the chastity of wife or sisters. Such abuses are so common that they should not normally rouse anyone to the pitch of intense excitement necessary for committing homicide. But in several of our cases, though it was these expressions that were reported in Court as the cause of provocation, I think probably many other unpleasant expressions were actually employed. Some Maria are sufficiently intelligent, when they are pleading provocation, to mention the things which they think would provoke the Court rather than the things that really provoked them.

Educated people are sometimes puzzled why the rude, coarse aboriginals should be so offended at a little bad language. But the truth is that there is a strict etiquette in these matters, and while a lot of filthy talk is tolerated provided the conditions are right, any breach of the rules will cause an explosion of temper that may end in tragedy. It is probable too that the abuse releases an instinct for revenge that is unconscious. Stanley Hall says:

> The instinct of revenge is very deep-seated, and not entirely eradicable. In abnormal cases it is instantaneous and perhaps unconscious. I have myself talked with perhaps a score of youthful murderers under sentence of death, who, I believe, were in every way as good by nature as I am, but who in an instant of fulminating anger struck the fatal blow, possibly harder than they knew or because a weapon was at hand, and killed, it may be, their best friend with a regret no less than

if sudden death had come without their agency, and with a self-reproach equal to that which they would have visited upon any wretch who had slain their friend. When we reflect that the entire administration of criminal law up to recent date was based upon vengeance, we cannot wonder that its impulse is so strong and passionate in the heart of man, and when we read the horror of some American lynching scenes, we realize that collective man can with impunity be as vindictive as those on whom we inflict the worst punishment.[1]

IV

RECIDIVIST CRIMES

The two examples of serious recidivism in our list where men committed double murders—that is to say, after being convicted of one murder and serving a sentence for it, they committed another shortly after release—give rise to serious speculations about the value of imprisonment as a cure for a disordered and homicidal mind. These cases, both of which can be classed as crimes of revenge, are so important that we must consider them in a little detail.

Murami Dhurwa was sentenced to transportation for life for murdering the Kandki of his village, and was released from jail in 1929. After his release he went to live jointly with his elder brother Hurra at Palnar. For about ten months everything went well. But then in the middle of December 1929 Dhurwa had a violent quarrel with his wife ostensibly for not keeping the house clean. He pushed her out of the door, and declared that he was going to kill his brother and his nephew, Wella, for not giving evidence in his favour at the trial at which he had been sentenced. He left his house and went to find Wella, though it was late at night. Wella was living in a hut nearby; he heard Dhurwa's threats and tried to escape. But he had hardly gone a few paces from the building when Dhurwa caught him and struck him a blow with a heavy stick that knocked him to the ground. Wella's wife shouted for help and his father Hurra ran to the rescue, but not before Dhurwa had given two more heavy blows. Hurra managed to disarm his brother, whereupon Dhurwa went away to a field-hut

[1] Hall, op. cit., p. 356.

and slept, but afterwards absconded. Wella was taken into the house by his wife, and the next day carried to the police station. But as they were going along the unfortunate man died.

Dhurwa's own version of the story differed considerably from this. He declared that he and his brother were not on very good terms for, while he had been in prison, Hurra had sold several of his cattle and when he had asked for the money, he had told him to get out of his house. He was trying, but without success, to get partition of the family property. On the night of the tragedy he had quarrelled with his wife for not lighting the fire, and for refusing to have intercourse with him. Soon afterwards his brother and Wella had come to beat him, and there had been a violent quarrel in the course of which he had, admittedly, killed his nephew. He had then gone to try to get jungle-medicine to treat Wella and his brother who had been slightly injured. This story would have been more credible if he had not, instead of getting medicines, absconded to Orissa and then to the Tea Gardens.

The Sessions Judge doubted the truth of either story. He considered that it was incredible that a man should live in close contact with a nephew and brother for ten months without revealing his anger for their failure to support him at his trial. Moreover, Dhurwa was on perfectly good terms with Wella after his release, and had even given him a cow and a bullock. It is probable that there was some deeper reason for the sudden flaring up of anger against Wella, and I am inclined to suspect that it was connected with the quarrel with his wife and her refusal to allow him intercourse. Supposing there had been some intrigue between the woman and the nephew, Dhurwa would have been outraged not only by his wife's infidelity but by the considerable danger that this unlawful relationship would bring upon the whole family. This would also account for the reticence of the witnesses who invariably try to conceal any kind of incestuous or unlawful relationship from the Courts. Even so the murder will remain a crime of revenge. With remarkable clemency the Judge sentenced Dhurwa to life-imprisonment and not to death.

V

Another double homicide occurred at Garmiri. Kadti Hunga was the owner of a plantation of sago palms and an irrigation tank, the fish of which he regarded as his own preserve. One evening at the beginning of November 1934 a group of men, one of whom himself had served a sentence for homicide, were distilling mahua spirit in a field. Somebody suggested that there might be something in one of the traps set by Hunga in his tank, and two of the men went to the place and brought back a handful of fish. They were at the business of distillation all night and at cock-crow they had two bottles ready. They roasted the fish for breakfast and began to eat and drink. Suddenly, as the first light of dawn came into the sky, Hunga appeared on the scene. It is always exceedingly annoying to have fish stolen from your traps, still more actually to see the thieves eating your fish and drinking the juice from your palm trees. Full of rage Hunga attacked the party. Three of the men ran away, but the fourth, Markami Dorga, was lying drunk on the ground. Hunga sat on his chest and killed him, probably by throttling him. Unfortunately the post-mortem was conducted too late for a definite opinion to be given. But those who saw the body shortly after death described a swollen neck, protruding tongue and coagulated blood which is not inconsistent with a death by strangling.

The three men who ran away told nobody what had happened, and Hunga himself kept quiet about it. The following evening, however, he was seen carrying Dorga's body over his shoulder to a tank, where he threw it into the water. Later that night he called the village elders together, admitted that he had killed Dorga and told them where they would find the body. He probably thought that he would be able to arrange matters with the village panchayat, and get off on payment of suitable compensation. But a report was made to the police and Hunga was arrested. He himself admitted attacking the men who had stolen his fish, but denied that he had carried the body to the tank or that he ever confessed the killing before the villagers. He was sentenced to transportation for life. But the

Appellate Court did not consider that the evidence was sufficiently definite to prove that Hunga really intended to kill his victim. Since Dorga was intoxicated he may have died more by accident than by design. Hunga's sentence was, therefore, reduced to one of five years. This was on 9 May 1935. On 12 April 1939, Hunga was released and went home to Garmiri where he found his wife Gangi awaiting him. The usual ceremonies of purification were performed; the villagers enjoyed a feast; Hunga was sprinkled with water in which gold had been dipped and he was then free to enter his house and assume once again his tribal privileges.

For three months everything went well. Hunga had his old mother in the house with his wife and two little daughters, Malla and Kosi, aged eleven and twelve respectively. But after a while the happiness of the house was clouded. Hunga had left a certain amount of money with his wife when he went to jail. He himself claimed that it was Rs 100, but this seems to me doubtful. At all events, there was a certain amount and the probability is that it was spent. Hunga began demanding the return of the money or at least a part of it, and named Rs 20 as the minimum which must be paid. He continued nagging his wife about this for a long time, and she retaliated by sulking and refusing to give him proper food. Hunga, who seems to have been an exceptionally early riser, generally took a meal very early in the morning, and on 18 July Gangi brought him his usual breakfast of rice and pulse. But a chicken had been killed and cooked the previous night, and Hunga demanded why he was not given meat with his rice, probably suspecting that his wife was again keeping food from him. Gangi replied that she had put some of the chicken aside for him, but that it had been eaten by a cat. Hunga got very angry and threw the rice at her and slapped her twice. She went out of the room muttering that she would tell her brothers and get the panchayat to see that he was sent back to prison.

This was to an ex-convict a very terrible threat. Hunga got out his knife, and went to the front of his house, standing there for a little while and looking round to see if there was anyone about. But his house was in a lonely place,

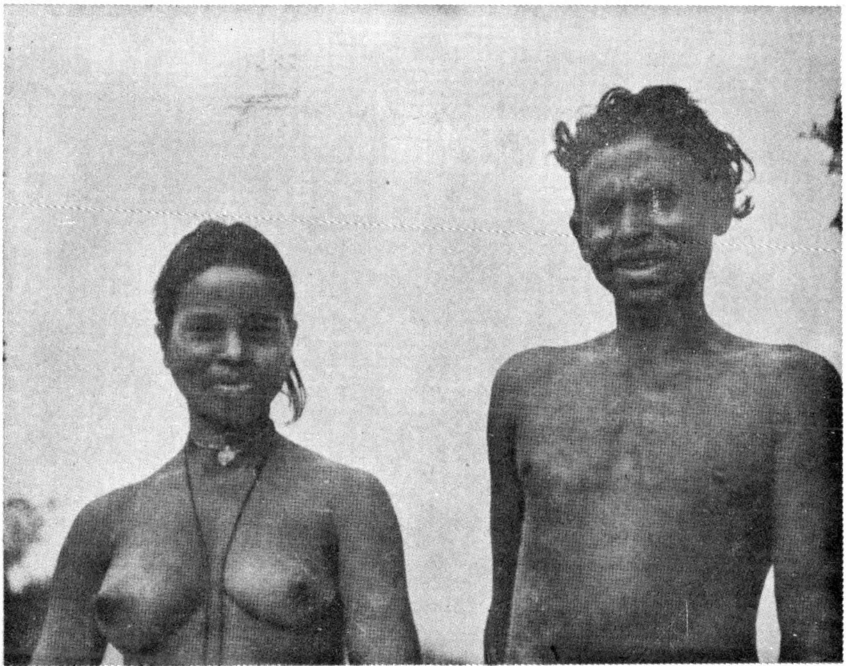

(*a*) Bagori and Jimme, who tried to kill her co-wife, after her release from jail (p. 114)

(*b*) Attami Gutte (p. 198)

(*c*) The lucky Doga (p. 198)

PLATE XXIII

(*a*) Sori Bhima, who feared his victim was a sorcerer (Case No. 19 and p. 67)

(*b*) Vedta Sukra, who believed his uncle to be a sorcerer (Case No. 96 and p. 67)

(*c*) Kartami Bira, who also feared his victim as a sorcerer (Case No. 19)

(*d*) Habka Masa, jealous of his wife

PLATE XXIV

and there was only one building, belonging to his brother, nearby. At this time of the year everyone was busy in the fields. Hunga therefore caught hold of his wife by the hair, threw her down and prepared to cut her throat. She tried her best to snatch the knife from his hand, but was unable to. The two little girls, Malla and Kosi, who had been sitting in the kitchen, came screaming and tried to save their mother. They cried for help, but there was no one to hear. As they tried to pull their father's hands away from their mother, they themselves got slightly injured. Then Hunga put his knee on Gangi's waist and sat above her holding her hair by one hand, while he sawed through her throat with the knife in exactly the same manner as the priest, at a Maria festival, slowly cuts through the neck of a dedicated pig. When he had cut almost right through the throat and was sure that Gangi was dead, he picked up a rope and went behind the house.

A little while later Hunga's mother, who had been to fetch water, returned to the house. She saw Gangi lying dead and Kosi beside her weeping. The child said that her father had gone behind the house with a rope, and the old woman hurried round and found her son hanging from a rafter of the house, his feet about a cubit and a half above the ground. The knife covered with his wife's blood was lying below. She picked it up and cut through the cord, and Hunga fell to the ground unconscious but still breathing. He recovered, but only to be sentenced to death and hanged. The clothes of Hunga and Gangi, partners in this unnatural tragedy, were buried together and an earthen tomb was raised above them.

CHAPTER THIRTEEN

THE CRIMES OF WOMEN

I

It is notorious that women are everywhere less criminal than men. 'The proportion varies, however, greatly in different countries. In France it is usually about 4 to 1; in the United States it is about 12 to 1; in Italy and Spain the proportion of women is very small. In Great Britain, on the other hand, the proportion of criminal women is extremely large, especially for the greater crimes.'[1] In Bastar the proportion is 23 men to 1 woman.

Havelock Ellis points out that woman is protected from crime by certain physical and psychological characteristics—her physical weakness, sexual selection, domestic seclusion, prostitution and maternity. Among Maria women, however, the only one of these forms of protection to operate is maternity. Maria women are protected by considerable physical strength and are as capable of striking a murderous blow with an axe as are the men. Since every Maria woman is married, sexual selection is of no assistance in removing from the place of danger and temptation the more degenerate and abnormal types.

As far as the domestic seclusion of women is concerned, the Maria situation resembles that in the Baltic provinces of Russia of former days, where the women shared the occupations of men and the level of feminine criminality was comparatively high. In England also, which has taken the lead in enlarging the sphere of women's work, 'the level of feminine criminality has for half a century been rising'. The Maria woman is not only free to assist her husband in the tasks of daily life, but she also frequently participates in those very occasions which are regarded as most provocative to murder, the drinking parties when large quantities of rice-beer are consumed. There is no prostitution among the Maria. But on the other hand women do not, as in Europe, fall out of the social ranks.

[1] Havelock Ellis, op. cit., pp. 261 f.

For the Maria (as for the European woman) maternity is the great protection. The reason for the low incidence of homicide among Maria women is possibly connected with the strong aboriginal belief that it is supernaturally dangerous for a woman to take life. This is the ultimate reason why there are no women priests, for the priest has to offer sacrifice. Maria women are not supposed to kill goats or even chickens. They are not permitted to join in hunting. The only pursuit of the kind which is not taboo to them is fishing—but fish are cold-blooded creatures.

It will be noted, however, that the number of Maria women who commit suicide is almost as high as that of Maria men.

II

Five of the 100 homicides were committed by women, and in one of them the woman was helped by a man. Two of these were typical women's crimes arising out of annoyance and exasperation over comparatively small matters. In the first case two women, both of whom had been married to the same man and were now widows, were living together. The older widow was so tiresome and so continually nagged the younger that at last the girl could stand it no longer, and gave her three blows with an axe whereon she died. In the second case, a man and his wife were collecting red ants for food when they heard the cries of a child in extremity. They went to the place and found a little girl about ten years old lying on the ground with her neck broken. She had been killed by her step-mother for not doing what she was told. The older woman had climbed up a tree and was picking the leaves and throwing them down. She called to the child and asked her to bring her basket closer so that she could drop the leaves directly into it. When the child disobeyed, her step-mother came down from the tree and beat and kicked her, then twisted her neck till she died. Both the older woman and the girl were weak and hungry for want of food. There was no rice in their house and they had been living on mahua for days. Fatigue and hunger played their part in this tragedy, as so often happens.

In 3 cases wives murdered their husbands. If this seems a large percentage, it must be remembered that in no fewer than 18 cases did husbands murder their wives. Tati Hirma had three wives. One was dead and the other two were living at the time of the tragedy. The youngest wife Mase was frequently beaten by her husband, who said she did not work properly and ate too much. Their constant quarrels attracted the notice of the villagers, and a panchayat was held which fined them four annas each. One day in January 1940, when the two wives were reaping the rice crop together, their husband went to the field and beat Mase. Late that night when everyone was asleep, the girl got up and killed her husband with an axe. The injuries were severe. There were several fractures in the skull, the face was mutilated and the brain congested. The Court found that the girl had received great provocation, her body had many marks of injuries and it was shown that sometimes she was so severely beaten that her whole body would be swollen, and she would have to foment her injuries with hot water. She had a baby only five months old, and so she was given the terrible mercy of life-imprisonment.

The murder of Marvi Bododi by his wife and younger brother is considered in detail in Chapter Seven as a typical carefully premeditated but clumsily executed crime of elimination.

III

The murder of Tati Mundra by his wife Pande at Bodenar on 25 October 1935 was the sequel to a long tale of unhappiness and cruelty. Pande was deserted by her first husband, who went away to the Tea Gardens leaving her behind, and she was persuaded by her mother's sister, with whom she had taken refuge, to marry Mundra, a thing she herself claimed she never wanted to do. During the first part of their association, Pande and Mundra lived, if not happily, at least in peace. Then Pande's daughter by her first husband died, and she began to feel more and more distaste for the husband whom she never seems to have really loved. She made several fruitless attempts to escape from him. But every time he pursued her and brought her back. Then he would beat her ferociously and helped by his relatives would rub into the wounds the juice of the marking-nut (*Semecarpus anacardium*, Linn.). This juice is a powerful irritant and when applied to the skin desiccates strongly, raising black blisters. Months after Mundra's death the marks of injuries were clearly visible on the unfortunate woman's body.

The last week of Mundra's life was fully occupied in chasing his wife. It appears as though he was really fond of her or at least really desired her in a sadistic manner, and he probably got considerable pleasure out of torturing her. On 20 October he went with his father to Lakhopal where they had heard Pande was hiding. They sent a villager ahead to call the girl, and she came trembling out of the house and hid below a tree. Mundra and his party then forcibly took her home to Tikanpal. That same night she ran away again. On the third day Mundra set out once more in search of her. They heard that she had again gone to Lakhopal and this time, when Mundra found her, he decided not to go home but to take her to a Siraha at Killepal in order to get her exorcized of the evil spirit which, he had decided, was the real cause of her continually leaving him. This is sometimes done when a cow refuses to stay with the herd or fails to return to its own shed at night. The Siraha is called in and divines what ancestor or godling is causing the trouble, whereupon suitable remedies are adopted. Sometimes these remedies may be unpleasant, including the burning of chillies under the nose, beating with an old shoe or making the patient drink urine.[1] It is little wonder that poor Pande regarded this suggestion with alarm.

On the evening of that day a witness remembered meeting an unknown man and woman on the boundary of Kaklur

[1] How severe these remedies sometimes are may be seen in the circumstances of a case at Mandla in 1925. A Rajput youth became strange in his manner after witnessing a melodrama and his trouble was diagnosed as spirit-possession. He was first tied to a pole in the courtyard. Then his elder sister fell into a frenzy; she swallowed a live bit of coal, declared she was possessed by Kali, and sacrificed her little daughter to that goddess in an attempt to restore her brother's sanity. This remedy failing, the unfortunate youth's hands were burned and he was tied naked in a place generally used by a harmless lunatic with a local reputation for sanctity. Here he died of exposure.

and Bodenar. The man was carrying an axe and told him he was travelling from Tikanpal to Killepal, and he asked for and obtained a cucumber to eat for supper. The witness noticed that the woman looked angry and sat at some distance, refusing to speak to her companion. Later that same evening the villagers of Bodenar saw a man carrying an axe and cucumber and followed by a woman enter the village, and they allowed them to sleep in the village Rest-house. The following morning they discovered the man lying dead with a deep wound going right into the brain. The woman had disappeared.

Later Pande described the continual torture and mutilation to which she was subjected by Mundra. She said that on the night of the tragedy, in the Rest-house Mundra had forcibly attempted to have intercourse with her and she had prevented him. He had declared that if she did not consent, he would cut her to pieces with an axe. They then lay down separately and both tried to keep awake, she in order to prevent him from approaching her in her sleep and he to ensure that she did not run away. But at cock-crow, exhausted by his long journey, he fell asleep and Pande killed him with the axe and made her escape. She was sentenced to transportation for life but the Sessions Judge made a strong recommendation for mercy, and in appeal her punishment was reduced to one year's imprisonment.

In this murder several factors operated simultaneously. There was the desire for revenge for years of cruelty. There was the imperative necessity for Pande to eliminate a man who would not leave her alone, and who would neither allow her to live happily with him or to go anywhere else. There was the fear of treatment by the Siraha. There was the extreme fatigue and exhaustion of her attempted flight, the misery of her capture, the further long journey with little food, and finally a long night's vigil.

IV

Dislike of the husband may equally result in suicide when the woman is weaker or the social odds against her are too heavy. Budri did not love her husband and whenever she was taken to his house ran away from it. After this had happened several times, she hanged herself. Kunjami Burji, a widow, was desired by Konda who sent seven men, according to custom, to bring her to his house. In spite of her remonstrances, she was taken forcibly, but managed to escape with her three little children and hanged herself in the house while they were asleep. A young girl, Poyami Pande, was given to her mother's brother's son in marriage. After the feast, the couple were shut up together in a room as usual for the consummation of the marriage. But Pande objected, fought her way out of the room, and ran home where she was thoroughly scolded for such improper conduct. That night she hanged herself.

CHAPTER FOURTEEN

CRIMINAL LUNACY

CRIMINAL lunacy is not a serious problem in Bastar.[1] During the 22 years from 1919 to 1941, only 8 criminal lunatics were sent to the Mental Hospital at Nagpur. Two of the 8 were released cured, and 6 remained. More recently from 1935 to 1941, 17 persons were examined for insanity in the jail at Jagdalpur. Five of these, all murderers, were sent to Nagpur; five were found to be falsely pleading insanity and were convicted of violent crime; one was found to have committed a murder while insane, but was released as cured in 1937. The others were sent in for observation as harmless lunatics under the provisions of the Lunacy Act.

Of the 6 criminal lunatics sent to Nagpur, only 2 were Bison-horn Maria. But in 2 other cases Bison-horn Maria, who were convicted of culpable homicide not amounting to murder under Section 304, showed marked psychotic characteristics.

Marvi Bhima was a melancholic and murdered his wife in a fit of manic-depressive insanity. For two days before the tragedy he had behaved very strangely, walking in and out of the house and going round and round it; and it was actually while the relatives were calling the village elders to deal with the matter that he went into his house and stabbed his younger wife Kondi in the stomach with an arrow. After stabbing her he tried to pull the arrow out, but finding this difficult he pushed it right through her body and removed it from the back. In the meantime the village elders were on the way to the house, and when they got there they saw Bhima wandering about with a bow and arrow in his hand. They sent the unfortunate woman to the police station where she expired while making a dying declaration. No one dared to go near Bhima. But the next morning he went into a neighbour's house and they hastily

[1] It is often said that mental disorders are very rare among primitive people. This has been questioned, but little evidence has yet been accumulated. See E. Winston, 'The Alleged Lack of Mental Diseases among Primitive Groups', *American Anthropologist*, Vol. XXXVI (New Series, 1934), pp. 234 ff.

closed the door and bolted it from outside. When the headman got there, he found Bhima hiding inside a large bamboo bin used for storing grain. The villagers kept him locked up until the police came and took him away.

Before the Court Bhima admitted stabbing his wife, but declared that he did not properly remember why he did so. Everybody testified to the fact that he had been very fond of Kondi and had always treated her well, though for the whole year his behaviour had been strange. After the murder he showed no sign of realizing what he had done, and during his trial he wept not because he had killed his wife, but because he feared 'that in his absence his cattle were being distributed like fowls'. He tried to escape from the Court two or three times during the trial, for he was filled with fear that he would be thrown into a pit, and begged the Judge that he might be hanged or given any imprisonment rather than that. The medical evidence was that Bhima was suffering from melancholia. He was acquitted of the charge of murder, but was detained under Section 471 of the Criminal Procedure Code.

'The periodic mental disorders of epilepsy', says Sullivan, 'are divisible, according to their relation to the characteristic paroxysms, into those preceding the fit, or pre-epileptic disorders, usually in the direction of morbid irritability, those following the fit—post-epileptic dream states or maniacal outbursts of longer or shorter duration—and those occurring in lieu of a fit, or possibly after a very slight and unobserved attack of petit mal. Criminal conduct, and particularly acts of homicidal violence—for homicide is *par excellence* the crime of the epileptic—may occur in connexion with any of these disordered conditions. Its most frequent and characteristic form is the homicide committed in the phase of obscured consciousness which may follow or replace a fit or an attack of epileptic vertigo.'[1]

Hemla Chewa was an epileptic, and his left hand was a fingerless stump. On 18 January 1922, as he was going through the jungle near Hirana, he say a Halba boy about sixteen years old cutting fire-wood. He had never seen the boy before, and there was no suggestion that he had any relations with him. In the Court he produced a story of

[1] Sullivan, op. cit., p. 133.

being chased through the forest by three men and said that as he was running away he met the boy and seized his axe and killed him with it. Later the same evening he assaulted and injured a woman with his axe, and hit her nephew when he ran to her assistance. Chewa was tied up by the villagers but escaped during the night, and went to his uncle's house in the same village. The next morning he was again caught and taken to the police. In the Court he showed complete indifference to his trial, and talked throughout in a low tone. He was acquitted of murder, but was detained in jail as a lunatic.

Another epileptic who exhibited the characteristic signs of obscured consciousness and amnesia was an elderly man named Khotlu who killed his wife Mase on the evening of 12 December 1920 at Kawargaon. For a year before the tragedy he had been getting attacks every Sunday. He used to shiver uncontrollably, froth at the mouth, suffer violent convulsions and fall to the ground unconscious for two or three hours. At such times he had the delusion that a rebellion was about to take place and he would call on everyone to run away. Sometimes he himself armed with a stick would run into the jungle. On two occasions he had to be tied up, and was taken first to Torwa and then to Pondum to be treated by medicine-men.

Khotlu's wife Mase was nearly as old as himself, and had borne him ten children. They were apparently on the best of terms. But on the day of the tragedy, which was a Sunday, when they went out with their little boy to cut the kosra crop in their fields, Khotlu fell down in a fit. After lying unconscious for some hours he got up and shouted 'Run, run, the Bhumkal (Rebellion) is coming'. He told his wife to go home at once. But she said that their work was not finished and she would first pick some leaves and then come. Khotlu accused her of being in love with someone whom she wanted to meet in the forest. At that she agreed to go with him. He began to push her along and, as she was walking home before him, he shot her with an arrow from behind.

The woman somehow reached the village, and died three days later. Khotlu stayed out in the fields and in the evening came and sat in his house. When he was asked the following day where his wife was, he said she had gone to fetch water. Presently he pointed at something and said that it was his wife coming. When he was taken to see the dying woman, at first he declared that she was not his wife at all, then later insisted that he had no recollection of the incident.

The case of Poriami Kosa is one in which we approach very near to the boundaries of insanity, although the Court considered that he was sufficiently responsible and sentenced him to seven years' imprisonment. He was a man who was regarded as almost imbecile by his fellow Maria. He was incapable of ploughing his fields or of buying things in the bazaar. His wife seems to have treated him as a grown-up child. He suffered from some form of paralysis. On the day of the murder, shortly before sunset, when 'the sun was only three bamboos above the horizon', Kosa asked his wife to lie with him. But she refused and abused him, taunting him with his illness and saying that he would never get better. He then attempted to have congress with her forcibly, and she resisted. In the struggle her wooden combs and cloth fell to the ground, and Kosa full of rage stabbed her with a small pointed knife on the face and neck. She ran for about forty paces and fell dead to the ground.

Kawasi Chamru had a curious fit of madness which lasted several days. On the first day he wandered about the jungle. On the next he climbed up a tree and sat there all day. On the third day he killed two of his bullocks and rubbed their blood on his body. Nothing then happened for several years. But shortly before his tragedy he again began to act strangely. He had always been on good terms with his wife. But now he developed delusions that she was unfaithful to him. One day he suddenly began to beat her. Holding her by the tuft of her hair, he struck her three times on the head with a heavy bit of wood from a plough. She fell down and Chamru went on beating her till she died. Then he dragged the body into the house and, pulling a handful of grass from the roof, lit it and set fire to the building. Everything there, all the clothes, grain and the dead body, was destroyed. Chamru took a bamboo pole in his hand and sat under a mango tree in the jungle, where he remained until he was arrested.

It is possible that in this case some important evidence was suppressed by the witnesses, for there was a suggestion that the murdered woman had committed incest with her brother. The fear of excommunication and fines would be sufficiently strong to induce everyone to keep quiet about this. On the other hand, it is equally possible that the suspicion of his wife's infidelity was a delusion of Chamru's disordered mind.

Other Maria have been content to take their own way out of the world, when the psychotic disturbance became too strong for them. Many different symptoms are recorded as preceding such suicides. Baiha Ganga, for some days before his death, refused to eat and when people approached him attacked them with his stick. Bongi Maria was subject to periodic attacks of insanity ; he tried to kill himself three times before he finally succeeded. Others displayed a marked narcissistic attitude, wandering aimlessly in the jungle, refusing to talk or work ; such were Saradu, a northern Muria, who used to wander naked, Nari Maria, Pakli, a little girl about ten years old, and Marvi Mundi, a woman who had suffered since childhood from attacks during which she refused to eat and wandered about aimlessly, neglecting the dozen children she had borne.

There is finally the strange and sombre case of Markami Hirme, mother of four children and about to bear a fifth. In her pre-pubertal period she had been subject to epileptic fits, but was treated by the local Siraha, and was believed cured. On 22 October 1935, at her home at Gonderas, the epilepsy recurred, and she became 'strange in her behaviour'. She was in the eighth month of pregnancy. Two days later, when her husband was out watching the crops, and her eldest daughter had gone for water, she hanged herself from a rafter of the house in the presence of her three little children.

Now such a death is the most dangerous in the world. The woman who dies in pregnancy or childbirth is known throughout India as the Churelin or Churin ; in Bastar she is often called the Ondar Muttai, the Old Bee Woman, who attacks men with the fury of a swarm of bees. Hirme's husband and the village elders seem to have been unable to decide what to do. Not one of them dared to touch the corpse, and it remained hanging for two days in the house. Then, so the villagers declare, the foetus of the unborn child automatically discharged itself from the womb. By this time the necessary ceremonies of protection had been performed, and the body was cut down.

CHAPTER FIFTEEN

THE HOMICIDE'S BEHAVIOUR AFTER HIS CRIME

I

THE normal behaviour of a Maria after he has committed homicide is to do nothing at all. He may run away into the jungle for a few hours. He may go to see a friend in another village. But in the great majority of cases, he either stays at home quietly or he returns home in a very short time. It is unusual for him to try to abscond, though this was done by 4 of the 117 persons involved. In 81 cases the accused confessed after being arrested by the police, and in 9 cases he voluntarily gave himself up.

TABLE TWENTY-ONE

BEHAVIOUR OF HOMICIDES AFTER THE CRIME IN 117 INSTANCES

Attempted to escape	6
Absconded to another Province . . .	4
Attempted to conceal crime	
By making it look like suicide . .	6
" " an accident . .	1
" " a tiger-kill . .	2
By burying the bodies . . .	3
By arson	2
Attempted to implicate others	4
Himself tried to commit suicide	1
Persuaded or threatened villagers to hush up the matter	12
Gave himself up	9
Confessed after arrest	81
Denied the crime	36

The few cases, therefore, where a Maria homicide has tried to evade the consequences of his crime are of special interest. It cannot be said that the Maria are very expert at concealment. Sometimes there are clumsy attempts to make the murder look like suicide. This was done in each of the three throttling cases of 1933. In the first, the murderer after throttling a young boy tied a cloth tightly

round his neck, and strung him to a tree. In the next, where according to the medical evidence the murderer strangled a girl with a thin rope, he tied the body to the branch of a tamarind tree, but so carelessly that she was not found hanging but sitting on the ground. In the third, Ujji Poda tied a rope round his victim's neck and broke it. He then tied the broken end to the roof of a field-shed and left it dangling, the idea being to suggest that the man had hanged himself, but that the rope had snapped and allowed the body to fall on the ground. Poda then bribed everybody to make a report of suicide to the police.

Again, when Poyami Masa stabbed his wife with an arrow, his idea seems to have been to suggest suicide; but unfortunately for him he did not do his work properly and the poor woman lived long enough to tell the villagers the truth.

In two other cases the murderers arranged the bodies of their victims to look as though they had been attacked by tigers.

In three cases the murderers attempted to hide the body. In one, the concealment was done so clumsily that marks of blood and every trace of a violent crime was left on the scene of the crime. In another case an attempt was made to suggest that the deceased had met a natural death by drowning, and in another a report was made that the dead man was an epileptic and had killed himself by falling in a fit onto a stump of wood.

The Maria's attempts to put their crimes on to innocent people are less discreditable than they appear. The idea seems to be that, if an obviously innocent person is accused, he will be able to clear himself in Court, and the police may then drop their investigation and both the innocent and guilty will escape. In 1940, in a village near Aranpur a man was arrested for shooting someone with an arrow, and the prosecution witnesses actually testified that they saw him do so. He denied the crime, and presently another man went to the police and confessed that he was the real culprit. But there was no evidence against the second man and both persons were acquitted. The following year at Aranpur when Barse Chewa was arrested for the murder of his father-in-law, his relatives tried to involve Chewa's brother in the case. They declared that the brother had gone to a Siraha, and had asked him to perform sacrifices which would protect him from the consequences of the crime of which he was the real culprit. It was easily proved, however, that he could have had nothing to do with the matter, and it is probable that the Aranpur people were hoping by this trick to secure the release of both the brothers. This will explain other attempts to involve young men in crimes of which they were obviously innocent. In one case the accused, a youth of only eighteen, tried to involve his brother, though in the end he confessed his crime before the Court. In another, the villagers tried to force a young man to admit the crime and the youth's own father actually took him to the police station for this purpose. The Sub-Inspector refused to accept his confession.

In the Gumiapal murder, however, where the real murderer was the Gaita of the village, the people combined to protect their priest and put the blame on an innocent man. They forced the Kotwar to implicate him and make a false report. When I met the murderer fourteen years afterwards in jail, he was still insisting on his innocence and that the real murderer was the man whom he had tried to implicate so many years before.

But these attempts to shift responsibility are uncommon. It is remarkable how quickly, once the police have arrived on the scene, a Maria admits his guilt, and in 81 of our 100 cases such confession was made.

We should not perhaps assume that these confessions are necessarily evidence of the truthfulness and simplicity of the aboriginals. They may be, but we would do well to take into account the judgement of Sir Cecil Walsh.

> The Indian police are past masters in detective work amongst their own kith and kin, and are endowed with exceptional gifts of insight into the mentality of the average uneducated villager. They are without scruple, and extraordinarily clever in their methods of extracting information. To take what is probably a fairly frequent example, they will tell the man as soon as he is arrested that his only chance of escape is to make a full and candid statement. The majority of men, in such circumstances, are cowardly, and only too ready to sell their associates, if they think by doing so they can purchase immunity. When the statement has been made, the next step is

(*a*) Poriami Hirma

(*c*) Poriami Ganga

(*b*) Poriami Hunga

PLATE XXV
The Pinna Bheji Tragedy
(Case No. 76 and p. 209)

(*a*) Miriami Doga, exasperated by a creditor (Case No. 64)

(*b*) Kuhrami Tonda, the dwarf who revenged himself on a bullying younger brother (Case No. 33)

(*c*) Vetti Hirma (Case No. 99)

(*d*) Vetti Rupe, who killed a man in a drunken quarrel (Case No. 100)

PLATE XXVI

> simple. The accused man is told, 'But this is no good to me as it stands. I must have corroboration. No judge will act upon the statement of a guilty party, unless it is corroborated by some independent fact, and unless your evidence is made acceptable to the court how can you be given a pardon?' This absolutely correct statement of the law may itself be corroborated by the simple method of reading to the accused extracts, perhaps embellished by the wily officer, from the printed instructions issued to the police, in which the principles on which the courts act in requiring corroboration are carefully explained. The simple-minded villager finds no difficulty in following this argument, and proceeds to give chapter and verse, describing the places in which the loot, or the weapon used for the murder, can be found. When this happens, how can one suppose the man to be innocent?[1]

This does not mean that the police are corrupt or unduly oppressive. The tricking of a criminal into an admission of his crime is applauded in many famous detective stories. M. Poirot was an adept at this particular art and so have been many others of the great detectives of fiction. It is probable that unless some such methods were used a majority of Maria criminals would go unconvicted, for it is notable that, while 81 accused out of 117 confessed after arrest, only 9 gave themselves up voluntarily before it. In more than one case the accused took the police to the scene of his crime and himself provided them with all the clues and proofs they wanted, and then afterwards, probably on the advice of the defending counsel, withdrew his confession.

II

The number of cases where even the villagers have been ignorant of the real author of a murder are so few that it is worth discussing one of them in detail.

Goge, a burly, rough, quarrelsome man of about fifty years was the headman of Kasturpal. He had three wives. On 4 March 1922, his two elder wives went to another village to drink rice-beer. His younger wife was sleeping in the kitchen, and he himself on a cot in his house was alone except for his little daughter who was on the ground

[1] Sir C. Walsh, *Indian Village Crimes*, pp. 30 f.

beside him. About midnight someone came quietly into the house and stabbed him, making a deep wound on the right side of the neck and killing him instantly.

The youngest wife was wakened, not by any cry from her husband, but by the noise of a man running past her room. It was a dark night and she could not see who it was. She thought nothing of it, and turned over and went to sleep again. But a little while afterwards the two senior wives returned and when they entered the house they saw the cot covered with blood and a great pool on the floor being eagerly licked up by a dog. They cried for help, and a few of the neighbours with torches of flaming straw gathered to see what had happened.

Then the three wives sat down together to discuss who could have been the murderer. There is, I think, something at once pathetic and bizarre in the picture of these three women, each of whom had linked her life to the dominating and far from agreeable personality now lying dead before them, sitting round the fire at midnight and wondering which of their friends or neighbours could have hated their man so bitterly as to murder him.

Their suspicions first fell upon a neighbour called Guddi. A little while previously Goge's son had killed one of Guddi's goats, and the two men had quarrelled. They had made friends again, but within a week of the incident two of Guddi's children had died. Guddi declared that Goge had killed them by his magic, and had gone so far as to say at a bazaar that one day he would kill his enemy. Two days later, therefore, a report was made to the police, and in order to implicate Guddi properly the two elder wives declared that they were in the house at the time of the incident and that Goge had declared before he died that it was Guddi who had injured him. One of the women said that she had actually seen Guddi running away with a spear in his hand.

Guddi was arrested, but investigation showed that he had never left his house that night, and there was no evidence against him. He was released and the police had to continue their search. For five months there was no clue to the identity of the murderer, and apparently not even the villagers knew who it was.

But Guddi was not the only enemy that Goge had made. Indeed it appears that the dead man, as a result of his rude and dominating ways, had so many enemies that it was impossible to choose between them. A few days before the murder, a man from another village had come to him to report that a cow and a bullock had been stolen. He asked Goge in his capacity of village headman to discover the thieves. Goge sent for a man called Mado who was in the service of Oyami Kola as a Kabari farm-labourer. When Mado came, Goge tied his hands together and beat him with a stick. But Mado declared that he was innocent of the theft and since nothing could be proved against him he had to be released. Goge, however, insisted on his belief that Mado and Kola had taken the cattle and eaten them. The next day Goge went to Kola's house and again beat Mado while Kola hid himself indoors. After that Mado disappeared. Two days later Goge came to the house again, this time with three or four companions for the purpose of beating Kola. But his wife warned him in time, and he was able to hide in the garden. Goge once more accused Kola and his servant of stealing the cattle, and declared that, if he could have got Kola then, he would have beaten him to death. For the next two days Kola remained indoors, afraid to venture out for fear of being attacked. At last he decided that such an existence was intolerable, and he went quietly out of the house at night and killed Goge with his axe.

Kola is one of the few Maria criminals who acted with intelligence. Immediately after the deed he washed his axe, and saw that there were no blood-stains on his person. He buried the axe in a rat-hole near his house. He swore his wife to secrecy, and neither of them said anything, they went nowhere, they did nothing. They kept quiet. No suspicion fell upon Kola, nor would it have done but for the fact that he was unable to bring himself to come forward and help the police in their investigations.

Kola had taken a line which in a city would have been entirely successful. He decided to keep quiet, have nothing to do with the affair, and show no interest in it. But that is not the way to behave in an aboriginal village. In a place where so little ever happens, where life is so dull, where the humblest visitor is a momentous break in the monotony, for a man not to be present to listen to all the absorbing details of a police investigation shows that he must have something on his mind. Kola's absence from the investigations made some of the neighbours suspicious, and they began to talk. One of them went to Kola and began to discuss the murder. Kola with incredible folly said that he knew who the murderer was. It was someone from outside the village, he said, and when he was asked how he knew, he declared that there were two murderers, one of them being the original suspect, Guddi, and the other a stranger. He knew about it because, he said, he had been present at the time, standing outside the house and had seen all that had happened.

Talk continued and in due time reached the ears of the police. A constable came to Kasturpal and questioned Kola and his wife. He repeated his original statement, and was brought to Jagdalpur. Here, as the record says naively, 'he was questioned again and again' until at last he took the entire blame on himself. He was taken back to his village, and showed the police where the axe was buried. At his trial he maintained his confession, but claimed that he was afraid that Goge was going to kill him and had acted in self-defence. He was sentenced to life-imprisonment.

It is hard to understand how Kola, five months after his crime, should have lost his nerve and involved himself in the case just because somebody expressed a suspicion of him. His conduct up till that moment had been technically flawless. But it appears to be a characteristic of the aboriginal criminal to break down at the first hint of pressure.

CHAPTER SIXTEEN

THE ATTITUDE OF SOCIETY

I

THE SANCTION OF MYTH

THE place of myth in sanctioning tribal custom and inspiring and controlling tribal action has become a commonplace of anthropology. How far then is murder regarded with approval in the mythology of tribal India ? To the aboriginal mind the supernatural world is populated with beings whose conduct, if they were on earth, would speedily lead them to the gallows. The revered and honoured Dead behave to the living with a spitefulness and cruelty that they never showed on earth. The clan-gods and village deities are irascible, touchy beings, ready to take offence over the most trivial matters, greedy and exacting. The Supreme Being himself appears in a far from creditable light. He is jealous of mankind. He despairs of getting sufficient souls for his kingdom, and kills men by treachery and deceit. According to Birhor[1] and Asur[2] legend he burns the first man and woman alive in a furnace for no other reason than that he dislikes the smell of their smithy. The Kharia tell how he destroyed men by flood and fire, being annoyed because they cut down fruit-trees.[3] A Kol story from Bonai shows the Supreme Chando so exasperated at the sight of the parents of mankind enjoying sexual intercourse that he killed them out of jealousy. A Kuruk tale describes how Mahapurub destroyed his own children for making too much noise. It was from their dead bodies that the world came into being.

In Juang mythology, history begins with a cowardly and deceitful murder by the gods, who created the world from their dead victim's blood and bones. The Bhuiya story of creation is on the same lines. The son of the first human couple is murdered by a tiger sent by Dharam Deo. His head becomes the sun, his chest the moon and his blood gives the red earth its colour.

1 S. C. Roy, *The Birhors* (Ranchi, 1925), p. 402.
2 Verrier Elwin, *The Agaria* (Bombay, 1942), p. 101.
3 S. C. Roy, *The Kharias* (Ranchi, 1937), p. 415.

Death comes into the world by the treachery of the gods. The Baiga describe how Bhagavan grew tired of men, but did not know how to kill them. So he gave Nanga Baiga itch and the old man began to scratch. But he was unable to reach the small of his back, and one day when he picked up a stick to scratch himself there, Bhagavan turned it into a cobra and it bit him and he died.[1] The Juang say that formerly men did not die because they did not sleep, and Bhagavan had to send a woman to sell them curds mixed with sleep-medicine. When they ate the curds, they slept and died. The Bhuiya story describes how so long as Jug Budha and his wife were living, no one died and the world was becoming over-populated. So the Supreme Being sent a centipede to bite them, and thus introduced death into the world.

The Muria too, in the north of Bastar, associate the coming of death with the murder of a son.

> In the Middle World no man died, and Mahapurub wondered how he was to get souls for his kingdom. He had a son. He killed him and prepared to carry him out for burial. But when his wife heard of it, she ran weeping to the place and, taking her son from him, sat with the corpse in her lap. Mahapurub said, 'We must bury the child, don't be foolish'. But she said, 'No, I'll never give him to you'.
>
> Mahapurub then planted a jamun tree behind her. One day some of the berries fell to the ground before her. She picked them up and as she ate her mouth was reddened with the juice. Mahapurub came again and said, 'Give me the boy. You are a witch, you are eating his flesh.' He brought a mirror and when she saw her reddened mouth, she thought she really was eating her son. She wept bitterly, but gave the body to Mahapurub. He buried it and from that day, death has been in the world.

A similar sacrifice accounts for the origin of the sun and moon. The Muria, in a story which is known in a slightly different version to the Bison-horn Maria, describe how after the great wooden circles for the sun and moon were made, there was the problem of how to put life into them. Mahapurub had a son, and Lingo declared that only by killing him and giving his blood to the sun and moon to

[1] Verrier Elwin, *The Baiga* (London, 1939), p. 329.

drink, would they become alive and be man and woman. One day while Mahapurub was working in his fields, his wife put the child in a swing and went for water. Lingo stole the child and brought him down to earth. He sacrificed him and offered his blood to the sun and moon and they became alive.

Both the Baiga and Muria have stories to account for the disappearance of human sacrifice.

> Now Nanga Baiga and Nanga Baigin had nothing to sacrifice for the steadying of the world. So they took their own three sons and daughters in a *kawar*, and were carrying them along. Then they met a jungle hen. 'Where are you going?' she asked. And when she heard, 'You mustn't kill your own children. Take two pairs of mine. Offer one pair, and keep the other for breeding.' So said the jungle hen. Then Nanga Baiga lifted one son and daughter out of the *kawar* and left them with the hen, and put the chickens in instead.
>
> A little later they met a sow. She also begged them not to sacrifice their children, and gave two pairs of sucklings in exchange for two more of the children. Then they met a barking deer, and made a similar exchange.[1]

The Muria story runs as follows:

> The Muria was thinking, 'How am I to worship the earth for I have nothing to give her?' He had one daughter. He covered her whole body with soot to make her black and forced her to walk on all fours like a black cow.

[1] *The Baiga*, p. 315. 'At Nasik, in the Deccan, when cholera appears, a woman of the Mang (menial tribe) is solemnly led out of the city as a scapegoat. She remains outside the city bounds till the next day, when she bathes and returns. The ceremonial, which closely resembles that of bringing a victim to a shrine, doubtless implies an earlier rite of human sacrifice.

'Another rite resembles that of the self-immolation of pilgrims, who used, in former times, to fling themselves in the name of Siva, over the cliff known as Bhairava Jhamp, near the famous shrine of Kedar Nath in the lower Himalayas. This rite has now been commuted into the paying for the service of a bedi or rope dancer, who slides on a wooden saddle upon a cable hung over a precipitous cliff as a means of propitiating Siva.

'In the form of the "Bihunda" rite the same custom prevails in the Punjab, on the River Sutlej.

'In Baroda also, at the worship of Vagh Deo, the tiger god, a man is covered with a blanket; he bows to the image and walks round it seven times. During this performance the worshippers slap him on the back. He then tries to escape to the forest, pursued by children, who fling balls of clay at him, and finally bring him back, the rite ending with feasting and drinking. The above are instances of attenuated forms of the custom of human sacrifice and immolation which has become intolerable under the conditions of modern society.' —Haikerwal, op. cit., pp. 66 f.

> Then he went to the jungle to worship Mother Earth. On the way he met Lingo driving a cow. Lingo said, 'O man, where are you going ?' 'I am going to worship Mother Earth.' 'What are you going to sacrifice ?' 'I have nothing to give but my own daughter and I am going to sacrifice her.' Then Lingo said, 'Give me your daughter, and I will give you my cow'. From that day the Muria have not offered human beings to the Earth Mother but, taught by Lingo, have sacrificed their cattle.

A Bison-horn Maria account of creation tells of the great deluge and how the earth came into existence from mud that dropped from the hairs of the great boars that then lived in the world. There were two deities, Irisirma and Markaraja. They had two daughters, Iro and Palo. The girls both wanted to marry Koyabhimul, but the parents were unwilling and tried to kill the boy. They first sent a great snake to bite him as he returned from the jungle. But the girls warned him in time, and told him to invoke the name of their father and the snake would be unable to harm him. The parents then tried to kill him by asking him to sacrifice a chicken, planning to behead him as he bent down to do so. But the girls again warned him, and the boy said to Markaraja that he must first show him how the sacrifice was to be performed. As the older man bent down, the boy picked up a sword and beheaded him. 'In those days there were few gods and so there were few deaths on earth. The mortality on earth has increased because of the great increase in the number of deities.'

We have already seen how the origin of magic among men is connected with a human sacrifice and cannibalism. The Maria are acquainted with similar stories of the origin of the sun and moon through the sacrifice of a living being. Some of the Maria iron-smelters describe how at the beginning they were unable to extract iron from the ore. They killed a Maria and put his body into the furnace, after which their craft prospered.

Maria folk-tales are full of the usual murders, treacheries and deceits. But it is worth noting that generally these are attributed to outsiders and members of other castes. The Maria themselves usually appear virtuous and honourable.

I do not suppose anyone was ever incited to murder by these stories and legends. I doubt if anyone would ever consciously quote them as justification for his acts. But they do give an amoral background to the life of the tribe. This, combined with the character of the gods, does not help men to behave better. Budtha killed his wife because she did not give him chicken for breakfast. But in tribal belief a hundred godlings and ancestors have killed and tormented men because of some irregularity in offering them their beloved fowls.

II

THE ATTITUDE OF SOCIETY: CO-OPERATION WITH THE POLICE

Throughout tribal India in the old days it was probably the universal custom for the villagers to try cases of homicide on the spot, to impose a penalty and to demand suitable compensation.

It is noted in the Kurnool Manual that in former times the Chenchu headman used to 'dispose of murder cases, the murderer, on proof of guilt, being put to death with the same weapons with which the murder was committed. Captain Newbold, writing in 1846, says that, passing through the jungle near Pacharla, he observed a skull bleached by the sun dangling from the branch of a tamarind tree, which he was informed was that of a murderer and hill-robber put to death by the headman. In the time of the Nabobs, some of the Chenchu murderers were caught and punished, but the practice seems to have prevailed among them more or less till the introduction of the new police in 1860, since which time all cases are said to be reported to the nearest police officer '.[1]

An interesting account of the attitude of tribal society to murder in Assam is given by Hodson.

> Murder within the clan is so rare an event that I have no information concerning the attitude of these groups towards the offender in such a case. The murder of a member of another clan or village would occasion a feud which would only be ended with the slaughter of a member of the murderer's clan or village, and it is known that some of the worst village feuds have originated in this manner. Accidental homicide is punished among

[1] Thurston, op. cit., Vol. II, p. 28.

> the Tangkhul by fine, amounting to six cows. At Jessami in the Mao group the offender has to make a short sojourn away from his house, but not necessarily outside the village; while at Liyai he is banished from the village. At Mao his punishment is seven years' banishment from the village and a fine of five cows. At Maikel banishment for one year and a fine of five cows, while murder ensuing in the heat of passion in a quarrel is punished with seven years' banishment and a fine of ten cows. The Mayang Khong people exact only a fine of one cow in cases of accidental homicide. Both the Chiru and the Marring impose a heavy fine in such cases, part of the fine being compensation to the relatives of the dead man and the rest being consumed by the village in the course of the settlement of the matter.
>
> In some cases the weapon or other lethal instrument is forfeited to the relatives—a proceeding reminiscent of the law of Deodand.[1]

In former years adultery was commonly punished, so far as the male offender was concerned, with death and this proceeding gave no occasion for a feud. Among the Tangkhul theft was at one time punished with death, if the offender was caught in the act. Nowadays a fine is held sufficient. Arson is penalized and is considered so serious that even when it is accidental a heavy fine is demanded.

In Bastar also it was formerly the custom for the people to take the law into their own hands and where necessary to pay compensation for doing so to the local authorities. In fact, the older Maria still remember how in the days of their grandparents compensation for murder was paid to the Jia (the high priest) of Dantewara or to the Nengi and Hikmi (State representatives) at Mailawada. A very old man at Harmamunda described how 'In the old days when a witch was caught, her hands were cut off; and she was taken to the Nengi and Hikmi who were paid eight female calves. If a man was found practising black magic, his teeth were first knocked out with a large bone,[2] and then the bone itself

[1] T. C. Hodson, *The Naga Tribes of Manipur* (London, 1911), pp. 106 f. For an account of the attitude of society and 'judicial murder' in Papua, see F. E. Williams, 'Group Sentiment and Primitive Justice', *American Anthropologist*, Vol. XLIII (New Series), pp. 523 ff.

[2] In a review, M. B. Emeneau notes that 'the Kotas of the Nilgiris believe that Kurumba sorcerers who step out of line should have their front teeth knocked out. The reason is that they are thereby prevented from saying spells correctly'.—*American Anthropologist*, Vol. XLVII, p. 164.

was pushed into his mouth until he died'. The idea was that he had done his evil with the purpose of 'eating' or gain and so he was given a bone to eat. When this happened, the Nengi and Hikmi received eight male calves. 'Sometimes the witch or sorcerer had all their teeth knocked out, their mouths were burnt with hot oil, and they were banished from their village. With this mark upon them no one would shelter them. Yet another method of dealing with a witch was to tie her up in a sack and throw her into the river.' In another village I was told how a witch was wrapped up in straw and burnt alive.

An old man at Dhurli described how his brother had been killed by a witch's magic. When the Waddai confirmed this, his father killed the witch and paid compensation of four female calves to the Jia.

At Phulpar the headman said that in the old days they used to break the teeth of a witch, shave her head, cut her forehead with a broken bangle and so drive her from the village. Similarly I was told in several places in Konta Tahsil that the people used to cut a witch's nails, shave her head and drive her away. They would confiscate her property and often kill her. There has never been any doubt whatever in the minds of Maria with whom I have discussed this matter that a witch or a sorcerer ought to be punished with death, and that the public were perfectly justified in taking the law into their own hands in a proved case of witchcraft.[1]

There are probably many cases never discovered by the police that are settled by the Maria panchayat. In others, after everything has been settled by the panchayat, the police have discovered that a crime has been committed. There were as many as 12 such cases out of our 100. And

[1] An interesting parallel is furnished in a note by the late Rai Bahadur Hira Lal on a Report by a certain Captain Sinnock about conditions in the Surguja State in 1818, of which he was then in charge. A landholder named Parbal Sahy had ordered a witch to be put to death. During his trial the Court asked him, 'Do you know that he who is the author of murder commits a great crime?', to which he replied, 'I know that it is a very great crime to commit a murder, but in my country, Surguja, it is no crime to kill a witch'. Sinnock reported the most drastic witch-tests, including the ordeal by water and a test wherein the suspect had to spout milk from the mouth onto a pipal leaf.—Hira Lal, 'Witches and their Ordeals', *Man in India*, Vol. VI (1926), pp. 295 ff.

they are instructive. For example, when Mundra killed his wife the villagers fined him a feast of rice and a calf, and then assisted him in cremating the corpse. When Koliha killed Bondki, the wife of Dasru, a panchayat was held by the Pargana Manjhi, and the husband of the murdered woman was given five rupees, a bullock, a pig and some rice. The panchayat received twenty rupees, of which the Pargana Manjhi and the village Peda took five each, the Kandki (headman's assistant) four and the Kotwar one. The villagers then decided to hush up the incident, and it only came to the ears of the police through an informer. When Kartami Hirma killed his baby daughter while he was beating his wife, the panchayat demanded a fine of twentyfive rupees in consideration of which they agreed to hush the matter up. The accused paid five rupees on account and promised the rest within a month. The panchayat even seized the stick with which the beating had been done. Then the Kotwar reported that the child had been still-born.

When Poriami Handa was killed, the villagers forced his widow to accept compensation from the murderer and to keep the matter a secret. But she told what had happened to her brother-in-law, and he reported the matter to the police. In another case a group of men who had been involved in a robbery killed two of their number to prevent them giving them away. The headman was the cousin of one of the murderers. He called the people of the village together and persuaded them to agree to say nothing about the incident, and it was only through the efforts of the father of one of the victims that the matter came to light. Even then the headman attempted to bribe the police. In this case the only reason for concealment seems to have been the friendship of the headman for one of the people involved. A similar reason seems to have influenced the villagers in another murder. When Miriami Harma fell into a rage at being accused of theft at a panchayat, he snatched his baby daughter out of the arms of his wife, and holding her by the legs dashed her on the ground, killing her immediately. Possibly the members of the panchayat feared that they would be involved, and the next day the murderer and the Kotwar went to the police station and reported that the child had been bitten by a cobra.

Where the murderer is a man of influence in the village, such as one of the civil or religious headmen, he may attempt to force the people to conceal his crime. Manjhi Banda was the Peda of Turri village, and he said that it was his own brother he had killed and it was nobody else's affair. He even forbade the ferrymen to take the body across the Indrawati, and had it buried himself. It is probable that the villagers were influenced by the circumstances of the case. The murder occurred as a result of a quarrel about the partition of the family property which the dead man demanded. But local opinion seems to have been that, since the two brothers were married to two sisters and were thus practically one family of which the elder brother was the patriarchal head, the dead man was wrong in demanding a separate share. Ujji Poda was a well-to-do man and persuaded the villagers to make a false report to the police. Here too there was probably a general belief that Poda had acted rightly in killing the man who had interfered with his wife's chastity. When Gunda was killed by his son, the villagers hushed up the matter partly because the murdered man was the clan-priest of the Hemla Clan, and his son automatically succeeded him, and partly because of the justifiable nature of the crime. Even the Court considered the murder so excusable that it awarded a sentence of only one month's imprisonment.

In another case the murderer so terrorized the village that nobody dared to go to report the crime. At first the villagers refused to cremate the corpse. But the murderer threatened to kill the headman and burn him with the corpse, and insisted upon it being cremated. It was only after a week that the Peda was able to slip out of the village and make a report. When Oyami Masa of Khutepal killed his junior wife by beating her, he first of all told the villagers that the woman had died of fever. But when they examined the body and found marks of beating, Masa, who was the Waddai of the village and a very domineering and influential man, prevented them from making a report and insisted that the body should be cremated immediately. It was not till three weeks later that any report was made at the police station, and by this time, of course, it had become impossible to prove that Masa had intended to murder his wife or had used sufficient force to kill her. He was, therefore, sentenced to only one year's imprisonment: his presence of mind probably saved him from the gallows.

An ingenious attempt to hoodwink the police occurred at Jhoriabadhan in 1923. After the mysterious disappearance of a little boy aged two-and-a-half years the police came to investigate, and the villagers took the constable to the thrashing-floor whence the child had disappeared, and there showed him a boy about six years old. They told him that this was the missing boy and that he had been found wandering in the fields. Even the child's own mother declared that this was the lost boy, and since all the members of the family as well as the villagers supported her, the police went away. There is no doubt, however, that a child did disappear and it is probable that he was offered as a human sacrifice.

TABLE TWENTY-TWO

ILLUSTRATING THE KIND OF ASSISTANCE GIVEN TO POLICE IN 100 CASES

Information withheld from police	12
Homicide reported by villagers	79
Accused arrested by villagers	25
Accused gives himself up to police	9

In one case, but only one, a prosecution witness was so troubled by his family that he committed suicide. On the whole, however, the Maria appear to co-operate with the police very well. In 88 cases out of 100, they assisted in some way or other. Sometimes they reported the matter at the police station. Sometimes they themselves arrested the murderer and kept him in custody until the police arrived. They co-operated by assisting at the inquest which is held in a village when the police arrive to investigate a suspicious death. In one case the villagers took an active and dangerous part in pursuing a convict who had escaped from jail with the result that one of their number was killed.

This was the exciting pursuit of Markami Mundra in 1934.

Mundra was convicted in 1933 and sentenced to two years' imprisonment for an act of violence. On 3 May 1934, he escaped from jail with another convict and a proclamation was issued for their arrest. A Sub-Inspector of Police went at once to Gudra, Mundra's own village, and told the people that a reward of fifty rupees had been offered for his capture, and some constables went from village to village looking for him. Very daringly Mundra in his prisoner's clothes went to his house in Gudra, and stayed there till his mother came home from a bazaar. Thence he went to a Kalar's house near Nayanar. The police heard that he was somewhere about, and without knowing that Mundra was hiding there, went to the house to get fire to light their cigarettes. Mundra seeing them and supposing that he was discovered rushed out with a knife in his hand, and tried to stab one of the constables. But they caught him and tied him up with the help of the villagers. They took him to the Kuakonda police station, which they reached at dawn. Thence they went on to Dantewara, which they reached late at night and put up in the Kotwar's house. They tied Mundra's feet to the leg of the cot on which one of the constables was sleeping, and his handcuffed hand to a pillar. But while they were all asleep, Mundra managed to escape again. This time he went to his maternal uncle and got his handcuffs broken. Then dressed in a small loin-cloth and carrying a bow and arrow he went to his house and took away his wife Kase.

Meanwhile the police went back to Gudra and with the help of the villagers searched the surrounding forest. For eight days the search went on, the Maria taking a leading part in it. At last they got information that Mundra had been seen in someone's field. They again beat the forest and at last found Mundra and his wife. Mundra threatened them with his arrows and managed to escape. But the villagers caught his wife and brought her home. Another week passed with Mundra lurking in the jungle, and one day when Kase went to work in the fields, he took her away again. The Maria, led by Markami Bhima, their headman, again searched for him, but without success, until at last they found him and his wife on the Kopli Hill. Mundra turned upon his pursuers and shot at one of them, his arrow hitting the ground a little in front of him. Once again the search-party succeeded in capturing the unfortunate Kase, and she was beaten and tied up inside her house with a large party of Maria guarding her.

During the night the woman wept loudly, and attracted by her cries Mundra came and stood before the house and said that he would kill the men who were pursuing him and troubling her. He accused his fellow-Maria of doing more than the police for his arrest. Then he struck a beam of the house with his axe in token of revenge and went away. After some days—it was now over two months since he escaped from Dantewara—Mundra again went to look for his wife, but was unable to find her. Markami Bhima the headman, who had been threatened with death by Mundra, had been taking many precautions. But Mundra somehow managed to get into his house at night and killed him by shooting him at close range with an arrow. A week later Mundra went into the Madras Presidency. His hiding-place was betrayed by a woman who met some Maria from the original village who were still searching for him, and the police managed to arrest him on 2 February 1935.

The most remarkable thing about this case was the very large part taken by the Maria in assisting the police. They were no doubt influenced by the reward of fifty rupees that was offered, but even so their help was remarkable and Mundra greatly resented it.

III

Why do the villagers conceal murders from the police ? We should not too hastily attribute this to a merely savage absence of the civic instinct. There are many other reasons. First and foremost they still consider that they should settle everything themselves. They believe that it is only in a tribal Court that the real facts can be known. We have seen that they are generally unwilling to testify against a powerful priest or magician who might revenge himself on them. They are equally unwilling to assist the police where they believe a murder has been justified.

Then they fear the annoyance and expense of having police subordinates quartered on them and the expense and waste of time of having to go to a distant Court, especially at the more busy periods of the agricultural year. Again the

(*a*) Kalmumi Masa (Case No. 17 and p. 126)

(*b*) Markami Wango (Case No. 44 and p. 127)

(*c*) Markami Nanda, who was employed to beat up a landlord (Case No. 74 and pp. 152ff.)

(*d*) Murami Dhurwa, twice imprisoned for homicide (Case No. 69 and pp. 157f.)

PLATE XXVII. Tragedies of the Serving Marriage (pp. 125ff.)

(*a*) Veko Dome, who was very hungry (Case No. 98 and pp. 145f.)

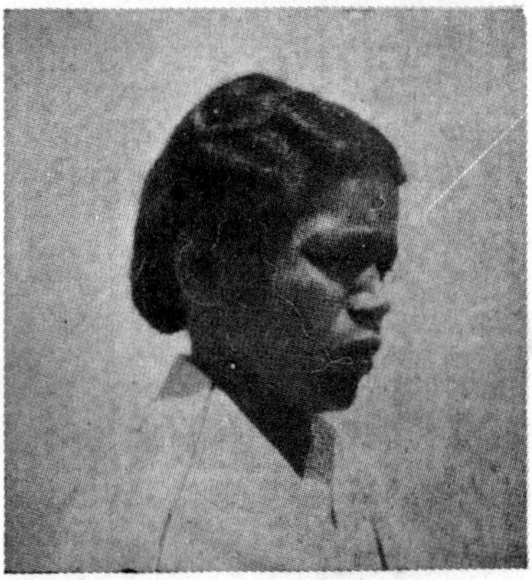

(*b*) Kuhrami Hirme who, hungry and exhausted, killed a child of ten (Case No. 32)

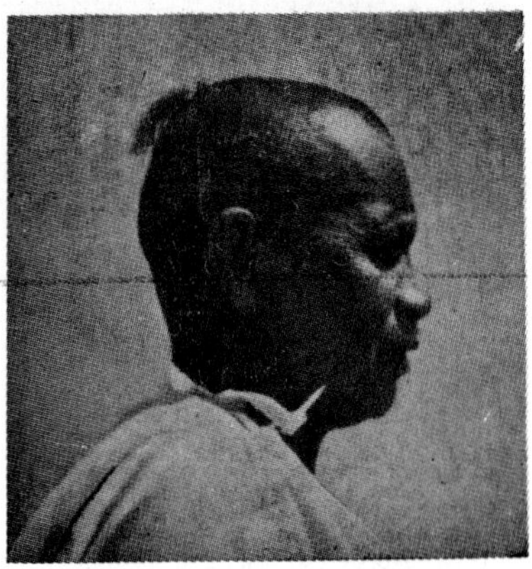

(*c*) Marvi Mundra, who killed his wife at the end of a long day (Case No. 61 and p. 145)

PLATE XXVIII

real reason for a crime is often something which the Maria dislike revealing in Court and which they despair of making outsiders understand. Another powerful factor is the supernatural danger—and the expense of avoiding it—of a post-mortem examination, and of allowing the corpse to be buried outside the proper territory of its clan.

Memories of past oppression die slowly and Grigson has a remarkable passage on the conflict between State and people in former times. He points out how in the old days in Bastar (as in many parts of India at the present time) everything conspired to limit the authority and lower the prestige of the tribal elders. He describes the extreme inconvenience to the villagers of a police investigation.

> A badly trained police, often singularly lacking in common sense, would descend on a village and waste days in pointless investigation of petty cases, expecting not only to be fed on rice, mutton and poultry by the villagers during their stay, but also to be provided with stores of grain under the old bisaha system to take away with them at the end of the investigation. Villagers would be compelled to carry the supplies thus forcibly taken from them to the police station, perhaps two or three days' march distant, and would rarely be given even the nominal payment prescribed under the old bisaha rules. Then would follow a protracted trial at the still more distant tahsil headquarters, ten witnesses being summoned where three or four would have been ample; and probably all these witnesses at the end of the trial would have to accompany the police party back to the police station to carry their impediments, and might be kept even longer as 'athpaharia begar' labourers to clean the police office and lines and do domestic work for the constables.

Even today when the Bastar police force has been trained in traditions that are in many respects admirable, it is impossible to keep a check on the conduct of all subordinates, and their very presence in a village is disturbing to the aboriginals. Grigson continues:

> It is not surprising that, as the result of these methods of dealing with the aboriginals, their panchayats tended to co-operate as little as possible with the State; their object became to conceal crime from the police and in general to comply with State requirements only so far as was necessary in order to avoid trouble, and, above all, visits of subordinate State officials to their villages.

> The records of murder and other trials show many cases of the village elders meeting and deciding to hush up a crime, especially if it had occurred at harvest or any other busy agricultural season, rather than have the whole life of the village community disorganized by police investigation, committal proceedings and Sessions trial. Such crimes may have come to light later through the panchayat reporting them at their own convenience, or through the widow or other relative of a murdered man being dissatisfied with the compensation which the murderer had been ordered to give, while in some Parganas informers arose who subsequently used their supposed prestige with the police to become petty local tyrants. Conversely on occasions panchayats, disgusted with the failure of the police to investigate thefts or with the acquittal of guilty persons by the Tahsildars, took the law into their own hands and had the thieves killed.[1]

I make no apology for quoting Grigson at length on this subject, for it was largely due to his efforts that a new tradition was established in Bastar, and that the Maria began, however slowly and imperfectly, to co-operate with the administration. Even so I doubt whether they will ever be able to overcome the tribal and religious objections to revealing their inmost thoughts in the public Court.

This fear of the outside world is revealed in a number of examples where Maria have committed suicide rather than be involved in police inquiries and legal proceedings.

The aboriginal is not alone in finding litigation and contact with officialdom trying to the nerves. Hunga of Kothiagura was involved in a cattle-theft case and believed himself badly treated by the constable investigating it. He prepared a petition to the Superintendent of Police and, wrapping it carefully in a parsa leaf,[2] set out to Jagdalpur to present it. But on the way, his fears, his grievance, his sense of lost prestige overwhelmed him, and he hanged himself from a parsa tree by the roadside.[3]

[1] Grigson, op. cit., pp. 284 ff.

[2] *Butea frondosa*, Roxb., the 'Flame of the Forest'.

[3] The case of Saradu, a young Maria landlord of Bermakot, in 1933, belongs to the bad old days before the taking of free supplies and labour had been prohibited. An Excise Sub-Inspector came to the village to inquire into a case of illicit distillation. He does not seem to have received all the supplies he wanted, and so he threatened the landlord, who came of a leading Muria family, with prosecution on some false charge. Saradu hanged himself rather than face the indignity and disgrace.

Marvi Mundra of Cholnar had some of his cattle stolen and reported the matter to the police. The case proceeded normally, and Mundra was summoned as complainant to the court. The accused called two defence witnesses, a matter which seems to have shocked Mundra profoundly. He, being simple and honest himself and knowing his case to be true, seems to have expected it to be settled in his favour immediately. In the evening, under the great trees of the travellers' camp at Dantewara, he expressed his concern to his companions and while all were asleep went away and committed suicide.

In case No. 1, Lakhmu of Erpund, an old timid Maria who may have himself been involved in the crime, was called by the police as a prosecution witness against his step-son. The boy's mother was so angry at his being willing to give evidence against her son, and she and the family abused the old man so much, that before the matter came to trial he hanged himself.

Another case, this time of attempted suicide, occurred in connexion with a police investigation as recently as 1941. An elderly Maria, Poyami Masa by name, who lived in the beautiful village of Kaklur among the mountains, had a quarrel with his nephew Kosa. Kosa struck the old man with his axe, and was sentenced to imprisonment. While in jail, in order to revenge himself, he made a report to the Administrator that his uncle had murdered a Banjara gypsy some years before, had placed his dead body in the village temple, and had given a feast to the villagers who had hushed up the whole affair. The police investigated the matter and found that actually seven years previously an unknown Banjara had died in the village, and his body had been quietly disposed of by the people in order to avoid the bother of a police inquiry. No one ever knew who the man was, nor was his body ever found. But Poyami Masa was so alarmed at the arrival of the police that he hanged himself on a branch of a tree behind his house, but was cut down by his son before he died. At his trial he was acquitted, the Sessions Judge finding that there was no real evidence against him.

The extreme care that is needed in dealing with primitive people, who may easily misinterpret official action, is seen in a deplorable incident that occurred among the Chenchu about ten years ago. 'It was the mahua season and the Chenchu were in the process of distilling liquor when two policemen arrived in the village and arrested the *peddamanchi* and three other men for illicitly distilling liquor. Unused to dealing with aboriginals they failed to reassure the other people that nothing very serious would happen to the four offenders, and apparently even made them believe that more policemen would come and arrest all the villagers. This threat caused, probably much to their own surprise, a general and immediate stampede, and so terrified were the Chenchu that they did not even stop to pick up their small children, but left them wherever they happened to be, and fled into the jungle. The whole day they dared not return to the village, and when they stole back in the evening they found that several of the smallest infants had died from exposure to the burning sun. Yidgaru (Tokal) says that altogether eight children perished on that occasion, and though this may be an exaggeration, it is certain that the child of his brother, who was one of the arrested men, died at that time. Only two of the four men were found guilty and condemned to one month's imprisonment, and strangely enough both died of fever within eight days of their return from jail.' [1]

IV

BEHAVIOUR TOWARDS THE RELEASED CONVICT

When a murderer comes out of jail, before he is admitted to the ordinary privileges of tribal life and sometimes even before he is allowed to enter his house, ceremonies of purification must be performed. These are of two kinds. The first is a straightforward ceremony to purge a man from the defilement of having been in jail and in the hands of the police. This is probably a Hindu idea,[2] and is connected with the fact that in jail prisoners must take food from members of any caste. It is likely that they may be beaten by

[1] C. von Fürer-Haimendorf, *The Chenchus* (Hyderabad, 1943), pp. 267 f.

[2] It is said of a Hindu Sessions Judge in the Central Provinces that after passing sentence of death he would break the pen with which he wrote the judgement and destroy the clothes he wore. He would not eat till he had bathed and undergone a ceremony of purification.

constables, who again may be men of low caste, and they are almost certainly forced at some time to wear handcuffs, which is regarded by most Hindus as degrading. A term of imprisonment involves, of course, culture-contact in its most concentrated form, and we need not be surprised to find aboriginal prisoners bringing back from Jagdalpur Hindu notions of this kind.

The ceremony, it is interesting to note, bears no relationship at all to the kind of crime that has been committed. For stealing a cow or for the illicit distilling of mahua liquor a man has to undergo the same purification as if he had committed a brutal murder. Even if he is acquitted, the jail contagion is on him and he must free himself of it.

The ceremonies vary from place to place. At Jabeli, where they have had a lot of experience of this sort of thing, the Maria told me that when a man returns from jail he is not at first allowed to enter his house, but must remain outside and the family gives him his food at a distance. He must then go to his Waddai and give him five rupees for some of the water in which his clan-god has been bathed. The priest sprinkles him with this and gives him a little to drink. He sprinkles some of it over the house. Then the released prisoner gives a feast of beef or pork to the village, he is allowed to go into his house, and from that day 'everybody forgets all about it'.

Sometimes the water must be brought from Dantewara. Hemla Bakka, for example, had to get from the Jia water in which the goddess Danteshwari had been bathed. When Doga came out of jail, the Gaita heated a bit of gold in the fire and touched his forehead, mouth, wrists, knees and toes. He dipped the gold in water and sprinkled it over the body. In Pogu Bheji, the priest burnt with a bit of gold the murderer's tongue, the back of his neck and the upper part of his left arm. He made a fire above the gold with branches of the mango, dumar, karanji and mahua trees and sprinkled the hot ashes over his head. Then the people washed him with ghee, milk and haldi water. When he had given a feast he was free of the contagion of the jail.

When Nendi Muya of Dhanikarka was flogged for stealing a cow, he had to sacrifice a pig and a white chicken to Mati Deo, and bring water from the shrine of Lakshmi Devi at

Kuakonda. When Telami Dhurwa returned from jail after killing a man in a drunken quarrel, he offered his clan-god Uru Maru, a pig, a cow and a hen, and had to undergo the usual ceremonies of purification.

Apart from these ceremonies, however, the fact that a man has served a sentence for murder has singularly little influence on his social position and domestic happiness. It is true that imprisonment, if it is for a very long term, sometimes acts as an automatic divorce, and women feel that they are at liberty to marry again. But generally wives wait for their husbands to be released, as I found Deve, the wife of Kawasi Borga, waiting for her husband at Doriras. Borga, ten years before, had gone to jail with a life-sentence for killing his uncle. His wife had all the time been well looked after by the villagers, and I found her house substantial and prosperous. Her two sons had been successfully married and were carrying on the business of their home with the help of their wives.

People, however, are sometimes afraid to marry a released murderer. Doga of Jabeli must be one of the luckiest young men alive, for after being sentenced to transportation for one murder he was released after three years; whereupon he is said to have killed his wife, was sentenced to death and again got off on appeal. He came to see me armed with a ferocious-looking axe, which had actually been put in evidence at one of his trials as the weapon with which he had committed murder. He was trying to get a new wife, but without success. 'They are all afraid of me,' he said, 'for fear I might kill them as well.' But he thought he might possibly get a widow. Another youth who found it very difficult to get a new wife was Hemla Bakka, who killed his wife for committing adultery, and got three years' imprisonment for it. At Aranpur all the girls were frightened of the charming Gutte, who had been in jail for killing a man in a drunken quarrel after a cock-fight. They thought if they displeased him he might murder them too.

At Khutepal, Oyami Masa, who was imprisoned for killing his junior wife, seems to have suffered no loss of prestige on account of it. He is a Waddai, and when I was there he went over to Tikanpal to offer sacrifice on behalf of that village.

At Muler I visited the widow of Ido Deva, an unpleasant quarrelsome fellow who had recently been hanged for murdering one of the most popular men in the village. In spite of this, his widow was well treated. She was not excommunicated and was allowed to share in the usual feasts. But she always remained inside her house, and generally refused to talk to people; the headman told me that there would probably be some difficulty in getting her two sons married, for people would say, 'After all, their father was a murderer'.

The relationship between the families of a murderer and his victim is always a delicate one, and Frazer has collected many examples from all over the world in illustration. The Uraon make sacrifices to the angry ghost of a murdered man, and sometimes even reckon him among the ancestral spirits of his murderer. Roy records that two Uraon, related to each other as cousins, had a quarrel over a piece of land; and one of them, in a sudden fit of anger, thrust his axe into the bowels of his companion. The man, thus struck, at once ran to his assailant's house and, pressing his wounded stomach with his hands, sat down at one corner of the hut and exclaimed, 'Here I establish myself', and then ran out again to the field in dispute and dropped down dead. To this day, the descendants of the murderer propitiate the murdered man's spirit. After the harvest, the first sheaf of paddy from the field where he fell dead is offered to his spirit at the same corner of the house where he sat down before his death. The descendants of the murdered man too are allowed access to the spot in order to make similar offerings.[1]

I have not found this custom in Bastar, though that does not mean that it does not exist. But I have found everywhere an anxiety that there should not be any enmity between the families. Compensation is often paid to the victim's widow or family, and the murderer's family may contribute to the expenses of the funeral. Both families should always have a feast together. In Gamawada the family of an imprisoned homicide, Barse Mata, gave every kind of help to the relatives of his victim: among other

[1] S. C. Roy, *Oraon Religion and Customs* (Ranchi, 1928), pp. 69 f.

things they provided a pot of rice-beer and a pig for his funeral rites.

V

BEHAVIOUR TOWARDS THE DEAD

The reaction of society to violent crime may be seen from the funerary arrangements that are made for both the murderer and his victim.[1]

In the great majority of cases these arrangements are complicated by the fact that the corpse of the deceased is not available. It is generally taken to headquarters for post-mortem examination, and when a man is hanged in jail his body is disposed of by the prison authorities. This does not mean, however, that the funeral ceremonies are omitted. Clothes and other property belonging to the dead are brought back from the Magistrate's Court or from the jail, and these are used to represent the corpse. When Markami Deva killed his wife at Darbha the people brought her clothes, necklaces and armlets to the village. These relics were not brought into the house, but were put outside in the yard. The usual funeral drum was not beaten, but the relatives gathered and the brother of the husband (the husband himself was in police custody) put haldi and oil on the things, and a relative by marriage carried them in a basket to a pyre which had been prepared outside the village. Men and women walked behind throwing seeds of rice, maize and pulse mixed together in the basket.

The pyre was under a tree over which a great camel's-foot creeper was growing. They carried the basket round it seven times. Relatives put small pieces of cloth upon it in the usual way and removed them. They hung a bit of cloth on the tree. Then they lit the pyre and went away. They did not erect an uraskal, though here they said that they would

[1] Everywhere in India the ghost of a murdered man or a suicide is dangerous. The Lushai think a victim's ghost will haunt the murderer and drive him mad.—J. Shakespear, *The Lushai Kuki Clans* (London, 1912), p. 76. Both the Lushai and Lakher perform ceremonies to make the dead man's ghost harmless and to ensure that it becomes the servant of the slayer in the other world. If this is not done, the ghost may blind, lame or paralyse the man who killed him.—N. E. Parry, *The Lakhers* (London, 1932), p. 213. Frazer gives many examples from other parts of the world.—Sir J. G. Frazer, *The Fear of the Dead in Primitive Religion* (London, 1936), Vol. III, pp. 103 ff.

have done so if they had been able to afford it. When Doga of Jabeli killed his wife, but was acquitted on appeal, no ceremony was performed for the dead woman at the time. But when Doga returned home, he himself made a small pyre and carried his wife's clothes and ornaments in his own hands, and thus performed the usual ceremonies.

The day after the burning of the pyre two men go to inspect the ashes. When Oyami Anda was hanged they found 'signs of hanging'—the marks of a rope—among the ashes.

The funeral drum is not beaten for the ceremonies of a man who is hanged or of his victim or when somebody commits suicide. Otherwise the ceremonies are largely the same as usual.

After Kadti Hunga was hanged for murdering his wife Gangi, the clothes of both murderer and victim were put together and covered with earth, and a small pillar of cotton-wood was erected nearby.

Sometimes the dead man's clothes are not brought to the house, but are kept outside the village for fear that they may bring the angry ghost along with them. At Killepal and other villages it was the custom to burn the clothes at a cross-roads outside the village.

In the Konta Tahsil, the Maria have a custom of making a small doll or image to serve as a corpse. An unpleasant, quarrelsome fellow called Ido Deva committed a murder at Muler and was hanged. After his death the villagers did not fetch his clothes from the jail but when the fact of his hanging was confirmed, they cut a bit of the gongum tree 'about the length of your forearm', dressed it up in some of Deva's old cloth, put a pair of his earrings where the ears might be, and one of his necklaces round the 'neck'. Then just as if it was a real corpse they put it on a bier, covered it with a cloth and carried it out to the pyre (which was in the ordinary cremation-ground) and burnt it. At the head of the pyre they placed a forked saja branch and hung a cow's tail upon it. When I went to the cremation-ground I saw Deva's ashes still fresh and only a few yards away an older pile of ashes for the man he had murdered. Nearby still lay the pots and a specially-made basket for offering rice to the offended ghost.

Sometimes the corpse is cremated near the menhirs. At

Aranpur I saw a large pile of ashes and half-burnt logs of wood in front of the uraskal stones erected in memory of members of the Barse clan. These were the remains of the pyre for Barse Chewa who had recently been hanged. In this case it was considered of ill omen that, although two attempts were made to burn the pyre, a lot of the wood remained unburnt. In other villages, however, we were told that such ceremonies must not be performed in the neighbourhood of the menhirs.

There seems to be no objection to erecting an uraskal or danyakal stone either for murderers or for their victims. At Palnar an uraskal was mounted for Mulami Bella. At Dugeli an uraskal was erected for a murdered man. In other villages such as Metapal (where there is no uraskal for Banjami Irma who was murdered by his own son) or at Gandarguda (where there is no danyakal for Rawa Hirma) the absence of these memorials is said to be due to the fact that the deceased were poor men and their relatives could not afford them. But at Dugeli, Kunjami Pandu told us that an uraskal for a murdered man can only be erected after the case against the murderer is settled. When his own brother was murdered, he did not at first erect a stone for him, and he was continually troubled by the restless ghost who came in dreams to reproach him for not 'mingling his soul with the dead, and for his failure to give him a stone'. Once Pandu did this, he had no more bad dreams.

The ceremonies of erecting a menhir for a murderer are exactly the same as for anyone else. When the villagers were carrying the stone for Mulami Bella at Palnar, they halted and put it on the ground, and the women of the house threw rings on to it. Afterwards the women eagerly collected these rings, for it is considered very lucky to wear them.

On the forest road between Palnar and Jabeli there is a row of the flat memorial stones called danyakal, and at one end a tall carved wooden pillar and a large earthen tomb. The tomb, the pillar and one of the stones are in honour of Marvi Oyami Masa who died in jail while serving a sentence for the murder of his uncle. Masa was a very important man in Jabeli. He was rich, he was the Waddai of the village and he was a Siraha medicine-man. His death seemed to be far more important to the villagers than that of the man he murdered. The stone next to his is for Marvi Buta who was also sentenced for this murder and also died in jail. But there was nothing at all in honour of the murdered man.

The erection of a carved memorial pillar is probably the greatest honour that the Maria can pay to the dead. It is the equivalent of being buried in Westminster Abbey. Masa's pillar is a very fine one. It shows him as a Siraha sitting on a swing: a streamer of untidy hair blows out from his head. Another carving shows him mounted on an elephant. Another portrays him riding on a horse attended by his wives. All round him are the symbols of his life; deer and tigers represent his love of the chase; axes, swords and knives symbolize his valour and enterprise; two men carry a pot of rice-beer in memory of his drinking prowess.

The business of keeping the ghost of the murderer or his victim quiet naturally greatly exercises the minds of the village medicine-men and priests. There is danger either that the ghost will cause trouble among the other ghosts of the family, and thus by annoying the ancestors may bring trouble upon the living: or it may inspire another member of the family also to commit a murder; or it may return and simply make itself troublesome. At Phulpar, after Pandu had been hanged and the usual ceremonies performed, the village priest sacrificed a hen near the pyre saying, 'Now we make your home here: live here with your ancestors peacefully'. If they fail to do this, they said, they think someone else in the house will also commit a murder. Then they erected a saja pole and after sacrificing a cow to appease the ghost of the dead man, each relative in turn picked up the cow's tail, saluted it and hung it on the pole. The Waddai went to a corner of the room where the Pot of the Departed was kept, sprinkled liquor there and addressed the ghost: 'Live now with your sons. Do not go to your daughters. Care for the people of your house. See that your children prosper.'

Often, after the ceremony of burning the clothes and ornaments, a man sits in the house of the deceased and the ghost comes upon him. He is led out to the pyre, and there he buries a *bhut kukri*, a ghost hen, to ensure that the ghost will not come to the house and trouble its relatives.

The ghost of the murderer or his victim becomes a Mirchuk.

Sometimes it is supposed that this Mirchuk possesses a man and makes him commit a murder. At Gudra, when Kawachi Linga returned from jail after serving a homicide sentence, a black chicken was sacrificed to the Mirchuk of his victim. But the chicken refused to eat the rice that is always offered to test it before it is killed, and the people thought that this meant that Linga would be possessed by the spirit of his first victim and thus be driven to commit another murder. To avert this danger they sacrificed a pig and a cow, and only then readmitted him to their society.

The Mirchuk, whatever its origin may be, may be employed by a witch as her familiar and servant. She gets control over it and uses it to assist her in her wicked designs.

The Mirchuk is very quarrelsome, and the spirit of a man who has been hanged must not be mingled with the other ancestors in the Room of the Departed, for it is sure to cause trouble. So the Mirchuk is generally located outside the village under a large stone, in an ant-hill or in a mahua tree. At Dhurli we were told that, when Telami Hunga was murdered, his ghost was kept apart, for he was a student of magic and such persons turn into Rao Bhut. For such no uraskal should be erected, nor should the ghost be mingled with the other Departed.

Indeed it is often held that the ghosts of the slain and of executed criminals should not be 'mingled with the Departed' and nothing should be put for them in the sacred Pot in the ordinary way.[1] When the boy Ando was murdered by his uncle Irma, this precaution was taken. Ando's ghost still roams the village, an axe in its hands, seeking vengeance. Irma's ghost is said to have possessed itself of the rope with which he was hanged and people were afraid it might use it to hang the other Departed of his clan or to steal their cows.

It is very dangerous for a murderer to see the ghost of his victim while he is in jail, perhaps because it is impossible there to perform the proper ceremonies of protection. Pandu

[1] Mateer reported that in Travancore the ghosts of executed murderers were regarded as specially dangerous and were believed to haunt the place of execution. To prevent this the executioner used to cut off the criminal's heels with a sword or hamstring him as he was thrown off.—S. Mateer, *The Land of Charity* (London, 1871), pp. 203 f.

of Chichari described how this happened to three of his fellow-prisoners and they all died. Boti of Telam suffered a similar visitation and was ill for a whole year.

In several places I found that a house or a village had been moved from its original site after a murder had been committed there. At Aranpur, for example, the house in which Chewa killed his father-in-law was destroyed, and a new house was built elsewhere for the widow and other members of the family. At Doriras the whole village was shifted from its former site in the year following the murder of Kawasi Boti. Muler village also was shifted after the murder of Rawa Harma.

VI

The funeral ceremonies of a suicide are performed in the same way with the clothes and ornaments taking the place of the corpse. When Masa's younger wife hanged herself at Samgiri, her body after the post-mortem examination was buried at Dantewara. Her clothes and ornaments were taken out to a cross-roads and cremated according to the customary ritual. Her scythe, rice-husker and winnowing-fan were placed at the spot, but the scythe was picked up and carried home by one of her husband's relatives. Next morning they went to inspect the ashes and found distinct marks of hanging. A chicken was used to divine the cause of death, and it indicated that the woman had been angry and committed suicide in a fit of temper. The tragedy was in fact due to the girl's complaint that her husband did not pay her enough attention. The chicken's neck was then twisted, the head removed, split into through the beak and thrown away.

In Borgum village, the wife of Markami Pide committed suicide because she was in love with another man and did not care for her husband. The body was taken to Dantewara for the post-mortem and buried there. The clothes were taken back to the village and burnt outside together with her mat, winnowing-fan, rice-husker and sickle. The next day the Priest of the Dead put rice and roots round the pyre. He made seven small piles of rice and brought a chicken saying, 'You were angry and put an end to your life; now become cool and rest in peace here and trouble none of us, for this is your home'. When the chicken had pecked at the rice, he twisted its neck and threw it on the still-burning pyre. A pig and a cow were then sacrificed and an uraskal erected the same day. After returning to the house they made a rough drawing with flour of the garden and of the house with its various rooms on the floor. On this pattern they again offered rice to a hen saying, 'We have now made a house for you; don't stay outside any longer, but remain here'.

The ghost of the suicide, like that of a murderer, becomes a Mirchuk and lives in an ant-hill. If the Mirchuk gets angry, it may possess a member of the family, and he too may commit suicide unless the proper offerings are made at once. The suicide's ghost may also come to the village and cause trouble in a variety of ways. As we have seen elsewhere, the Mirchuk is often used as a familiar by witches. It is most important that the soul of a suicide should not be 'mingled with the Dead'. In some villages they say that this prohibition is absolute. In Dugeli, they said that they should wait a year. A menhir should not be erected. A remarkable double suicide at Khutepal illustrates the danger of ignoring these rules. Bandi, the headman of this village, had two wives. One day they quarrelled, and the elder wife hanged herself in a rage. Her funeral ceremony was performed as though the death had been a natural one. Her soul was mingled with the Dead, and an uraskal memorial pillar was erected for her in the place used by other members of the clan. It is believed that, when this is done, the suicide's ghost quarrels with the other ghosts of the clan and annoys them. In this case the angry Dead so troubled the wife of Bandi's younger son, who was living in the same house, that she too committed suicide after a quarrel with her mother-in-law. This second suicide was regarded by the villagers as the immediate result of having erected a memorial pillar and mingled the soul of the elder woman with the ancestral Dead. When the girl's ceremonies were performed, therefore, they carefully burnt her clothes in a place away from the usual crematorium and, although they gave her an uraskal, they did not sacrifice a cow or hang its tail in the usual manner round the stone.

At Dualkarka, however, they said that an uraskal should

never be made for anyone who commits suicide or is killed by violence. Here they described how, when the members of the household in which a suicide has occurred are feasting at the close of the funeral ceremonies, they suddenly feel as though somebody is strangling them, and to get rid of this unpleasant feeling they have to go to the village boundary and make the usual offerings. If the dead man has been killed by a tiger or has been murdered, the relatives feel that they are being mauled by some great animal or that an unseen hand is belabouring them with a heavy stick.

CHAPTER SEVENTEEN

THE ABORIGINAL PRISONER

I

How do the Maria get on in jail? This is a question that only a Jailor can answer, but I have been told by those responsible for aboriginal prisoners what an appalling ordeal prison life is for people accustomed to the great freedoms of the hills and forests. 'If a Maria is sentenced to a long term of imprisonment,' says Grigson, 'he will beg to be hanged rather than be confined within walls: and few of the wilder Bison-horn Maria survive long imprisonment.'[1] The grim forbidding walls, the stone beds, the rule of silence, the attitude of suppliant and obsequious deference before officials, the absence of any kind of recreation, the lack of all religious comfort, the denial of human companionship, the appalling monotony oppress and crush them. The Maria is perhaps insensitive to mental suffering, but on the other hand he has no reserve of philosophical or intellectual fortitude to draw on in a crisis. To him life with a woman and daily intercourse with her, a good supply of tobacco, the rough simple food of his village and the not infrequent stimulus of alcohol are perhaps the only necessities of existence. But they are necessary, and many prisoners have told me that they missed these things far more than the restraint upon their liberty.

How do the prisoners themselves look back on their experience? I will attempt to discover this by quoting their own sayings. Markami Doga said, 'I felt very sad in jail, and my thoughts were always in my house'. Another man said that he was continually worrying about his children and who would look after them. Another was distracted lest in his absence his cattle would be distributed like fowls among the neighbours. Many of the prisoners with whom I talked in jail had an extremely sad and pitiable look. I particularly remember the suffering on the face of Habka Masa who had

[1] Grigson, op. cit., p. 96. Since this was written, improved conditions in the Jagdalpur jail have increased the life-expectation of all the prisoners.

killed his wife, and of Marvi Kuma who described how much he missed his wife and children and was always wondering whether they got enough food to eat. Vetti Rupe told me that he was continually thinking of his family. Dasru, himself a magician, was worried because in prison there was no Siraha to consult about the various untoward things that happened. The three men who had been sentenced from Pinna Bheji and whom I met after their release said: 'The worst thing was we always were thinking of our cattle and our homes, and to feel that we had got into prison by accident. We could hardly eat for the memory of our children.'

These aboriginal prisoners are remarkable in not finding sex a problem while they are in jail. This statement will probably be received with incredulity by many of my readers. I can only say that I have gone into the matter as fully as anyone could who was not himself a jail official or a prisoner setting out to investigate this particular point. The jail officials, who know their people at least as well as officials elsewhere, some of whom have had very long experience, have told me that cases of homosexuality are unknown and that even masturbation is not practised by the aboriginal prisoners. When I have discussed the same matter with released convicts they have all said the same thing, and I am inclined to believe them, because they have shown no reticence in speaking freely and even coarsely about other sexual matters. I think it is possible that the Maria who in his natural state is, as far as I can discover, completely innocent of any kind of sexual deviation simply would not think it possible that any substitute could give him satisfaction or indeed could be practised. The thing just would not occur to him.[1]

What is generally believed is that medicine is put in the food. I do not suggest this is so, but it is what is supposed. One after another has described how he never got any erection at all while in jail, and several people have found themselves impotent for a time after their release. Barse Mata of Gamawada declared that he had never even felt

[1] It would be hard to imagine a greater contrast to this than, for example, the conditions described by J. F. Fishman in his *Sex in Prison* (London, 1935).

desire while in jail. Boti of Telam declared that the doctor had made them all impotent by medicine put in the food. On the other hand, Pandru of Chichari said that he frequently suffered from erections in jail and from nocturnal emissions. Naturally, however, the worst thing about jail-life is the deprivation of the company of women, though many Maria would modify this by saying that it is rather the whole family atmosphere, houses, children, cattle as well as the wife, that was missed. When I asked one youth what jail-life was like, he said, 'No wife, no bazaar, no children, no family'. But the thing that most oppressed him in jail was the silence.

The food in jail is good, better than the prisoners get in their own homes. Since 1935, a special effort has been made to improve the health of the prisoners among whom at one period there had been a rather heavy mortality. The result has been highly satisfactory. There was only 1 death in 1938, 2 in 1939 and 4 in 1940. Accommodation in the jail is for 308 prisoners and the daily average is between 210 and 230. Special measures are taken against respiratory diseases, notably influenza. Phyrnoderma (toad-skin), which was one of the chief causes of reduced vitality among aboriginal prisoners, has been practically banished by the prophylactic administration of meat and cod liver oil. The ex-convicts generally grumble at the food and declare that they are continually unwell, but all reports agree in saying that they actually eat heartily and keep very fit. I think the real fact is that the food is unfamiliar to them and that many of them suffer from nervousness and a general psychic depression which makes them feel wretched, even though their actual bodily health is excellent. Several prisoners have declared how they long for roots and the gruels prepared in the ordinary way at home.

The work given to the prisoners varies. Some of the Maria work in the kitchens, and it is interesting that the Hindu prisoners respect their social status and agree to eat from them. Ghasia and Panka are not admitted into the jail kitchen. Maria and Muria do not do sweepers' work in the jail,[1] though when a man is hanged Maria prisoners deal

[1] But I believe that Gond prisoners in the Central Provinces are made to work as sweepers, a thing that should never be allowed.

with the corpse. Short-term prisoners, suitably shackled, are allowed beyond the walls to work in the gardens of the Palace and the higher officials. Other prisoners learn to make baskets and chiks. But the main prison industry in Jagdalpur, as throughout India, is weaving. Some of the Maria have become experts at this art. I was told that Kunjami Malle and Marvi Tibru were excellent at it, and that Murami Dhurwa of Palnar was so good that he was sent to Raipur for training. In 1940 the receipts from jail industries exceeded Rs 10,000.

Unfortunately no aboriginal prisoner is able to take advantage after his release of the training he receives in jail. For weaving is regarded as the monopoly of the low caste Ganda and Mahara, and no aboriginal will ever degrade himself by practising it. Should he do so, he would be excommunicated, he would be unable to marry his daughters and he would be forbidden access to his clan and village festivals. I have constantly inquired about this and especially as to whether there is any reason behind it. Nobody seems to know the origin of the taboo. It may date from the days when the aboriginals did not use cloth at all, and regarded it as something foreign and alien. It may have simply come into being because of the Maria's dislike and scorn for the particular castes which practise weaving. It is not impossible, of course, that the Mahara and the Ganda themselves have encouraged the idea so as to enjoy the monopoly of trade. If all the Maria ex-convicts were to set up looms and make their own cloth, the existing weavers would be hard hit financially. I met one Maria who had tried to carry on his weaving work after a term in jail. But there had been such a commotion about it that he had to abandon the project.

It is a pity, I think, that some art or craft could not be taught to aboriginal prisoners, not only in Bastar but throughout India, which would be of value to them after their release. In five, ten or fifteen years a man could become an expert carpenter or wood-carver, a first-rate cook, an admirable market gardener. The Maria do learn a little gardening but they might do more, and carpentry on a large scale would be invaluable. For the aboriginal blacksmiths, whether they be Maria Lohar in Bastar or Agaria and Asur in central India, a certain amount of training in blacksmithery might lead to their introducing new technical methods into the work of their tribe. Basket-making, rope-making and so on are all very well in their way. But the profits to be made from such work in remote aboriginal villages, where there is no one to buy at a proper rate, are pitiable, and few people can make such business pay. This is seen very clearly among the Juang, a few of whom have had to fall back on basket-making for a living and have become some of the most pathetically impoverished people in all India.

II

The question of dreaming among criminals was studied by De Sanctis who is quoted by Havelock Ellis. He specially investigated the contents of the dreams with reference to their emotional content.

> The former class dealt with quarrels, falls from a height, persecutions, fearful visions, often of mystical character, and were frequently concerned with the sexual sphere; while the latter class merely repeated the unimportant events of the day, or insignificant scenes from past life. A special inquiry was made in regard to dreams dealing with the crime which had led to imprisonment; 22 acknowledged such dreams, 16 men and 6 women; while, however, the majority of the men's dreams concerning their crimes were emotional, the majority of the women (4 out of 6) experienced no emotion in dreaming of their crimes. The rarity of emotional dreams generally was very remarkable, only a third of the criminal dreamers having often such dreams, and many of those who dreamed of their crimes without emotion were murderers. The conclusion reached by De Sanctis is that the criminal, or at all events the criminal guilty of crimes of blood, during the nights following the deed and during imprisonment, sleeps quietly and deeply, unless special causes (such as disease, nervous conditions, egoistic preoccupation, or the state of the weather) interfere with natural conditions. The habitual sleep of criminals resembles that which De Sanctis has found usually among old epileptic cases and imbeciles. Idiots have a similar dreadless sleep, and De Sanctis points out a probable connexion between an unemotional dream-life and a general anaesthesia of sensibility in the waking life. There undoubtedly exists a small class of hyperaesthetic and emotional criminals, who exhibit their characteris-

> ties both waking and sleeping, but they form a very small proportion of criminals. On the whole, the dream-life of criminals shows that they are insensitive and unemotional, true imbeciles in feeling and partly so in intelligence.[1]

The dreams of Maria prisoners mainly agree with this. The aboriginal theory of dreams is that the *jiwa* or soul leaves the body in sleep and goes out to seek adventure. The dream is what it sees as it goes to and fro about the world. In prison the soul takes every opportunity to leave the confined and frustrated body, and goes home to visit the family or roams abroad in search of variety. Barse Mata said : 'In my sleep I really feel as though the soul was leaving my body. It runs to the house and sees all my people there.' Another man described how his wife came and slept with him in his dream, and how he would go out and see his family and his dead father whom he had murdered. But, he added, his father never reproached him for what he had done. Boti described how he saw dances, bazaars, his relatives and wife and children. Marvi Kuma said that his soul frequently went home to visit his wife. Muchaki Dasru sees his wife and children at night. He sits up and wants to weep. But on another occasion he finds, as he said, that 'the dream is the chutney of sleep' and by its help he has been able, in spite of imprisonment, to see all that is going on in the outside world. Munda sees girls, fighting cocks, horses (which are bad), snakes (which are good). His soul constantly seeks rice-beer and tobacco. Vetti Rupe said that he saw his family in dreams, and sometimes a witch or a sorcerer. 'Even now our enemies can trouble us from outside the jail.' He said that he found dreams alarming, for in the ordinary way if a Maria has an inauspicious dream, he can make suitable offerings and free himself of the danger. In the jail there is no shrine and no chaplain for this purpose.

Very tender experiences between husband and wife occur in dreams, and one boy described how his young wife came to him in sleep and gave him the food he loved and slept with him. More moving still, reminding one of a famous incident in Browning's *Ring and the Book*, was the experience of a boy who killed his wife in a drunken rage. 'When I

[1] Havelock Ellis, op. cit., pp. 152 f.

saw her dead, I wept and was very sad. I killed her by mistake. It was not from the heart.' He went on to describe how she still came to sleep with him in dreams. She, his victim, catches him by the hand and says, 'Come. Why do we stay here in this prison?'

But normally it is considered extremely dangerous to see in a dream the ghost of the person you have murdered, or to be visited by the Departed. Pandru of Chichari described how he had a dream in prison in which two people were pressing his shoulders very hard when suddenly a third man came and pushed them aside. These two people represented the Departed, and the man who pushed them away was a friendly ancestor who thus saved him from a serious illness. He said that while he was in jail three of his fellow-prisoners saw in dreams the ghosts of the men they had killed and all three died. Boti of Telam was also visited by the ghost of his victim, and as a result he was ill for a whole year. This suggests a strongly emotional element in dreams about violent crime.

This is a convenient point to refer to the very interesting dream seen by Pandru shortly before the fatal quarrel with his brother which led to murder and imprisonment. In his dream he saw an Anga clan-god and a drum and village trumpet. The clan-god stood for the corpse of the murdered man being taken out for burial and the drum and trumpet suggested that the people were weeping and mourning. In *The Muria and their Ghotul* I suggest a close connexion between the uses of the Anga clan-god and the corpse for purposes of divination. The Anga, which is carried on the shoulders by four men and in many cases resembles a bier, is a suitable harbinger of doom.

A Jailor of thirty years' experience told me that usually the Maria murderers went to their fate bravely and seldom had to be dragged or forced. They were asked to say *Ram Ram Ram* as they went to their death. The executions have a profound effect on other prisoners. Doga of Jabeli was condemned to death and was confined in a solitary cell next door to Marvi Chewa. He told me how terrified he was when Chewa was hanged, since he knew that the same fate was in store for him. All night before his execution, Doga listened to the unhappy man weeping and heard the struggle as he was dragged out of his cell by the warders. The Maria from Pinna Bheji described to me how terrified they were when the nephew of the Zamindar of Bhopalpatnam and his two companions were hanged. The Zamindar's nephew went to his death crying *Ram Ram*, but at the gallows he lost control of himself and covered the presiding Magistrate with the foulest abuse.

CHAPTER EIGHTEEN

CONCLUSION

I

THE reader who has examined the many different crimes recorded in this book cannot fail to be struck by the astonishing innocence of many of them. Compared to the dark and complicated wickedness of so many European murders, compared to the fundamental savagery of the actions of such men as Palmer or Orsini, most of these crimes appear almost accidental. In some cases the culprit regards himself as an executioner rather than a murderer. He believes his act to have been entirely justified. In others simple people despairing of making their cause understood in the courts, which use another language and whose ways and outlook are so different from theirs, take the law into their own hands. But of criminals, in the real sense of the word, there are few. Few of the convicts in the Jagdalpur jail would be fit heroes or villains of a detective story.

No one should suppose that, because this book is concerned with violent crime, the Maria themselves are equally preoccupied with the subject. There are a great many Maria, at least 175,000 of them. They live scattered over a vast area half the size of Holland. There are on an average only 12 true homicides every year. The great majority of the people live quiet, peaceful, hard-working lives. Even on the most uncharitable evaluation, their addiction to violence is only remarkable when compared to their immediate neighbours, who are some of the most pacific and gentle people on this planet. It is no doubt true that the Maria are jealous, quick-tempered, passionate, revengeful. Their faults and their virtues are those of strength, not of weakness. It is from such a tribe that we might look one day for creative genius, for positive, explosive, advanced ideas.

It is sometimes debated in Bastar whether anything can be done to wean the Maria from violence. I doubt it. For example, an important cause of murder is fear of witchcraft and magic. Eliminate this fear, and the number of murders will decrease. But the belief in witchcraft can only be removed by education. And how is the Maria to receive the kind of education that will achieve this end? Even if schools were opened all over southern Bastar, they would only be little village schools which would teach up to an elementary standard and be staffed by schoolmasters themselves semi-educated. In the last ten years I have had a wide experience of village schoolmasters, and I do not know a single one who does not believe in magic and witchcraft as firmly as any aboriginal. Those acquainted with the small towns of central India will agree that even university graduates and men holding responsible positions in Government service are equally affected by the belief. Education, in fact, would do nothing to lessen the fear of witchcraft. It might, on the other hand, stimulate other kinds of crime. Not a few educated aboriginals take to blackmail, impersonation and cheating once they have gained the power that literacy gives them.

Another important cause of homicide is alcohol. Suppose prohibition was introduced. Would this reduce the amount of violent crime? I think it most unlikely. In the first place the Maria, angry and resentful, would tend to co-operate less and less with the administration in preserving law and order. Illicit distillation would begin everywhere. The brewing of rice-beer, which can be done in the secret part of a house, would be very difficult to detect. An endless procession of short-term prisoners convicted for excise offences would come from Jagdalpur to infect the Maria area with criminal ideas picked up from other prisoners.

Jealousy and the desire for revenge is probably the third most important cause of murder. I know of no method by which these passions can be eradicated from the human heart. It must, however, be remembered that Maria jealousy is the great safeguard of the Maria home. The women are chaste and faithful not only because most aboriginal women at this stage of development are so, but because of the terrible danger of infidelity. When we move to the more gentle tribesmen of Mandla or Bilaspur we find little jealousy and very few murders, but a woeful lack of attachment to the marriage bond and a marked indifference to female chastity.

Interference in the life of a tribe is almost always attended by disastrous results. I have already quoted von Fürer-Haimendorf's account of what has happened among the Chenchu. This could be paralleled by similar situations in many parts of the world.

Propaganda by officials on tour designed to impress upon the Maria the value of human life and the wrong of taking it; some means of making the civil courts more readily accessible in order to remove from the tribesmen the temptation to take the law into their own hands; and special attempts at the annual Dassara festival, when thousands of Maria come in to Jagdalpur to honour the Maharaja, to influence the headmen to set their face against violence; these would probably improve the situation a little.

How far would deterrent measures influence the Maria? Comparatively few death sentences are passed or executed. Out of 117 persons convicted on our list, only 21 were sentenced to death and only 18 were hanged, although 75 were convicted of actual murder under Section 302. If the death sentence were imposed more frequently, would it deter the Maria from murder? When I have discussed this with the people themselves, they have declared that it would not. They say that they commit murder for only two reasons. The first is accidental, when they are drunk or when they give someone a beating without intending to kill and the victim dies on their hands. The second is when a man is driven to such despair that he decides to destroy his enemy and himself at the same time. Here murder becomes a sort of suicide. But the people think, and probably rightly, that in neither of these cases would fear of the death penalty have any effect. I myself would not venture on an opinion. But I think that, if the death penalty is to be given at all, it should be given consistently and that wherever a premeditated murder has been proved, it should follow as a matter of course. In some villages, the Maria suggested that the headman and Kotwar should be very severely punished whenever they fail to report an act of violence. So long as the people think that they can kill and then, by paying compensation to the panchayat, can avoid punishment, there is definite encouragement to crime.

But in the main I think the Bastar tradition, which is merciful and lenient, is wise. Indeed Sir Cecil Walsh, discussing violent criminals in the United Provinces, goes so far as to say:

> I have sometimes wondered whether such men ought to be punished at all, beyond being bound over to keep the peace. If three stalwart and useful cultivators happen to lose their lives in a sudden village fight, those who caused the deaths are generally guilty of murder, but it seems harsh and uneconomic to hang three more, to send another six to transportation for life, and to break up and ruin several homes. Of course, the magistracy, which enjoys a good deal of control over the police, is responsible for the peace of the district, and a magistrate who did not take the only steps open to him under the codes to punish such disorder and destruction of life would be transferred, and probably black-marked. 'Grievous hurt', which includes knocking out a tooth and involves severe, rigorous imprisonment, the equivalent of hard labour, is almost invariably inflicted. It has always seemed to me that these cases are punished with terrible severity. There is certainly no relation between the moral gravity of the offence and the punishment usually awarded, and imprisonment is absolutely no deterrent, so that severity loses much of its value. Personally, I tried to treat these cases when they came before me on appeal with leniency, and went out of my way to encourage others to do likewise. I think this principle is sound, though it has no application to deliberate brutality, which, in England, used to be treated too lightly. But the point is, as it seems to me, that the presence amongst criminal statistics of these cases of loss of self-control in sudden quarrels between illiterate people is misleading to anyone who seeks to draw an inference from figures in an attempt to form an opinion of the criminal instincts and tendencies of a community.[1]

II

Not only in Bastar but throughout India, there is urgent need for reform in the treatment of the aboriginal prisoner. There will have to be, of course, the most drastic and far-reaching changes before the present penal system of India is brought into line with that of civilized administrations. But

[1] Walsh, *Indian Village Crimes*, p. 12.

I suggest that the aboriginals, here as everywhere, present a rather special problem and might be considered separately.

In jail, the aboriginal, as we have seen, suffers in acute and subtle ways. His ordinary life is so free; his needs are so few and simple yet always fulfilled; his life depends so entirely on certain stimulants to existence that without them he quickly loses the desire to live and, even though he survives his sentence, he comes out of jail with his faith broken and his nature permanently twisted.

The aboriginal prisoner everywhere has no religious consolation, even on the eve of his execution. He does not even have the emotional outlet that the European prisoner gets from singing hymns in Sunday chapel. Although his life is full of the fear of hostile supernatural beings and of his ancestors who may be deeply offended with him for his crime, he has no means of propitiating them in the proper manner. If he has an ill-omened dream in prison, if a god or ancestor appears to him and makes a demand of him, there is nothing that he can do about it. It would be a good thing in Jagdalpur, if criminals, on the eve of their execution, were allowed to visit the temple of Danteshwari, tutelary goddess of Bastar, and make a suitable sacrifice to her.

The aboriginal depends greatly on his recreations. These are entirely stopped in jail. In Europe and America the authorities have realized the futility and danger of such a deprivation. Is there no way by which aboriginal prisoners in certain places should be allowed the singing or dancing that is so dear to them?

What is really needed is a special prison for aboriginals only, to which all those with, say, sentences of more than seven years should be sent from every part of India. It should be situated among the hills, and run more as a camp than an ordinary prison. The aboriginals should be taught crafts which will be useful to them after their release, not occupations like weaving which are taboo. They should be given, as far as possible, food to which they are accustomed. If there were only aboriginals, it would be possible to arrange for their own priests to perform sacrifices at the time of the great festivals and whenever it was necessary to make some private act of propitiation. Regular times could be set apart for corporate singing and for dancing—which incidentally is splendid exercise and in tribal India takes the place of organized games and physical training. I cannot see the point of depriving long-term aboriginal prisoners of the thing which many of them value as the chief comfort of their hard existence, tobacco. For men whose lives are obviously ruined and broken, some concession in this respect could do nothing but good. In any aboriginal prison the rule which makes a convict stand before an official in a penitential attitude, with head bowed and hands held before him, should be abolished. Nothing should be done to make the aboriginal servile and obsequious. His spirit should be re-created, not broken. There is in him a great fund of natural innocence on which to build.

For what great areas of crime and semi-criminal human activity are untouched by these simple aboriginals! Unnatural vice is unknown to them. Rape is extremely rare. Infanticide and abortion is so unusual as to merit special record. They are almost entirely ignorant of cheating and blackmail. They do not tread the mean and devious ways of untruth.

These tribesmen—and it is important to emphasize this for the Maria—do not cheat and exploit the poor and the weak. They are mostly ignorant of caste and race prejudice. They do not prostitute their women or degrade them by foolish laws and customs. They do not form themselves into armies and destroy one another by foul chemical means. They do not tell pompous lies over the radio. Many of their darkest sins are simply the result of ignorance. A few of them are cruel and savage, but the majority are kind and loving, admirable in the home, steadfast in their tribal loyalties, manly, independent, honourable.

APPENDIX ONE

TABLE OF 100 MARIA HOMICIDES

No.	Name of murderer	Name and relationship of victim	Date of crime	Section of I.P.C. and sentence
1	(*a*) **Banda of Hitulkudum** (*b*) **Pandru of Erphund**	Two victims, a Sikalgir and a Mahara, both petty traders	Feb. 1921	(*a*) 302. Death. Executed, 13.10.21. (*b*) 302. Death. Executed, 13.10.21.
2	Barse Chappe of Gamawada	His senior wife, Sukhi	4.5.32	304. 7 years. Died in jail.
3	Barse **Chewa of Aranpur**	The father of a wife who had left him, Tati Pandu, a Maria blacksmith	25.10.40	302. Death. Executed.
4	Barse **Dhurwa of Gamawada**	His younger brother, Barse Bododi	18.5.35	302. Transportation for life.
5	Barse **Kama**, 35, of Michenar	His wife, Hungi, 30	12.9.25	302. Death. On appeal, life imprisonment. Died in jail, 20.12.26.
6	Dudhi Bhima of Pordem	His uncle, Marvi Deva	27.9.30	302. Transportation for life. On appeal, 10 years.

Brief history of the crime	Attitude of the murderer and of society
The two traders had about Rs 100 and were going from village to village to buy cattle. Banda and Pandru persuaded them to go to the Indrawati for fish and there killed them with axes and robbed them. They buried their victims in the sand and the crime was not discovered for a fortnight.	An old man, step-father of Banda, gave evidence against him. He was abused by his wife and hanged himself. Pandru's young brother was chief witness for prosecution. Both confessed, but in Court partly retracted.
Chappe was a sick man, supposed to be possessed by a spirit. Went to Siraha for treatment and camped in open hut. Had delusions that Sukhi was giving him contaminated food. Asked both wives to have intercourse with him in hut. They refused. Three days later he asked Sukhi, and when she refused he beat and killed her.	Confessed to the murder, but claimed it was because Sukhi was trying to outcaste and poison him.
Chewa married Bandi, Pandu's daughter. A year later Chewa's house was burnt down: Bandi was suspected and sent home. After two years she married again. Chewa demanded compensation from Pandu. There were many quarrels and at last Chewa shot Pandu while he was asleep.	Chewa tried to prove an alibi. A relative tried to implicate another man. In 1939 a similar trick had saved two men in a neighbouring village.
The two brothers were living together. Dhurwa sold a bullock but failed to give Bododi any share of the money. This annoyed Bododi who frequently asked for it. On day of tragedy, he demanded a rupee and Dhurwa called him into an inner room and shot him with an arrow.	Dhurwa admitted the deed, but claimed first that it was done in self-defence, then in mistake for a thief.
Hungi, eight months pregnant, had brought home bamboo shoots and was resting. Kama came in tired from grazing cattle and demanded food. Hungi answered sharply and Kama killed her with an axe as she was lying on the mat.	Kama ran to jungle and hid up a tree. Manjhi persuaded him to come down and the villagers tied him up and called the police. Kama confessed.
Uncle and nephew lived on opposite sides of a field which they cultivated jointly. Original owner abandoned field when his father died. In 1926, Deva fell ill and his father died, so he too left the field. Bhima cultivated it for 4 years and thus became the legal owner. Deva returned and claimed the land, but Bhima refused. Then Deva began ploughing the land and Bhima killed him.	Bhima confessed, but though evidence proved the murder was done with an arrow, he insisted that he beat his victim with a pestle—which would not have shed blood.

7	Guma Hunga of Toinar	Burgi, a supposed sorcerer	10.3.27	302. Transportation for life.
8	Habka Doga of Nerli	His friend and creditor, Muka	28.4.33	302. Transportation for life. Died in jail, 27.7.34.
9	Habka Masa of Halur	His wife, Pakli	10.7.39	302. Transportation for life.
10	Hemla Bakka of Arbe	His wife, Jimme	21.8.37	302. Transportation for life. On appeal, 5 years.
11	Hemla Chewa of Ronje	A Halba boy of 16, a complete stranger	18.1.23	Acquitted, but detained as a lunatic.
12	Hemla Mundra of Talnar	His father, Hemla Gunda	13.5.28	304. One month.
13	Jhoria Hunga of Kosalnar	An old man, Hemla Mukka, whose wife was his patient	25.7.34	304. 7 years.
14	Kadti Hunga of Garmiri	A farm servant, Markami Dorga	5.11.34	302. Transportation for life. On appeal, 5 years under 304. Released 12.4.39.

Hunga left his village because he believed Burgi was bewitching him. One day Burgi visited Toinar and Hunga, afraid that he had followed him to do further mischief, killed him with his axe.	Hunga confessed.
Muka gave three friends drinks of mahua spirit in the liquor shop at Kameli. One bottle was divided between the four. On their way home Muka demanded Re 1.4.0 as rent, but Doga's real debt was only As 4. There was a quarrel and a fight and Muka was killed. The Judge did not consider Doga was drunk.	Police were informed at once. Doga confessed.
Masa supported his old parents at Hallur. His wife, to whom he had been married three years, went to her mother's house for the Pen Karsita festival. Masa went too, but Pakli refused to return with him. Her parents went from place to place as coolies : Pakli accompanied them and Masa followed. After 6 weeks of this, in a little hut, on a night of heavy rain and a strong wind, there was a final quarrel. Pakli used very coarse abuse and Masa killed her.	After killing his wife, Masa returned home to see to his old parents and the affairs of his farm which had suffered by his absence at the start of the rains. He confessed after his arrest.
Bakka suspected his wife of an intrigue with her *elder* cousin, a serious tribal offence, and indeed claimed that he had caught her in actual guilt. There was a family quarrel, and Bakka got enraged and killed Jimme with a bamboo pole.	Bakka confessed, but claimed there was serious provocation.
Chewa was an epileptic. He met the boy in the woods and killed him with an axe. The same evening he assaulted a woman.	He confessed, but claimed he was mad and could remember nothing. The villagers arrested him and tied him up.
Gunda kept the wives of his two sons and drove his own wife and the sons from his house. He refused to divide the property. Mundra beat his father in a quarrel, and Gunda was on his way to report him when he was killed.	The villagers, considering Gunda had only got what he deserved, hushed up the matter and reported a death from smallpox. Mundra confessed after his arrest.
Mukka's wife was a leper. Mukka took her for treatment to Hunga, a Siraha-magician. One day he called him while he was resting and Hunga refused to go. Mukka abused him and Hunga, indignant at the insult to his sacred office, killed him.	The villagers reported the matter. Hunga confessed after arrest.
There was a mahua-liquor party in the evening out in the fields ; four friends were there. They stole fish from Hunga's traps. Hunga found them eating it and beat them. All ran away but Hunga caught Dorga and killed him by twisting his neck. Dorga had previously stolen juice from Hunga's sago palms.	Hunga threw the body into a tank, but admitted the deed to the villagers. Later he denied this.

15	Kadti Hunga of Garmiri	His wife, Gangi	18.7.39	302. Death. Executed.
16	Kadti Pandu of Molasnar	Aitu, an 11 year old boy, son of Pandu's wife's sister	6.1.33	302. Transportation for life.
17	Kalmumi Masa of Dugeli	His mother-in-law, Hungi, and his wife, Kohale	21.5.32	302. Transportation for life.
18	Kartami Aitu of Bara Badam	His 'brother', Kartami Chule	20.12.34	302. Death. Executed
19	(*a*) Kartami Bira (*b*) Sori Bhima of Nayanar	Bira's own brother, Kosa	25.12.35	(*a*) 302. Transportation for life. (*b*) 325 with 109. 5 years.
20	Kartami Hirma of Killepal	His infant daughter, 5 months old	10.2.37	304. 2 years.
21	Kawasi Borga of Doriras	His uncle, Boti	6.7.32	302. Transportation for life.
22	Kawasi Chamru of Nagul	His wife, Badhri	27.2.21	302. Transportation for life. Died in jail, 3.9.2[illegible]
23	Kawasi Handa of Pondum	An old servant of his father, Marvi Gutta	25.7.31	302. Transportation for life.

A chicken had been killed the previous night. When Gangi gave the morning meal, she said a cat had eaten it. Hunga threw the food at her and beat her. She threatened to tell the panchayat and send him back to prison. He took a knife and, despite the attempts of his two little daughters to prevent him, cut Gangi's throat.	After seeing his wife dead Hunga hanged himself behind his house. His mother cut him down and he was revived and arrested. He claimed that he was drunk, but this was proved to be untrue.
Pandu, who was fond of his nephew, wanted Aitu's cock for a cock-fight. Aitu refused, but they went together to the bazaar. On the way, Pandu tried to get the cock and throttled the boy during the struggle.	Pandu tried to make the death look like suicide. He denied the deed.
Masa was a Lamhada and his mother-in-law did not treat him well. He planned to go with his wife to live elsewhere. The two women tried to stop him. At last, when he was trying to remove his property from the house and Hungi obstructed him, there was a violent quarrel and he killed both women.	—
There was a long-standing quarrel between the two men over a sago palm. The murder was one of revenge and very cruel and deliberate.	Pleaded not guilty, though he admitted striking Chule once when gravely provoked.
Bira and Kosa used to quarrel about the division of land and cattle. Bhima feared Kosa as a sorcerer who had killed his children. Kosa suffered from yaws and was staying in an open hut. The two men beat him to death as he was sitting there.	They threw the body under a toddy tree to give impression Kosa had fallen. Bhima later confessed.
Hirma came home one evening with bamboos and demanded supper. Chule, his wife, said she could not give him any because there was no rice. She had the baby in her arms. Hirma lost his temper and beat Chule violently, breaking her arm, and hit the child by accident, killing her.	The panchayat demanded Rs 25 compensation and hushed up the matter. The Kotwar reported a child still-born. Hirma said he was drunk, but the Court decided this was an 'afterthought'.
Borga was headman ; P.W.D. work was in progress and more men were wanted. Boti, who used to do the headman's work for Borga, came to fetch them. Borga lost his temper and beat his uncle so heavily that he died by sunset.	Borga ran away. He confessed, but claimed he was drunk—a plea not accepted by the Court.
Chamru had once been insane. Was very queer and excited shortly before the tragedy. Seems to have suspected Badhri's relations with her own brother. One day he asked her to husk rice, she refused, and he beat her to death. Then he burnt the house above her body.	The Court considered the witnesses were all concealing something. Accused pleaded not guilty and said his wife burnt the house.
Handa quarrelled with his father whose cattle had done some damage to his crops, and beat him. Gutta intervened. Handa abused him, then went quietly away, got his axe, came back and killed him.	Handa confessed, but claimed he was drunk. No evidence of this, though he may have taken a little at a bazaar some hours before.

24	Kawasi Hurra of Dummam	A neighbour, Poriami Handa	23.7.34	304. 10 years.
25	Kawasi Kana of Dilmilli	His wife, Kawasi Chappe	20.2.38	302. Transportation for life.
26	Kawasi Hunga of Pedaras	His uncle, Kawasi Deva	26.1.28	304. 5 years.
27	Kawasi Koliha of Kapanar	Bondki, in mistake for his sister-in-law Hungi	24.5.37	304. 3 years
28	Kawasi Masa of Badam	His father-in-law, Marvi Kosa	19.11.36	304. 7 years.
29	Khotlu of Kaurgaon	His wife, Mase	12.12.20	Acquitted, but detained as a lunatic
30	(*a*) Kiske Nanda (*b*) Dirdo Bandi, nephew of Nanda (*c*) Kiske Kuma (*d*) Kiske Hirma, son of Nanda	Two men, fellow-thieves, of Gogonda	Aug. 1921	All sentenced to deat[h] under 302 and ex[e]cuted on 28.6.2[?] Father and son die[d] together.

A large party of men were ploughing someone's field and were rewarded by a feast. Hurra served the food and Handa complained he did not get enough. He attacked Hurra, who killed him, though probably he never intended to.	Hurra threw the body into a stream and threatened to kill anyone who gave him away. But later he confessed. Villagers tried to hush up the crime and forced the widow to accept compensation.
Kana came home late in afternoon after grazing cattle and asked for pej. His wife did not give it to him immediately, so he struck her on the head with his axe and killed her. Kana was rather dull mentally and had been treated by a Siraha.	Kana gave himself up to the villagers and they took him to the police. He said he and his wife were on good terms. 'I do not know what came over me. I was very hungry.'
On evening of the Bhimul Pandum, when everyone had been drinking landa, Deva went to bed, but was aroused by his nephew. They began to quarrel and fight, both drunk, and Hunga killed his uncle by twisting his neck. There was probably an old grudge about an unpaid bride-price.	—
Bondki and her husband came to the house to borrow a cow. They brought a pot of landa and everyone drank it. There was a sudden quarrel over Hungi's failure to provide food. Koliha shot at her, but the arrow struck Bondki instead. She was pregnant and died a fortnight later.	Villagers hushed up the matter, and compensation was paid. Koliha confessed.
A Waddai came for house-sacrifice and Masa invited Kosa and others to drink landa. He was drunk in the morning, slept till evening, woke and beat his wife for not feeding the Waddai properly. His father-in-law intervened and beat him in his wife's presence and, enraged, he killed him.	Masa confessed.
Khotlu, 55, was epileptic. Used to declare Rebellion was coming. Fond of Mase, 45, who had borne him 10 children. Had a fit in the fields and killed her while insane.	Villagers had him arrested. Khotlu denied all knowledge of the incident.
They had all been involved in a robbery of grain. Two were caught and were murdered to prevent them implicating the rest.	They buried the corpses. The villagers met and decided to conceal the murder. The accused pleaded not guilty.

31	Kuhrami Guddi of Mardum	Botse, a pregnant Mahara woman	20.4.38	302. Death. Executed, 5.9.38.
32	Kuhrami Hirme of Godpi	Her step-daughter, 10, Jimme	6.6.35	302. Transportation for life.
33	Kuhrami Tonda of Killepal	His younger brother, Kuhrami Gajru	28.9.39	302. Transportation for life.
34	Kunjami Gencha of Gumiapal	His father, Kunjami Makka	10.5.34	304. 10 years. In appeal, 4 years.
35	Kunjami Malla of Chilmalawa	His wife, Jimme	7.11.34	302. Transportation for life.
36	Lekhami Gagru of Alnar	A gambling crony, Thadgu Panka or Mahara	17.8.31	302. Transportation for life.
37	Manjhi Bande of Turri	His younger brother, Khotla Manjhi	24.7.27	302. Transportation for life. On appeal, 5 years under 304.
38	Markami Ganga of Potali	Marvi Masa	4.8.30	304. 1 year.

Guddi took Botse to a tank and sacrificed her to its deities. He cut open the belly and offered the foetus also. He sprinkled some of the blood on a neighbouring field and ploughed it in.	There was an attempt to make the murder look like a tiger kill. Guddi pleaded not guilty.
Hirme took the little girl with her to the jungle for leaves. Jimme did not obey her, and Hirme beat her and twisted her neck.	Villagers reported that Jimme had fallen from a mahua tree. The house in which the body was placed was burnt down. Hirme admitted she beat the girl but not that she twisted the neck.
Gajru was a very quarrelsome fellow and was several times fined by the panchayat for beating people. Tonda was a hideous dwarf, whose condition was aggravated by Gajru's bullying. At last he could bear it no more and killed his brother while he was asleep.	Tonda confessed, but later claimed he was forced to it by the villagers.
There was very little rice in Gencha's house and the family had agreed to eat only once in the evening. Gencha came home hungry, found nothing ready and smacked his sister for spending her time playing with the other girls and not cooking in time. Makka rebuked him, beat him and refused to let him get what food there was.	Gencha confessed, but did not intend to kill his father. 'He was very hungry.'
Malla and Jimme distilled mahua liquor in a field. They both got very drunk. As they were going home, Jimme fell and broke the pot and Malla beat and killed her.	Malla terrorized the people and made them cremate the body and say Jimme had died of small-pox. He denied everything.
There was a gambling dispute—everyone had drunk a lot of salphi juice and perhaps some mahua spirit as well. Thadgu beat Gagru, a serious matter for a Maria leading to his excommunication, and Gagru full of rage killed him.	Gagru gave himself up.
Khotla had long been demanding partition of the family property ; but the two brothers had married two sisters and Bande did not admit his claim. On day of murder, Khotla abused Bande who was an old man of 60 all day till late in the evening he met his fate.	Bande was headman of the village and insisted no report should be made.
Ganga and Masa had a dispute about land. They met in a liquor-shop. Ganga had had his drink, but there was none for Masa. Masa abused and beat him and in the heat of the quarrel Ganga killed him.	Ganga pleaded guilty.

39	Markami Hinga of Gumma	His brother, Markami Ganga	17.4.28	304. 6 years.
40	Markami Kola of Surnar	His younger step-brother, Markami Harma	10.5.37	302. Transportation for life.
41	Markami Masa of Adwal	Markami Handa, husband of the girl Bandi, who became Masa's mistress	30.9.23	302. Death. Executed, 4.4.34.
42	Markami Mundra of Gudra	Markami Bhima, a headman	20.8.34	302. Death. Executed.
43	Markami Turka of Potali Darba	His elder brother's wife, Kosi	16.10.35	302. Transportation for life. He died in jail.
44	Markami Wango of Hande Khodra	His betrothed, Marvi Paike	May 1936	302. Transportation for life.
45.	Marvi Aita of Paknar	A neighbour, Marvi Kamlu Masa	21.1.30	302. Death. Executed, 25.7.30.
46	Marvi Bhima of Kapanar	His wife, Kondi	4.10.39	Acquitted, but detained under 471 Cr. P.C.
47	Marvi Boti of Telam	His younger brother, Marvi Kosa	14.4.26	302. Transportation for life.

Hinga was a new Siraha and proud of it. One day Ganga abused him and his profession which was a financial liability in the farm. Hinga took the trident and chain from his hut-temple and stabbed him.	
The two brothers lived happily together. Harma sold Kola's drum for Rs 2.10.0 and only gave him Re 1. There was a quarrel over this and Harma slapped Kola and in the fight Harma was killed.	Kola gave out that Harma had gone to the Tea Gardens, and threatened to kill anyone who reported to the police. Confessed after arrest.
Handa had two wives. The younger, Bandi, 18, fell in love with Masa, 24. She eloped with him and Handa threatened to kill them both, but was killed first, while he was sleeping.	The villagers arrested Masa, and he confessed.
Mundra, who had been imprisoned for assault, escaped from jail and in the course of an exciting chase killed the leader of the pursuing Maria.	Perhaps because of Rs 50 reward, the Maria showed enthusiasm for Mundra's capture. He denied killing Bhima.
Two brothers lived together and shared their cattle though they had different fields. On the Korta Pandum festival, they all drank landa. Turka abused Kosi for not tethering the cattle properly or clearing the cow-dung. She answered him back and he stabbed her with an arrow.	The villagers arrested Turka, and he confessed.
Wango was a Lamhada serving for Paike. He suspected her of intimacy with a forbidden relation. After a violent quarrel with his father-in-law, he shot her.	Wango confessed and said he shot the girl when he found her having intercourse with her 'brother'.
Aita and Kamlu had quarrelled about the cutting of an embarkment. Aita pulled straw from Kamlu's roof and whistled in token of enmity, and shot him as he was coming home from the fields.	Aita denied the crime and said Kamlu fell accidentally on the arrow which impaled him.
Bhima suffered from melancholia and in one of his fits stabbed his wife with an arrow.	Villagers called the police. Bhima confessed, but said he could not remember properly.
Boti was in love with his younger brother's wife, a forbidden relationship. He took her to Jeypore, but returned and met Kosa in the jungle. There was a fight and Kosa was killed.	Boti went away to Jeypore, but he was arrested and confessed.

48	(*a*) Marvi Boti (*b*) Mase of Sirisguda	Mase's husband, Marvi Bododi, and his son, Hunga	30.9.40	(*a*) 302. Transportation for life. (*b*) 302. Death. On appeal, transportation for life.
49	Marvi Chule of Bara Gudra	His elder step-brother, Marvi Buti	9.7.34	302. Transportation for life. Died in jail, 17.3.41.
50	Marvi Deva of Gadhia	His daughter 4 years old. Tried to kill wife	8.1.26	302. Transportation for life. Died in jail, 30.1.27.
51	Marvi Hinga of Gariapal	His mother-in-law, Kawasi Mude	17.11.34	304. 7 years.
52	Marvi Hirma of Benglur	His cousin's son, a boy, Hando	17.4.32	302. Death. Executed, 30.9.32.
53	Marvi Hunga of Maroki	His nephew, Hemla Hirma	18.9.35	302. Transportation for life.
54	Marvi Joga of Phulpar	His wife, Pise	14.10.33	302. Transportation for life.
55	Marvi Kesa of Killepal	His father-in-law, Sori Hirma	21.9.23	302. Death. Executed, 28.3.24.
56	Marvi Khotla of Kodenar	A neighbour, Marvi Hurra	30.1.39	304 7 years.

Bododi was a Siraha. His wife wanted to get rid of him because he was poor and she wanted to live with Boti. She gave him oleander seeds in his food.	They both confessed.
Buti was a provocative person. He gave Chule land and charged double rent. Then he took the land away from him. Then he threatened to get his crop damaged by cattle. At last he quarrelled so violently that he got killed.	Chule confessed killing Buti, but claimed self-defence.
Deva suspected his wife's chastity. On the night of the tragedy he said he saw her with some-one. After food he asked her for tobacco (that is, intercourse). She refused and in rage he killed his child and tried to kill her.	Deva hid for a time, then be-ing hungry came home. He was arrested by the villagers and confessed.
Hinga's wife had fever and he took her to a Waddai in another village. He left her there and came home. Mude saw him and pub-licly abused him for neglecting her daughter. The insult so enraged him that he killed her.	The villagers arrested Hinga and he confessed.
Hirma promised a cock to Hando's father for the entertainment of a guest. Then he re-fused to give it. Hando took it forcibly. Next day, Hirma enticed the boy out of the village and killed him.	Hirma was a syphilitic. He confessed.
Hunga was 16, Hirma only 13. They had a sudden quarrel and the younger boy used a lot of dirty language. Hunga shot at him and killed him.	Hunga confessed.
Joga was suffering from swollen feet and went to Jabeli for treatment. Pise wanted to go home to look after the fowls. Joga said he would kill her if she did. Early one morning he asked her for water, she failed to get it, and he stabbed her with an arrow.	Joga ran away but was cap-tured by the villagers, where-on he lay flat with eyes shut. Said he could not remember what had happened.
Kesa had three wives; the youngest was Hirma's daughter, Mase. One day he beat her and she went to her father's house. He followed and found them all drinking landa. He asked Hirma why he had not sent Mase home: there was a quarrel and Hirma was killed.	Kesa and the villagers tried to put the crime on to a youth who was even persuaded to confess.
Many quarrels: Hurra's son stole Khotla's iron lamp; Hurra shot Khotla's pregnant cow which went into his field. On the day of Gaddi Pandum everyone drank landa; all day Hurra annoyed and abused Khotla and at last the latter beat and killed him. He was probably drunk.	Khotla confessed.

57	Marvi Konda of Bagmundi	A distant relative, Kunjami Bhima	3.11.30	302. Transportation for life. Died in jail, 11.2.33.
58	Marvi Kuma of Bastanar	His son, Marvi Konda	3.9.40	304. 5 years.
59	Marvi Mangru of Pakhnar	His neighbour, Kesa	22.2.26	302. Transportation for life.
60	Marvi Modu of Bara Gudra	His younger nephew, a boy of 12, Marvi Anda	9.9.38	304. 7 years. On appeal, 4 years.
61	Marvi Mundra of Munga	His wife, Kosi	30.10.32	302. Transportation for life. Died in jail.
62	(a) Marvi Oyami Masa (b) Marvi Gutta (c) Marvi Handa (d) Marvi Mundra (e) Hundami Doga (f) Marvi Tangra all of Jabeli	Marvi Masa, first cousin of Oyami Masa and clan-uncle of Gutta, Mundra and Tangra	27.4.30	All 302. Transportation for life. On appeal, (d) 3 years. (e) 3 years. (f) 4 years. The first 4 died in jail.
63	Marvi Paklu of Mutanpal	His wife, Dallo	16.7.39	304. 7 years.
64	Miriami Doga of Gampur	His elder cousin, Miriami Hurra	10.10.39	302. Transportation for life.

The two men went to a bazaar, came home and Konda slept all evening. When he woke, he tried to beat his wife and slapped Bhima's wife. Bhima objected and Konda took a pestle and killed him.	Konda confessed.
Konda came home hungry in the evening and asked his mother for food. It was not ready and his father abused him for demanding it. Konda picked up a stick, but the father struck first.	The family tried to hush the matter up by reporting that Konda fell on a peg in an epileptic fit, but the villagers made a report to the police and then Kuma confessed.
Mangru, a boy of 18, was the son of the village Pujari. There was a harvest feast and the Pujari started it without waiting for Kesa, one of the elders. There was a quarrel: Mangru thought his father was insulted. He lay in wait for Kesa and killed him as he was going home.	At first Mangru tried to put the crime on his brother, but later he confessed.
Modu and Anda were working in the fields. Modu rebuked the younger boy for not working properly, and Anda abused him and threw a clod of earth at him. Modu beat him with his fists and the boy died.	Modu tried to make the death look like suicide. Tied body to a small bhilwan tree, but this did not look convincing so he took it to a char tree.
Mundra and his wife worked very late and came home together. Mundra was impatient for his supper and there was a quarrel. He picked up a log from the fire and killed her.	Mundra gave a feast to the villagers and they agreed to hush the matter up. But after arrest, Mundra confessed.
Masa accused Oyami Masa of cattle theft. On the evening of the Wijja Pandum, all having taken landa, they went to Masa's house and beat him to death, doing the *sui* whistle.	They all confessed.
Paklu had an affair with Jimme. One afternoon he took her to a cave. Dallo followed and abused him and beat Jimme. Paklu beat Dallo, knocked her down and strangled her.	Paklu hid the body and threatened to kill Jimme if she reported the matter. Tried to make it look like a tiger-kill. Later, he confessed.
Hurra had given Doga two cows on hire and complained that for two years he had had nothing from him in return. One evening Hurra went to Doga's house and again demanded payment. Doga asked where he could get rice before the harvest and on a sudden impulse picked up a bit of wood and struck his creditor so hard that he died.	Doga gave himself up to the Kotwar.

65	Miriami Harma of Kindul	His baby daughter, 1½ years old	30.10.25	302. Death. On appeal, transportation for life.
66	Muchaki Dasru of Gumiapal	His friend, Poyami Harma	20.1.38	302. Transportation for life.
67	Muchaki Muda of Gogonda	Muchaki Harma	16.10.35	302. Transportation for life.
68	Mundru of Kosalnar	A friend, Raghu	16.4.32	304. 5 years. Died in jail.
69	Murami Dhurwa of Palnar	His nephew, Murami Wella	17.12.29	302. Transportation for life.
70	Nendi Hirma of Silakjori	His neighbour, Ganda	24.2.24	302. Transportation for life.
71	Oyami Kola of Kasturpal	His maternal uncle, Goge	4.3.22	302. Transportation for life. Died in jail, 25.7.34
72	Padami Guddi of Naktola	His mother, Pande	30.11.36	302. Transportation for life.

Two Maria were caught stealing rice. Before the village court, they implicated Harma. He denied the charge, but the villagers held him guilty and his uncle beat him. Harma seized his baby from his wife's arms and dashed her to the ground.	Harma went with the Kotwar to report his child had died of cobra-bite. Afterwards he confessed.
Dasru had borrowed a cart and bullocks and invited the owners to a landa party. Harma, his friend, came also. As they were drinking, Dasru and Harma quarrelled because Dasru said Harma had not paid him his Pujari dues. Harma went away and Dasru followed him and whistled and then killed him.	Dasru told the villagers that as he was their Pujari they should not report against him and he tried to implicate an innocent man. He pleaded not guilty.
Muda, a boy of 18, served Harma for 3 years as a Kabari farm-servant, and was married at Harma's expense. A few days before the Korta Pandum festival he stopped work and went to live with his father. On the festival day, Harma went and beat him. That night he stabbed Harma with an arrow in revenge. He was not drunk.	Muda confessed, but pleaded justification, that he had been beaten and that Harma was going to take away his wife.
Mundru owed Raghu a little salt. The two men drank mahua spirit together quite amiably, but then they quarrelled. Raghu attacked Mundru who snatched the axe from his hand and killed him.	Mundru confessed and pleaded drunkenness.
Dhurwa had been imprisoned for murder before : he was released in 1929. Ten months later he quarrelled with his wife and in his rage declared he would kill his nephew for not supporting him during his trial, which he did. The Court doubted this motive.	Dhurwa went away to Orissa and thence to the Tea Gardens. The villagers made the usual report. He did not confess.
Hirma was searching for a lost cow when Ganda, who seems to have been on bad terms with him, accused him of stealing his plantains. There was a sudden quarrel and Ganda was killed.	The villagers arrested and tied Hirma up. As he was being taken in a cart, he broke his ropes and escaped. He said the people had forced him to confess.
Goge accused Kola of stealing his cattle : he tied up and beat his servant, and Kola had to hide to escape punishment himself. At last in despair Kola went at night to Goge's house and killed him while he was asleep.	Suspicion fell first on another man. Kola evaded arrest for 5 months by doing nothing, but he roused suspicion by avoiding the police when they came for inquiries. At last he confessed.
There was a beer party to celebrate the kosra harvest. Guddi asked his mother for food ; she said she was busy and told him to ask his wife. She said she too was busy. Guddi got angry, picked up a hoe and beat and killed his mother.	He confessed, but pleaded that he was drunk and that he thought the hoe was a stick.

73	Pandru of Gudse	The village Siraha, Kosa	14.4.22	302. Transportation for life.
74	(*a*) Pandu (*b*) Nanda (*c*) Bhima of Phulnar	Nanda, Maria Thekedar (landlord) of the village	8.5.31	(*a*) 302. Death. Executed, 3.9.31 (*b*) 302. Transportation for life. (*c*) 302. Transportation for life.
75	Poriami Hirma of Garmiri	His lover, Mase	21.2.33	302. Transportation for life.
76	(*a*) Poriami Hirma (*b*) Ganga (*c*) Deva (*d*) Hunga of Pinna Bheji	Marvi Joga	5.3.38	304. (*a*) 7 years. (*b*) (*c*) (*d*) 5 years. On appeal, (*a*) 4 years. (*b*) (*c*) (*d*) 2 years.
77	Poriami Kosa of Morathpal	His wife, Gagri	4.2.32	304. 7 years. Died in jail.
78	Poriami Podiya of Pinna Bheji	His wife, Bandi	5.2.27	302. Transportation for life. Died in jail, 15.5.32.
79	Poriami Usodi of Gatam	Marvi Muka	25.3.35	304. Transportation for life. On appeal, 10 years.
80	Poyami Burka of Chhindgaon	His wife, Kosi	16.12.24	304. 7 years. On appeal, 4 years.
81	Poyami Chalki of Kodenar	Poyami Pitai	8.4.36	302. Transportation for life.
82	Poyami Kola of Gudra	Samaru, a Rawat	27.10.22	302. Transportation for life.

sago palm ceased giving juice. Kosa diagnosed Pandru's magic as a cause. There was a violent quarrel : Pandru abused Kosa and his god, plucked out his pubic hairs ; Kosa slapped him. Five months later Pandru shot his enemy.	Pandru hid in the jungle for a time, but returned next day and was arrested. He confessed.
Nanda and Pandu were on bad terms. Nanda used to accuse Pandu of stealing and once beat him. Pandu bribed the others to help him and tried to kill Nanda but could not get into the house. Next day they lured him into the forest and killed him.	All three confessed.
Mase, deserted by her husband, was in love with Hirma and became pregnant. The panch met and frightened her. She went to Hirma for help ; he proposed she should live with him as his wife. She refused and annoyed him and he throttled her.	He tied her up, apparently to make it look like suicide. Later he confessed.
The reason for this did not come out in court. The four men beat Joga with their fists and he died nine days later.	They denied killing Joga and claimed that he died of boils.
Kosa was a paralytic and almost imbecile. One day he asked his wife to have sexual congress with him : she abused him and refused and he stabbed her.	He confessed, but pleaded loss of memory.
Podiya was a young man, only married a year. He found his wife unfaithful and beat her nearly to death, then hanged her with a creeper.	He admitted the crime and thought it a proper punishment for his wife's infidelity.
Muka wanted to marry Usodi's younger sister, but the family objected. He twice tried to carry her off. Usodi killed him for it in a fit of rage.	He confessed.
Burka caught his wife in sexual intimacy with another man. He at once killed her and nearly killed the man.	He gave himself up to the village elders, who took him to the police.
On the Wijja Pandum day, Chalki's father was sacrificing. Someone brought his chicken too late. There was a quarrel and everyone was drunk. During the disturbance Chalki got his bow and arrow and shot Pitai.	Chalki confessed and pleaded drunkenness.
Samaru was having a drink in the liquor-shop at Dilmilli. Kola asked him for some ; Samaru said he had no money. There was a quarrel. Kola whistled and abused and later beat the Rawat to death with his axe.	Kola confessed, but said he was drunk and that the Rawat had kicked him. But in fact, Kola was angry because he could *not* get drunk.

83	Poyami Masa of Kumharsadra	His wife, Gadme	3.6.30	302. Transportation for life.
84	Poyami Panda of Killepal	A neighbour, Nanda	19.4.32	304. 3 years.
85	Punem Masa of Pusnar	Gaita Hunga, his father-in-law	15.8.34	304. 7 years.
86	Punem Pidga of Burji	His father, Punem Doga	22.3.36	302. Transportation for life.
87	(*a*) Sori Dhurwa of Mokhpal (*b*) Kartami Masa of Gudra	Marvi Poriami and Banda Kalar	1.8.37	(*a*) 302. Death. Executed. (*b*) 302. Transportation for life.
88	Sori Dome of Mokhpal	Her co-widow, Chule	9.11.32	304 5 years.
89	Sori Pandu of Mokhpal	Kamlu Hunga, his uncle	3.10.29	302. Transportation for life.
90	Tati Doga of Todka	His sister-in-law, Tati Hirme	27.5.37	302. Transportation for life.
91	Tati Mase of Kodenar	Her husband, Tati Harma	16.1.40	302. Transportation for life.

A Dhobi tried to seduce Masa's senior wife, Gadme. To get rid of him she told him to meet her at night. The younger wife told Masa. All day he brooded in rage and all night; he stabbed Gadme with an arrow just before dawn.	Masa tried to make it look like suicide. He pleaded not guilty.
Panda had suspected his wife of intimacy with Nanda for months. On the Mati Devi festival, when everyone had drunk landa, he caught Nanda and his wife together.	He confessed, and seems to have thought his action justified.
Masa owed Hunga eight annas rent. Hunga constantly demanded it. On the day of the tragedy, Masa tried to get the money, but failed, and Masa abused him and threw a bit of burning wood at him. In the ensuing quarrel Masa stabbed and killed the older man.	Masa confessed.
Father and son were living together amicably. One evening, they tapped toddy and drank it together. Over supper Pidga asked his father for a loan, but the old man refused, and the son suddenly lost his temper, got up and killed his father as he was eating.	Pidga confessed.
The two victims were on their way to the Kuakonda police station to report against the accused for cattle-theft. Dhurwa and Masa followed and killed them.	They hid the bodies under stones, but later confessed.
Chule and Dome were co-wives of Sori Deva. After his death, they continued to live together. Chule was old, suffered from yaws, a tiresome and plaguey woman. She grumbled at Dome for a year until in exasperation Dome killed her.	Dome denied the charge, and said the villagers were planting the crime on her.
Pandu had been playing his sarangi-fiddle at a landa party. There was a drunken quarrel, and Pandu tried to kill his uncle with an axe. He was prevented, so he got his bow and arrow and shot him. Pandu was notorious for his fits of rage when drunk.	He confessed.
Doga was the younger step-brother of Hirme's husband. After the latter's death, Doga expected the land and perhaps the person of the widow, over whom he had claims. On the day of the tragedy, he asked her for 'tobacco': she refused; and he killed her by stunning and then drowning her.	He left the body in a pool. Later, he confessed.
Mase was the youngest of three wives. Harma often beat her for doing no work and eating too much. The panchayat fined both. The beatings were very severe and after seven years she could bear it no more and took her revenge.	She confessed.

92	Tati Pande of Bodenar	Her husband, Tati Mundra	25.10.35	302. Transportation for life. On appeal, 1 year.
93	Uika Toka of Mundher	Telami Sika	1.11.22	302. Transportation for life. On appeal, 2 years.
94	Ujji Poda of Kaurgaon	His cousin, Kopa	3.8.33	304 5 years.
95	Vedta Hirma of Kodenar	Villa	11.6.25	302. Transportation for life. Released on special remission.
96	Vedta Sukra of Surguda	His uncle, Vedta Kola	4.1.41	302. Death. On appeal, transportation for life.
97	Veko Chamru of Nenganar	His wife, Hirme, his son Hando, 6, and his daughter Lakhmi, 10	28.10.36	302. Death. Executed, 3.6.37.
98	Veko Dome of Jamgaon	His aunt, Torka	25.11.22	302. Transportation for life. Died in jail, 11.4.25.
99	Vetti Hirma of Bara Satti	Rawa Hirma	8.12.39	304. Transportation for life.
100	Vetti Rupe of Parcheli	Kawasi Hirma	23.9.36	302. Transportation for life.

Pande's first husband deserted her. She then married Tati Mundra, and lived with him happily for two years. Then she began to run away to other villages. He would fetch her back, beat her and rub her with bhilwan juice. At last, when he was about to get her exorcised by a medicine-man, she killed him as he was sleeping.	She partly confessed.
Sika and others were stealing grain. Toka, a youth of 17, was guarding the fields and shot him, while the thieves were running away.	He confessed, but pleaded that he thought he was shooting at pigs.
There was a long history of love-intrigue between the younger Kopa and his elder 'brother's' wife. Poda showed remarkable forbearance but at last on unbearable provocation killed the youth.	He tried to make the death appear like suicide, and ordered and bribed everyone to make a report to this effect. Pleaded not guilty.
Villa wanted a chicken for sacrifice, as his son was ill. He asked Hirma who had not got one, then he went to another house and drank landa. Hirma's brother went by and Villa abused him for not giving the chicken: he replied and Villa knocked him down. Then Hirma came, struck Villa on back with his axe and killed him.	Hirma confessed and pleaded drunkenness.
Three years before Sukra's daughter died and Kola's magic was suspected. Then Sukra's son died and a Siraha diagnosed the same cause.	Sukra gave himself up to the villagers who took him to the police.
There was a long history of friction between husband and wife. Chamru at last strangled his wife and killed the children for fear they would say what they had seen.	He hung all three bodies in the house to make it look like suicide. Pleaded not guilty.
Everyone in the house was hungry. Dome had less food than anyone, Torka failed to bring him his food in the field and he struck her with his axe from behind.	Dome confessed.
There was long-standing enmity between the two men over land. Once they shot arrows at each other. Then there was a sudden quarrel over the theft of a pumpkin.	Hirma went to the police station and gave himself up.
There was a family landa party at the Korta Pandum festival, and in the course of it a quarrel arose between Rupe and his brother over a debt. They came to blows: Hirma intervened and was killed.	The villagers arrested Rupe. Rupe confessed, but said it was an accident.

APPENDIX TWO

TABLE OF 50 MARIA SUICIDES

No	Name, sex, age and place	Date	Brief history
1	Akali Modi, 18, of Kosalnar	14.8.38	He was a Lamhada and badly treated. Just before the tragedy his father-in-law scolded him for not tethering the cattle properly.
2	Alami Mata, 25, of Pahurnar	16.11.31	His dancing outfit was stolen. He was scolded by his father. He was unable to meet his girl.
3	Atami Kosa, 50, of Potali	31.1.35	He suffered from a painful ulcer and stomach trouble.
4	Baiha Ganga, 50, of Kukanar	22.6.32	He was regarded as mad and taken by his family for treatment to the Siraha.
5	Barse Chewa, 40, of Gamawada	23.7.34	He beat his wife and thought he had killed her.
6	Barse Konda, 35, of Hitawar	8.10.38	His daughter misconducted herself and he was defamed for it. He danced all night and hanged himself at dawn.
7	Budri (f.), 24, of Bodenar	8.1.33	She could not bear living with her husband.
8	Galle (f.), 19, of Goriapal	18.3.32	She was very independent of her husband, and when he tried to force her to cook against her will, she hanged herself.
9	Hunga, of Kothiaguda	17.8.37	He was accused of receiving stolen property, had lost his cattle and was troubled by the police.
10	Karti Kare (f.), 18, of Kosalnar	8.8.39	She was newly married, but after a quarrel ran away to another man. Her husband forced her to come home.
11	Karti Sukri (f.), 15, of Pondum	19.10.36	She was suffering from severe pains and undue prolongation of her menstrual period.
12	Kalmuni Boti, 40, of Pondum	22.5.33	His son had died.
13	Kawasi Deve (f.), 45, of Killepal	4.11.39	She was a widow living with her son and brother. They abused her for not working hard enough.

14	Kawasi Dulga, 30, of Dilmilli	22.1.37	He had two wives who were always quarrelling.
15	Kawasi Hurra, 21, of Sirisguda	4.6.40	His wife, whom he loved, did not care for him and was always running away and did not even cook properly.
16	Kawasi Marka, 50, of Maolibhata	29.7.38	He had been blind for seven years, and had long been gloomy and depressed.
17	Kome (f.), 20, of Kodher	13.8.32	She was a sensitive, quick-tempered girl. Her husband scolded her for not cooking in time.
18	Kunjami Baidi (f.), of Gadiras	3.3.39	She suffered from severe pains in chest and stomach.
19	Kunjami Burji (f.), 28, of Perpa	21.3.34	On her husband's death, a man who was her younger cousin claimed her. She was taken to his house, but escaped and hanged herself.
20	Kuhrami Pide (f.), 40, of Metapal	6.2.37	Mother and daughter (No 21) were very quick-tempered and specially resented any interference in household matters from Hurra, Pide's husband. One day Hurra found a calf had been killed by a panther. He scolded the women and they hanged themselves.
21	Kuhrami Pande (f.), 16, of Metapal	6.2.37	
22	Lakhmi (f.), 15, of Badrenga	9.11.40	She disliked her husband, tried to escape, but was always brought back.
23	Markami Hirme (f.), 35, of Gonderas	24.10.35	She was an epileptic. She hanged herself when eight months pregnant.
24	Markami Hunga (f.), 55, of Gongpal	1.5.37	She suffered from yaws and was very miserable.
25	Markami Kosi (f.), 35, of Rasawahi	11.7.37	The pain at menstruation drove her mad.
26	Markami Pandu, 50, of Parcheli	16.2.38	His wife scolded him for not thrashing the crop and for drinking too much. He may have been intoxicated at the time.
27	Marvi Dhodsa, 24, of Goriapal	17.5.39	He beat his sick wife for not caring for their child and felt very sorry for it.
28	Marvi Gutami, 22, of Katakanda	24.8.38	He loved his wife very much, but she was careless and used to leave him for her parents' house.
29	Marvi Mundi (f.), 45, of Oriyapal	9.11.32	She had fits of insanity from childhood.
30	Marvi Mundra, of Cholnar	29.12.35	He went to Dantewara as a prosecution witness in a cattle-lifting case, and got frightened.

31	Mate (f.), 20, of Kosalnar	17.8.35	She was beaten by her husband and his elder brother, and ran away, hanging herself on the banks of the Indrawati River.
32	Mundri (f.), 30, of Kaklur	26.11.32	She was a quarrelsome woman and used to run off to her parents' house. Her husband stopped her and she hanged herself.
33	Muke (f.), 40, of Bhejripadar	1.8.35	She had suffered acutely from pains in head and stomach. Her husband took her to a Siraha, but it did no good.
34	Nadi, 20, of Mandar	12.12.35	He had been insane since childhood.
35	Padami Dhudi, 42, of Naktoka.	2.12.33	His old mother used to scold him for not working properly ; he had severe headaches.
36	Pakli (f.), 10, of Takhapal	19.7.32	She was probably an imbecile. The Siraha had tried to treat her, but to no avail.
37	Poriami Bire (f.), of Kondre	21.9.36	Her husband was sick and she did not look after him properly. For this her son rebuked her severely.
38	Poyami Gupe (f.), 18, of Bastanar	29.7.39	She had been widowed and then became the second wife of a man. Her co-wife quarrelled and she ran away.
39	Poyami Hirma, 22, of Kokalpal	21.9.40	He was probably insane. He could not work properly.
40	Poyami Kosa, 15, of Sargipal	16.12.39	Someone took his clothes and he was greatly upset by the loss.
41	Poyami Lakhma, 45, of Gumiapal	25.12.24	He was ill. His two wives and a daughter died. He was sad and lonely.
42	Poyami Mangru, 50, of Dilmilli	20.7.33	He had leprous and very painful ulcers ; he could neither eat nor drink.
43	Poyami Pande (f.), 18, of Kawargaon	17.6.36	She hanged herself rather than sleep with her ' cousin-brother '.
44	Sori Deva, 25, of Kokalwada	9.6.39	His two cows died ; he quarrelled with his wife and beat her. She ran away. He felt repentant and miserable.
45	Sori Hirma, 60, of Korra	26.2.32	He injured himself at a festival and was a confirmed invalid.
46	Thadgu, 50, of Gadhia	30.4.40	He loved his son who was ill and took him to a Siraha, with no result.
47	Tiro (f.), 22, of Karka	6.4.39	Her first two babies died. Then the third got burnt and her husband beat her.

48	Veko Lakhma, of Haram	24.11.31	He was a Kabari bond-servant. He did not know how to pay his debt.
49	Veko Mukka, of Adhkariras	5.11.34	He was probably insane.
50	Wanjami Mase (f.), 22, of Pujari Palli	5.2.34	She was weak and lazy. She could not feed her baby properly. Her mother-in-law used to scold her constantly.

APPENDIX THREE

NOTE ON THE INDIAN PENAL CODE

The law dealing with offences affecting human life is fully set out in Sections 299 to 311 of the Indian Penal Code, and I will quote a part of this for the convenience of Western readers.

> 299. Whoever causes death by doing an act with the intention of causing death, or with the intention of causing such bodily injury as is likely to cause death, or with the knowledge that he is likely by such act to cause death, commits the offence of culpable homicide.
>
> 300. Except in the cases hereinafter excepted, culpable homicide is murder, if the act by which the death is caused is done with the intention of causing death, or—
>
> Secondly—If it is done with the intention of causing such bodily injury as the offender knows to be likely to cause the death of the person to whom the harm is caused or—
>
> Thirdly—If it is done with the intention of causing bodily injury to any person and the bodily injury intended to be inflicted is sufficient in the ordinary course of nature to cause death, or—
>
> Fourthly—If the person committing the act knows that it is so imminently dangerous that it must in all probability cause death, or such bodily injury as is likely to cause death, and commits such act without any excuse for incurring the risk of causing death or such injury aforesaid.
>
> *Exception* 1.—Culpable homicide is not murder if the offender, whilst deprived of the power of self-control by grave and sudden provocation, causes the death of the person who gave the provocation, or causes the death of any other person by mistake or accident.
>
> The above exception is subject to the following provisos:—
>
> First—that the provocation is not sought or voluntarily provoked by the offender as an excuse for killing or doing harm to any person.
>
> Secondly—That the provocation is not given by anything done in obedience to the law, or by a public servant in the lawful exercise of the powers of such public servant.
>
> Thirdly—That the provocation is not given by anything done in the lawful exercise of the right of private defence.
>
> *Exception* 2.—Culpable homicide is not murder if the offender, in the exercise in good faith of the right of private defence of person or property, exceeds the power given to him by law and causes the death of the person against whom he is exercising such right of defence without premeditation, and without any intention of doing more harm than is necessary for the purpose of such defence.
>
> *Exception* 3.—Culpable homicide is not murder if the offender, being a public servant or aiding a public servant acting for the advancement of public justice, exceeds the powers given to him by law, and causes death by doing an act which he, in good faith, believes to be lawful and necessary for the due discharge of his duty as such public servant and without ill-will towards the person whose death is caused.
>
> *Exception* 4.—Culpable homicide is not murder if it is committed without premeditation in a sudden fight in the heat of passion upon a sudden quarrel and without the offender's having taken undue advantage or acted in a cruel or unusual manner.

Exception 5.—Culpable homicide is not murder when the person whose death is caused, being above the age of eighteen years, suffers death or takes the risk of death with his own consent.

302. Whoever commits murder shall be punished with death, or transportation for life, and shall also be liable to fine.

304. Whoever commits culpable homicide not amounting to murder, shall be punished with transportation for life, or imprisonment of either description for a term which may extend to ten years, and shall also be liable to fine, if the act by which the death is caused is done with the intention of causing death, or of causing such bodily injury as is likely to cause death;

or with imprisonment of either description for a term which may extend to ten years, or with fine, or with both, if the act is done with the knowledge that it is likely to cause death, but without any intention to cause death or to cause such bodily injury as is likely to cause death.

Sir Cecil Walsh considered that these definitions were too complicated for the situations to which they were normally applied. 'The Indian Penal Code has always been considered a masterpiece of codification, and is the admiration of experts in jurisprudence. The beautifully moulded definitions of murder, and of culpable homicide not amounting to murder, set out every phase of thought through which a man's mind may pass when he is engaged in a fight and burning to defeat and injure his enemy. But men do not think aloud in a confused fight when they are "seeing red" and expecting every minute to be knocked out themselves. How are you to apply almost metaphysical processes of reasoning to the mental processes of half-mad savages, when you are not quite sure what the real facts are? In practice, these works of art in draftsmanship break down, and the simple English dichotomy of "murder" or "manslaughter" is to be preferred.'[1]

[1] Walsh, *Crime in India*, pp. 29 f.

BIBLIOGRAPHY

Adam, J. C. .. *Criminal Investigation* (London, 1924). This book is adapted from Hans Gross, *System der Kriminālistik*

Anatomy of Murder, The By various hands (London, 1936)

Beech, M. W. H. .. 'Suicide amongst the A-Kikuyu of East Africa', *Man*, Vol. XIII (1915)

Bjeere, A. .. *The Psychology of Murder* (London, 1927)

Bonger, W. A. .. *Race and Crime* (New York, 1943)

Cadogan, E. .. *The Roots of Evil* (London, 1937)

Cavan, R. S. .. *Suicide* (Chicago, 1928)

Cox, E. C. .. *Police and Crime in India* (London, 1911)

Crooke, W. .. *The Popular Religion and Folk-Lore of Northern India* (Westminister, 1896)

Dalton, E. T. .. *Descriptive Ethnology of Bengal* (Calcutta, 1872)

Durkheim, E. .. *Le Suicide* (Paris, 1897)

East, W. N. .. 'On Attempted Suicide', *Journal of Mental Science*, Vol. LIX (1913)

Ellis, Havelock .. *The Criminal* (London, 1914)

Elwin, Verrier .. *The Baiga* (London, 1939)

The Agaria (Bombay, 1942)

The Muria and their Ghotul (Bombay, 1947)

Myths of Middle India (Bombay, 1949)

Fishman, J. F. .. *Sex in Prison* (London, 1935)

Gault, R. H. .. *Criminology* (New York, 1932)

Green, L. C. and Beckwitch, M. W. 'Hawaiian Customs and Beliefs relating to Sickness and Death', *American Anthropologist*, Vol. XXVIII (1926)

Grigson, W. V. .. *The Maria Gonds of Bastar* (London, 1938)

Harada, Tasuku .. 'Suicide', *Encyclopedia of Religion and Ethics* (New York, 1922), Vol. XII

Haikerwal, B. S. .. *Economic and Social Aspects of Crime in India* (London, 1934)

Hall, G. S. .. *Adolescence* (London and New York, 1904)

Hart, Bernard .. *The Psychology of Insanity* (Cambridge, 1922)

Hollander, Bernard *The Psychology of Misconduct, Vice and Crime* (London, 1922)

Hooton, E. A. .. *The American Criminal: an Anthropological Study* (Harvard, 1939)

Crime and the Man (Harvard, 1939)

Jesse, F. Tennyson *Murder and its Motives* (London, 1924)

Keller, A. .. *A Hangman's Diary* (London, 1928)

Kinberg, O. .. *Basic Problems of Criminology* (Copenhagen and London, 1935)

Lombroso, C. .. *Crime: its Causes and Remedies* (London, 1911)

Macleod, W. C. .. 'The Distribution and Process of Suttee in North America', *American Anthropologist*, Vol. XXXIII (N.S.)

Michael, J. and Adler, M. J. *Crime, Law and Social Science* (London, 1933)

Mitchell, A. N. .. *A Grammar of Gondi* (Jagdalpur, 1943)

Page, Leo .. *Crime and the Community* (London, 1937)

Penzer, N. M. .. *The Ocean of Story* (London, 1924-28)

Reckless, W. C. .. *Criminal Behaviour* (New York, 1940)

Reik, T. .. *The Unknown Murderer* (Eng. trans., London, 1936)

Rose, H. J. .. 'Suicide', *Encyclopedia of Religion and Ethics* (New York, 1922), Vol. XII

Russell, R. V. and Hiralal .. *The Tribes and Castes of the Central Provinces of India* (London, 1916)

Sullivan, W. C. .. *Crime and Insanity* (London, 1924)

'Alcoholism and Suicidal Impulses', *Journal of Mental Science*, Vol. XLIV (1898). See also Vol. XLVI (1900)

Steinmetz, S. R. .. 'Suicide among Primitive Peoples', *American Anthropologist*, Vol. VII (1894)

Thomson, Basil .. *The Criminal* (London, 1925)

Thurston, E. .. *Castes and Tribes of Southern India* (Madras, 1909)

Tulchin, S. H. .. *Intelligence and Crime* (Chicago, 1939)

Von Hentig, H. .. *Crime: Causes and Conditions* (New York, 1947)

Walsh, Sir Cecil .. *Indian Village Crimes* (London, 1929)

Crime in India (London, 1930)

Westermarck, E. .. *The Origin and Development of the Moral Ideas* (London, 1912)

Zeleny, L. D. .. 'Feeblemindedness and Criminal Conduct', *American Journal of Sociology*, 1933

GLOSSARY

Bhut	..	A ghost or evil spirit
Danyakal	..	A cromlech, a flat stone put by certain clans for the tendance of the Dead
Gaita	..	The priest and religious headman of a village
Ghotul	..	The village dormitory of the Muria of northern Bastar
Gunia	..	A magician
Jawa	..	A gruel, called also *pej,* which is the staple food of the Maria
Jiwa	..	The soul
Kosra	..	A small millet, *Panicum miliaceum*
Lamhada	..	A youth who serves a period of years for his wife
Landa	..	Rice-beer
Mahua	..	*Bassia latifolia,* Roxb., the corolla of which is used for making liquor
Mandia	..	A grain, *Eleusine coracana,* used in the brewing of rice-beer
Manjhi	..	The petty chief or headman of a group of villages
Mirchuk	..	The ghost of a suicide, an executed murderer or a man killed by human violence
Paitu	..	A girl who comes of her own accord to co-habit with a man
Panchayat	..	A court of village elders
Pandum	..	A festival, usually celebrating the gathering and first eating of a crop
Peda	..	A village headman
Pen	..	A clan-god
Rame bird	..	The common Myna
Salphi	..	The Halbi word for the sago palm, *Caryota urens,* Linn.
Siraha	..	A medicine-man and diviner
Tahsil	..	A territorial division of a State or District, in charge of a Magistrate at whose head-quarters post-mortems are conducted and who commits prisoners for trial at Sessions
Uraskal	..	A menhir set upright for the tendance of the Dead.
Waddai	..	A clan-priest and medicine-man

INDEX

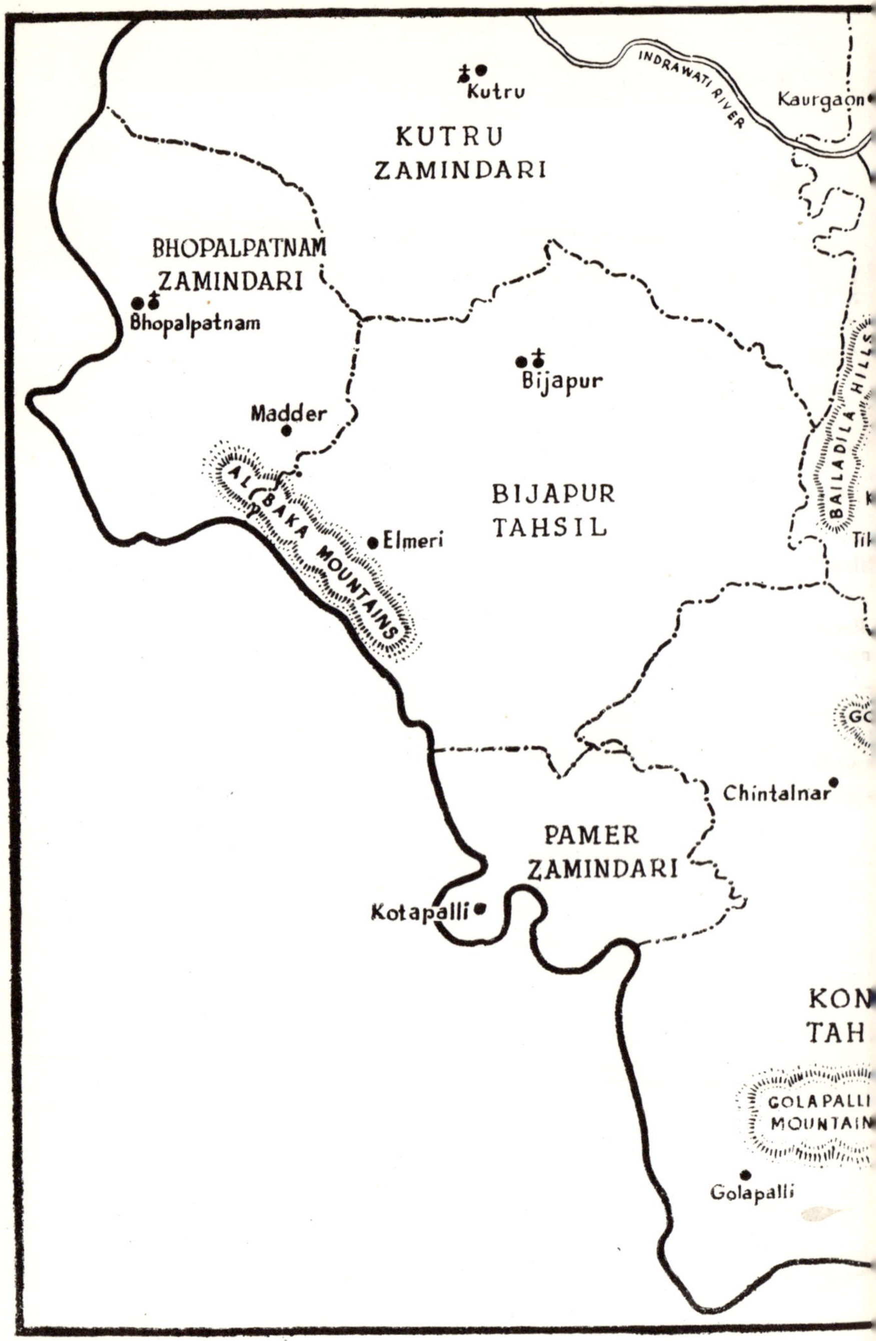

INDRAWATI RIVER
Kutru
Kaurgaon
KUTRU
ZAMINDARI
BHOPALPATNAM
ZAMINDARI
Bhopalpatnam
Bijapur
BAILADILA HILLS
Madder
AL BAKA MOUNTAINS
Elmeri
BIJAPUR
TAHSIL
Chintalnar
PAMER
ZAMINDARI
Kotapalli
GOLAPALLI
Golapalli